100
YEARS
SIMON &
SCHUSTER

DINNER FOR VAMPIRES

LIFE ON A CULT TV SHOW
(WHILE ALSO IN AN ACTUAL CULT!)

BETHANY JOY LENZ

Simon & Schuster

NEW YORK   LONDON   TORONTO
SYDNEY   NEW DELHI

100 YEARS
SIMON &
SCHUSTER

1230 Avenue of the Americas
New York, NY 10020

First Simon & Schuster hardcover edition October 2024

SIMON & SCHUSTER and colophon are registered trademarks
of Simon & Schuster, LLC

Simon & Schuster: Celebrating 100 Years of Publishing in 2024

For information about special discounts for bulk purchases,
please contact Simon & Schuster Special Sales at 1-866-506-1949
or business@simonandschuster.com.

The Simon & Schuster Speakers Bureau can bring authors to your
live event. For more information or to book an event, contact
the Simon & Schuster Speakers Bureau at 1-866-248-3049
or visit our website at www.simonspeakers.com.

Book text design by Paul Dippolito

Manufactured in the United States of America

1   3   5   7   9   10   8   6   4   2

Library of Congress Cataloging-in-Publication Data

ISBN 978-1-6680-6730-7
ISBN 978-1-6680-6732-1 (ebook)

This book is for you.

The Big House Family

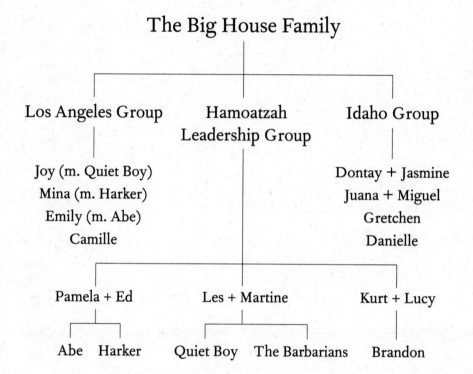

Los Angeles Group

Joy (m. Quiet Boy)
Mina (m. Harker)
Emily (m. Abe)
Camille

Hamoatzah Leadership Group

Idaho Group

Dontay + Jasmine
Juana + Miguel
Gretchen
Danielle

Pamela + Ed

Les + Martine

Kurt + Lucy

Abe   Harker

Quiet Boy   The Barbarians

Brandon

AUTHOR'S NOTE

From 1999 to 2015, I maintained detailed journals that chronicled the events described in this book. In an effort to uphold accuracy, I've had many conversations with others who were involved. I've mapped timelines, cross-referenced stories for reliability, and fact-checked to the best of my ability. There are real families still recovering today from these events. There are children who don't know their parents or relatives were involved and whose relationships with them would be forever altered if this information became publicly attached to them. Therefore, names and identifying details have been changed, and chronology, conversations, and characters have been modified or composited for clarity, brevity, or privacy.

The law does not define what does and does not constitute a cult. Other synonyms for what I believe I experienced include "high-demand group" or "high-control group." I have used the term "cult" informally throughout the book for ease of reference and to portray my personal experience.

Love does not dominate, it cultivates.

—*Johann Wolfgang von Goethe, "Das Märchen"*

ANGELUS: No weapons. No friends. No hope.
Take all that away and what's left?

BUFFY: Me.

—Buffy the Vampire Slayer,
"Becoming, Part 2," Season 2, Episode 22

DINNER FOR VAMPIRES

PROLOGUE

"I don't want to do this anymore. Maybe we need to separate for a while."

He was facing me when I said it, standing across the hotel room. He went quiet. Tense. I hadn't said the word "divorce," but it was close enough. His chest was moving in shallow breaths. He blinked a few times.

"And what about Rosie?" he said. "Who does she go with?"

Rosie. Resting on the bed between us, she rustled, still in her car seat alongside the suitcases we needed to pack for our flight back home to Idaho in a few hours. There she lay, eleven months of life and already full of turmoil. Her evenings were peppered with the sounds of her parents' bitter arguments, slamming doors, Mom crying in closets. On top of this, it took her six months to latch on to my nipple properly because she was born with a tongue-tie, so her introduction to nourishment was a mother weeping from pain, usually screaming into a pillow so she wouldn't be disturbed as I pushed through, bleeding into the milk. Yes, there were plenty of walks in the sunshine, naps on our chests, holding her father's thumbs as he cooed over her and blew raspberries on her tummy. That was her favorite. He could always make her laugh by doing that. She would gaze up at us, but we were the ones who were amazed at every little thing she did. There *were* good times. But more often we lived in a world of chaos.

I spoke quietly: "Well . . . I mean . . . I'm nursing her, so . . ."

He shook his head and let out a quick breath, then picked up a sweatshirt, balled it up, and threw it toward me with a growl.

It was only a sweatshirt. Before that, it was only a toy. Only a book. Only a cell phone. Only potted plants. Only a vintage rolling metal laundry basket colliding with a wall, ricocheting to the floor, and scaring our tough five-pound Yorkshire terrier so badly he shit himself right where he stood. He had *only* injured his hand punching holes in several of our walls and doors. A sweatshirt was really nothing.

My husband's father had encouraged his three sons from a young age to take out their aggression against women on the drywall and furniture, and he set the example himself. "Right in front of the woman, if needed," Les would coach, "so she can see how passionate you are about her and see how controlled you are to not harm her in spite of the fact that she makes you so angry." And boy, did I make my husband angry. Everything I did, said, thought—my very existence, it seemed.

He was especially angry with me lately, faced with moving back to Los Angeles, where we'd first met and where we'd spent these past few days looking at places to live and meeting new acting managers. Since marrying, I'd split time between our Family's home base in Idaho and the Wilmington, North Carolina, set of the hit TV series *One Tree Hill*, where, for nine years, I'd starred as Haley James Scott. The millions I made supported not only us but the extended Family's various endeavors, including a motel, a restaurant, and, most importantly, a ministry. Now that the show was over, I would have to go back to auditioning, which didn't happen in Idaho. The idea of leaving the Family was abhorrent to him.

That afternoon in our West Hollywood hotel he had been yelling at me for about an hour, which was standard. I was exhausted,

I had been exhausted for years. The therapist I had begun seeing around this time encouraged me to create some boundaries to help navigate these emotional storms. "Start with something simple," she'd advised. "Violence, for example. Physical violence around you is not acceptable. Ever." After that session, I told him this: "If you throw something across the room again, I'm going to immediately remove myself and Rosie from that situation and we can try talking again the next day."

He didn't like it. I believe his exact words were: "I don't agree to that."

In the split second after he threw the sweatshirt, I had to make a choice to enforce my boundary or not. I considered letting it slide and waiting until he really threw something heavy. I didn't want to make things worse. I could just let it go for now and we could talk about it later. I wanted to find a way to live separately for a few months, anyway. Go to counseling together and try to start over—just get away from his Family and their overbearingness for a little while. This thought tripped me up, thinking of them not just as overbearing but as *his* Family rather than *our* Family. That was a strange and surprising feeling. More surprising than the thought itself was how *right* it felt. But I didn't have time to consider what that meant. I could bring all this up plus the separation idea another time if I stayed. *Don't do it now, Joy. It was only a sweatshirt.*

Just then, I looked down at my daughter's face for the first time since the fight began, and I felt everything inside me shift. Her eyes were different. They were always deep and bright like little stars had landed in them. People frequently commented laughingly that they felt she was staring into their soul. In that moment, though, her big, wonderful chocolate eyes suddenly looked hopeless, almost dead. I realized she had just sat in the room for an hour as the air filled with her father's venom as it poured over us. Isn't that what kills plants in fifth-grade science experiments: isolating them in a room and yelling at them?

I picked up Rosie and held her to my chest. She was limp and looked so deeply sad. Maybe I was projecting. Maybe it was all in my imagination. Maybe God was present, like I'd known Him to be many times before, and He was somehow allowing me to see myself from a bird's-eye view. Whatever it was, my body went cold. And then it went very, very hot.

I had carried her for nine months, I had read the books on parenthood, I had delivered her myself after a twenty-hour labor, reaching down and pulling my daughter out of myself in the final moment. I nursed multiple times a day through the pain of her inability to latch. I got up in the night with her and then went to work at five a.m. with her. I prayed for her, fed her, changed her, took her to her doctor's appointments, spoke positive things over her daily—I did all the things mothers do. I think in that moment, though—seeing her light go out, knowing why, and knowing I was the only one who could do anything about it—that was the moment I actually *became* a mother. And that stupid sweatshirt became the heaviest thing he ever threw.

I began to gather my things. "I told you if you threw another thing I was going to leave with her for the night." I stated it pragmatically, holding a thread of hope that he might apologize.

I didn't even notice him move. He just was suddenly *there*. Over me, leaning in as I sat on the bed, his arms blocking me on either side, his breath hot in my face.

"If you leave," he spat, "I will get a lawyer and I will take her from you. I will fight for custody and I'll win. I will take. Her. Away from you."

My heart was a kick drum. He was so confident the girl he knew wouldn't leave. The girl he knew would stay because, in spite of the endless struggle and depression, she hadn't left. The girl he knew was committed to making the marriage work. She was trying to be a Godly, submissive wife. She knew she was selfish and just needed more healing—needed to surrender more. She knew, deep down, how much he'd sacrificed for her, how patient he was with her brokenness. The girl he knew needed him.

I knew that girl, too. I'd been living in her skin for ten years believing she was the real me. But where was the girl I used to be before? Before the downward spiral into normalizing abuse and handing over my autonomy not just to him but to our Family— no, to *his* Family. No, to a . . . to a . . . I wasn't quite ready to admit it. I was even more reluctant to use *that* word than "divorce." The word my estranged parents and former friends and coworkers had been using for years. The word that further isolated me from them but that I increasingly suspected was true.

He stood up, still glowering at me, then walked into the bathroom, slammed the door, and turned on the shower. I was lucky that he bet on me being paralyzed with fear, but I knew my window of time was short. I quickly scooped up Rosie in her car seat, grabbed my suitcase, and hurried to the rental car. Instead of driving to the airport, I let him take the flight home without us while Rosie and I crashed with a few old friends for the next week. Via text, he pleaded, then doubled down on scolding me for my insubordination, my selfishness, my heartlessness. Again, standard. And then he went cold. His messages became almost robotic, which only pushed me further away.

After a week with those old friends and phone calls with my therapist and parents, I was reminded of that other girl I used to be before. I was reminded I still *was* her, and finally I reached a place where I could say it.

I was in a cult. And I had to get out.

PART ONE

CHAPTER ONE

My first recollection of the American Christian-culture Crock-Pot I was baked in was around 1985: me, age four, sitting in the middle of the back seat bench in my parents' black Harvester Scout, where my tan, string bean legs stuck to the vinyl as I endured the seventeen-hour drive from south Florida to central Texas. With the metal seat belt heavy on my little waist—booster seats were a thing of the future—I pulled repeatedly on the cord that stuck out of the spine of my favorite doll, Melody.

Melody was the Christian version of Teddy Ruxpin or Cabbage Patch Kids. She had one song only. Pull the string and she'd sing, *Hosanna! Hosanna! Shout unto God with a voice of triumph! Clap your hands, all ye people, shout unto God with a voice of praise!* She was born out of the booming business catering to the charismatic evangelical movement that sprung up in the United States in the 1980s: Christian rock music, cartoon Bibles, kitschy cross jewelry, and dolls who praised the Lord.

My folks had come out of the Jesus Revolution hippie era, and were now in the thick of this new movement, having met at and graduated from one of the country's big charismatic Bible colleges. The story goes that Dad came out of the gym after losing a pickup game of basketball and saw Mom in the bursar's line to register for a class. He jumped into his '64 Mustang and rushed back to his dorm to grab the only cash he had—five dollars—so he could join her in line and have an excuse to talk to her. Mom (in her below-the-knee skirt) smiled at Dad behind her. He might have had a haircut to adhere to the conservative campus code, but he was still a hippie at heart. Dad saw her Bambi-ish face, said, "You look like you have stars in your eyes," and I was born in Florida three years later. We lived in the house of my dad's off-the-boat Australian grandfather in Coconut Creek with orange trees and Pompano Beach in the backyard. The heat was unrelenting, but the ocean was my playground.

Dad had graduated with a teaching degree, but there weren't any open positions nearby, so he picked up work where he could find it: painting houses, mowing lawns, reluctantly taking a risky job as a prison guard. Mom painted designs on white baby onesies and sold them for cash. Eventually they took a job as "house parents" in a home for troubled teen girls. It was free room and board, and, better yet, they saw it as a ministry opportunity. That lasted about a year, until one of the girls threatened to cook me. Mom had us out of there within the week, and they became determined to upgrade our life.

Dad had been sending résumés all over the country and scored a job as a high school teacher at a prestigious Christian school in Texas. And Mom was hired as the new secretary for the president of the biggest Christian music label in the country. So, Dad sold the Mustang and picked up the more family-friendly Scout. We packed up and headed out for Dallas, where there was also unrelenting heat but no ocean. Early on, I often dreamed of the swaying citrus groves and palm trees we'd left behind. I felt safe there under the humid haze. To this day I'd rather be hot than cold, and the smell of salt and oranges gives me an immense amount of comfort.

But life moves on, and so had we. A tiny apartment on the

outskirts of the city became home. I had a free ride to the private school, since Dad was teaching there, but I found making friends to be a challenge. It wasn't just the solitude of being an only child. I felt the profound disconnect between my life—riding to school in a truck with busted heat while warming my hands on the cigarette lighter or "World's Best Dad" coffee mug I'd made him in kindergarten—and the other kids'—who arrived at school in Cadillac Escalades and had new Magical Mansion Barbie Dreamhouses. My social life basically consisted of the singing Melody doll and our new cocker spaniel puppy, so I was extremely relieved to discover that Jesus would be my permanent friend.

In our home there were dinnertime prayers; frequent references to the moral guidance offered by Proverbs, Psalms, and the parables; and daily conversations about God. Dad had a New King James Bible that was bound with a leather so thick it belonged on a saddle. He read it with a highlighter and pen nearby, filling every inch of margin with impeccably written notations.

One night at my bedside, Dad finished reading to me from 1 Peter about Jesus taking our sins upon himself, closed that leather Bible on his lap, and said, "Do you know that God is so perfect that anything not perfect gets destroyed just by being near Him? Like a light being switched on in a dark room." Then he flipped the switch on the wall.

I ducked my head under the covers, giggling.

He smiled. "Look around! See any darkness?"

I peeked out and shook my head.

"Where'd it go?" he asked.

"The light ate it up!" I said.

"That's right," he said, tipping his head back the way he always did when he was pleased. "That's what God does for us. So long as we keep Him flipped on, He eats up all the badness."

It was simple, I understood it, and, eventually, I made my parents' faith my own.

My parents' new jobs didn't last. Over the next eight years we'd move to four different cities in Texas. This meant four different elementary schools for me and continued difficulty maintaining friendships. To add to that isolation, with each job change and new apartment, the tension between my parents had been growing. Raised voices, icy rooms, and slammed doors. Because of this volatility, constantly changing schools, and undiagnosed ADHD, I was a terrible student—fidgety and always daydreaming, unable to do my homework the way it was supposed to be done. I tried making it fun for myself any way I could: using different-colored pens, offering additional answers to multiple-choice questions, drawing pictures instead of writing sentences. My teachers were exhausted and frustrated, but luckily for me both my parents were great nurturers of creativity. They knew I just needed to be in an environment that turned my weaknesses into strengths. When I was seven, Mom brought me to a community theatre in Arlington, Texas, and I was cast as a munchkin in *The Wizard of Oz*.

It was perhaps inevitable that I'd become a performer. My family had a long history with the performing arts. My great-grandmother on my mom's side ran off as a teenager to join the circus and eventually wound up in vaudeville. My dad's parents, Doris and George, were also showfolk. She was a choir director and regional stage actress, and he was a regular on Broadway, appearing in the original productions of *South Pacific*, *Wish You Were Here*, and *Carousel*, and acting as stage manager for many more. In the attic of her New Jersey home, Grandma Doris had boxes—like *BUH-AHH-XES*—of playbills from shows they were in, plus original cast records, newspaper clippings, and handwritten notes from Broadway legends such as Shirley Booth and Joshua Logan. The scrapbook game in my family is strong. Family lore even has it that one day James Garner and Grandpa George were in an alley smoking a cigarette half past the end of a matinee, and Garner said, "Everybody's calling me to go out to Hollywood, but I don't know if I could leave the theatre." Grandpa George said, "Garner, if you don't get out of this rathole I will personally kick your ass," followed by an apparently convincing argument that led to James Garner packing his bags to try his luck in Hollywood, where his success carried through to his final role in Nicholas Sparks's *The Notebook*.

Upon further research, it appears James Garner never worked on Broadway as a young man. So, either his name got mixed up as the story was passed down, or Grandpa George was just full of shit—which, considering the fact he shacked up with a dancer from *The Jackie Gleason Show* and left Doris, my six-year-old dad, and his nine-year-old sister with severe physical disabilities, proooobably is the right answer.

I barely knew him, but Grandma Doris was a euphony of music and warmth. The times we'd visit her in Jersey, I'd swipe a Werther's butterscotch from the crystal candy dish on the upright piano, pull the string hanging from the upstairs hallway ceiling, climb the rickety stairs, and lose myself for hours in her attic. That highest point of the house had a single, dusty window and count- less saved props and costumes from old shows for me to get lost playing dress-up and soaking in the echoes of family history. I felt like I could understand more about who I was there, and I longed for family connection.

The Arlington community theatre gave me my first taste of really *belonging* somewhere. In the creative arts school there were dozens of rooms for rehearsals, costume making, set design, and dance and voice classes. People bustling everywhere and struggling to hear each other over the sounds of singing, clacking tap shoes, booming stereos, and instrument practices. I was invigorated by the smells of paint, sawdust, Aqua Net, and Pond's cold cream; hot lights and pure sweat.

On the big auditorium stage during opening night of *The Wizard of Oz*, I was supposed to hand off a prop to Dorothy and spontaneously decided my character would dislike Toto, so I recoiled from it and held my nose. The dog needed a bath anyway. I heard a ripple of laughs and realized I'd had an impact on the emotional experience of an entire crowd. A few more times onstage and I realized I could disappear from my problems at home and school and be anyone I wanted to be. On top of that, I was welcomed! My eccentricities like spontaneous singing, mimicking Lucille Ball, and daydreaming were things that got me in trouble at school—but they were an asset to me in acting. I went on to star in all the usual local theatre standards like *Annie, Gypsy, To Kill a Mockingbird*, and *Peter Pan*. I was becoming a valuable member of a community, and that was everything to me. At twelve I received a highlighted review in the *Dallas Morning News*, the first newspaper clipping of my own! Next, I was cast in my first on-camera role: the lead actress alongside a giant, costumed, singing songbook in a Christian movie. Think Barney the purple dinosaur, except a blue church hymnal. *Psalty's Salvation Celebration* is absolutely findable online. You're welcome.

Soon after that jump from stage to screen, I joined yet another new school, this one dedicated to TV and film, and my first trip to Los Angeles was arranged. Mom and I spent a week in a furnished Hollywood apartment going on every audition we could find. Apparently, I was getting good feedback from casting agents and when I got to the coveted final round of the *Mickey Mouse Club* auditions (the same year Britney and Justin were cast), I overheard Mom telling Dad over the phone, "She might really have a shot at this!"

It was very clear to me what I was meant to do with my life. It was clear to Grandma Doris, too. During one of my last trips to see her, after she'd been diagnosed with late-stage cancer, she gave me some career advice, speaking to me more as a mentor than as a grandmother.

"It's a hard life to be an actor," she said while I painted on her eyeshadow. Carole King played in the background on the stereo. *Doesn't anybody stay in one place anymore?* Beside us on the kitchen table lay a short, layered wig. We would put that on last. "It's hard to be rejected and always be competing. But there's nothing more glorious than being able to tell stories. I can't imagine having done anything else. It brought me so much happiness." She paused for a moment so I could apply her favorite pearly mauve lipstick from a silver tube. *It would be so fine to see your face at my door.* She pressed her lips together. "I have many regrets in life, but I don't regret one second I spent onstage." Then she hugged me close to her warm chest and looked into my eyes. "Sing your heart out, kiddo. One day your name will be in lights. I really believe that." *But you're so far away . . .*

When she died, she left the New Jersey house to Dad. Deep down, though, I felt it was also her gift to me: getting me closer to

New York City and putting me in proximity to real training and real casting and the real Broadway.

We left our life in the South and moved into the two-bedroom home where my father grew up. Dad got a job as an adventure co-ordinator/ropes course director at a mental health center, which basically meant he was leading group therapy on a grown-up playground. Mom got a job selling beige business phones with built-in shoulder rests—to whom, I'm not sure, but I was always uncovering boxes of phones in the house. With my big teeth, Texas twang, and frosty blonde hair, I checked into the same public school Dad went to and made exactly zero friends, at the demand of the queen bee who thought being nice and southern was weird. Using my acting skills, I quickly dropped the accent and adapted to "Jersey girl" for a while, until I realized the facade of brown lip liner, flannel shirts, and pitiful attempts to smoke cigarettes to impress said queen bee would only carry me so far. I decided, after taking an introductory French class, I felt more like a "French girl" inside, so I changed the spelling of my name to "Joie" and surrounded myself with everything that had to do with France: Catherine Deneuve and Juliette Binoche movie posters taped to my bedroom walls, *Les Mis* and Serge Gains-bourg in my CD player, and a steady rotation of berets. This also did not make me new friends.

I was lonelier than ever and deeply missed my Texas theatre community. Even though Mom was driving me into New York City multiple times a week for dance and voice lessons and audi-tions, it was still an hour and a half commute on a good day and too far to go for social meetups. My parents and I began attending a local church that had a Friday night youth group meeting, a sort of club within the church for tweens and teens. In an effort to keep me socialized, they insisted I attend, and that first night changed my life as I knew it.

I walked into a large rec room with fluorescent lights and about fifteen kids bustling around. I felt so comfortable onstage but so awkward in a crowd. I didn't know how to stand or hold my arms, who to talk to or what to talk about. Then, just as I was about to stuff my face with cheap pizza and find a corner to die in, from across the room I heard a resounding laugh. My vision was lassoed by a dishwater-blond boy with oceanic blue eyes. He came over and introduced himself in a voice too impossibly deep for his age. And the only thought running through my mind was: *I'm going to marry you.*

His parents were well respected in the church and community. It was a family of two boys, a middle sister, and a Weimaraner. They were happy and friendly, and the whole of them always looked like they'd just climbed off bicycles in Nantucket. Quickly, he and I became the very, very best of friends. We talked for hours every night, me taking advantage of the shoulder rest on the beige coil-corded phone in our living room. We both loved Jesus and the Dave Matthews Band. We had the same sense of humor. And he was the only other person I knew who hated cats. Since I didn't belong to a theatre community anymore, I decided *he* would be where I belonged.

I started traveling more for acting jobs, and although it took me away from Blue Eyes, I loved it. Mom would fly out with me to LA for weeks at a time to screen-test or film a pilot. I'd play Paul Sorvino's daughter, or James Franco's sister, or Ben Foster and Gabrielle Union's BFF. That last one was a comedy pilot set in the 1970s for CBS that we were all certain would get picked up, but Fox announced its fall lineup first, and CBS didn't want to compete with *That '70s Show*. Though my pilots weren't getting picked up, my name was circulating, and I was getting invited to fancy mansion parties where I recognized nearly every face I passed. It was exciting being one of the cool kids, considering how awkward I was used to feeling at school, but I never forgot what my dad said about keeping God's light turned on. I was sensitive to the underlying ego and darkness that seemed to accompany these kinds of Hollywood environments, where no one blinked if I was offered a drink from the bar and cocaine was passed around on trays. I didn't dare tell my parents these stories, but I confided them to Blue Eyes, a kindred spirit who shared my desire to make God proud.

Talking long-distance every night was too expensive during those trips, and email wasn't common yet (let alone laptops!), so he and I would write letters. We wrote to each other on anything—receipts, old homework. Once, he mailed me a letter written on a long strip of wallpaper he'd peeled from behind the bed frame in the hotel where he was vacationing with his family. In school, we passed notes endlessly. I'm surprised the tenth-grade Spanish class radiator didn't break down from all the paper we stuffed into it, hiding notes for each other to find later. In the summers, we'd drive in his little Volkswagen Jetta out to his family's Jersey lake house (not actually Nantucket, but lovely nonetheless), sit on the dock with our legs hanging over the lake, and plunge into all the big ideas of life.

He and his family were a burrow I wanted to hide in while my parents tried to superglue their crumbling marriage. They had split up once when I was younger but got back together for my sake. The years that followed were a swamp of bitterness and passive-aggressive dialogue. The full-fledged arguments would happen behind thin walls and closed doors, from which my mother would emerge with poorly veiled composure. If I ever asked, "What's wrong?" or "Are you guys okay?" her response was always the same, with upturned lips.

"Everything's fine!"

My mom had not inherited the family's acting gene, and in these attempts to protect me, she inadvertently led me into a loop of questioning my reality—a characteristic that was useful to me as an actress, and also useful to anyone who wanted to manipulate me.

When I needed to escape, Blue Eyes was there to listen and console. But I refused to cry in front of him. There was no way I was ever going to collapse into a heap of tears for him to clean up. Not like his cheerleader girlfriend did. Blue Eyes was, of course, the school's star athlete and was on again, off again with the head cheerleader, *as if that cliché needed help from them.* There I was, writing songs and poetry for him, weeping nightly into the neck of my aging cocker spaniel, and waiting patiently for him to realize he loved me back. I thought maybe my singing would win him over and joined the church's worship team (a Christianese term for the onstage band). Or maybe acting success would impress him. That year I had booked a few national commercials, a Stephen King movie called *Thinner.* I was brought in as Monica Keena's understudy for *The Devil's Advocate* because she had a schedule conflict, and I walked to set with the extremely kind and tall Keanu Reeves—only to have Monica arrive after rehearsal, which gutted me. And later I landed a small role on the daytime soap opera *Guiding Light* as the teenage clone—yes, *clone*—of beloved character Reva Shayne. But apparently none of that competed with turning cartwheels on the sideline of a football game.

Then one Saturday morning I was blow-drying my hair before going to Blue Eyes's house to rent a movie and hang out when my dad asked me to come into the living room. Mom was on a chair, crying. They told me they were getting a divorce. Mom proceeded to explain, confess, apologize, rationalize. After ten minutes, I said, "Can I go finish blow-drying my hair?"

They looked at each other and let me go.

Later, while browsing the French film section in Blockbuster Video, I told Blue Eyes, casually, "So, my parents are getting a divorce." And when the words left my mouth, my face went hot, my throat started to burn, and tears sprung up in my eyes. I'm sure he didn't know what to do any more than I did. He was just a dumb teenager like me. He tsked and said, "Ah, J, I'm sorry to hear that. You okay?"

I wasn't okay at all, but I said yes, still terrified for him to think of me as high-maintenance. I also refused to cry when I was kicked off the worship team a few weeks later—news my mom had to break to me while driving home from church.

"Apparently the pastors decided it's too confusing for you to be leading worship onstage while you're on a soap opera."

"Confusing? What's confusing about it?"

"Because soaps are 'tawdry,' which makes the church look like they endorse that kind of 'behavior.'"

Mom was fuming, and I felt my own shame and anger well up. "Do they understand what acting is? I'm just telling a story. And my character isn't even doing any of that stuff."

"It's not just that . . . With your dad and I divorcing, they just think it's complicated for the congregation."

I was quiet.

"It's fine," she said. "They were lucky to have you. Idiots."

While I did appreciate my mother's loyalty and fierce

protection—whether in this instance, or defending me against bullying stage moms who felt I was a threat to their daughters, or demanding the conservative middle school English teacher accept my research paper on Broadway (first denied as "too secular" a topic)—her overbearingness worked against me, too.

After Dad officially moved out and promptly remarried during my senior year, Mom and I had no buffer. One night, my mother and I were having one of our routine shouting matches. We didn't curse (good Christians didn't curse). I never said "I hate you," though I felt it often. But that night she had been chasing me around the house, into the bathroom even. I said "fuck." She slapped me. I screamed in her face, "Leave me aloooonne!!!!" Then I grabbed my keys and ran out to my car—an Eddie Bauer–edition Ford Bronco that I still wish I had, even with its busted air-conditioning.

She was on my heels, but I managed to get in and lock all the doors. With wild eyes, she banged on the windows and tried the handle. Then she stood in front of the car, crossing her arms and looking at me like, *Ha. Gotcha.*

She's so stupid, I thought. *Sit <u>on the hood</u> of the car if you don't want me to drive away.*

I pretended to put the Bronco in reverse but didn't actually shift gears. I looked behind me like I was going to back up, and she predictably ran to the back of the car to try to block me from that side. As soon as she moved, I peeled out.

I decided then to get the hell away from her as soon as I could, and apparently she felt the same. Mom met someone from California online. After six months they decided to get married when I graduated, and not a second later. The week of my commencement ceremony, he flew out to help her pack.

"This is unbelievable," she muttered at him on the day

they loaded boxes into the moving truck—the day after my graduation. She was looking at me, sitting in the middle of the living room, sketching a dress using the design software that came with our new Apple computer, courtesy of the money from my "sinful" *Guiding Light* gig. I was trying to keep my mind off Blue Eyes, to whom I'd said a brief goodbye at his graduation party by slathering my lips in Bath & Body Works wild-berry-flavored lip balm and finally getting up the courage to quickly kiss him. It was barely more than a peck, but I knew it'd likely be the last time we saw each other that summer, as he was traveling with his family and then headed to a midwestern college. So, I had to take the chance. He smiled and said thank you before we were swept back up in the frenzy of yearbook signings and congratulations. Then he acted like nothing happened.

"Joy, can you get off the computer and help me? I'm moving across the country here!"

"No, thanks," I said coolly.

California tried to calm her down. He was always trying to calm her down. "Just let her do her thing. If she wants to be disrespectful, she's graduated, she's an adult now, that's her choice."

Is that what I was? An adult? *Thank you for your time at our education factory. Now, please throw this hat in the air and go run your own life.* I looked around at our empty house. Dad's house. Doris's house. I squeezed the worn brown carpet under my toes.

"Well, you need to be out by Wednesday for the new owners," she said, heading to the truck with a box that had a beige phone cord hanging out of the bottom. "And you'd better get started, because I won't be here to clean up after you."

It was time for me to find a new place to belong.

. . .

I had already been thinking of moving to Manhattan—hoping to finally fulfill the destiny Grandma Doris envisioned for me—and that decision was solidified when I got a call from my manager saying *Guiding Light* wanted to bring me on as a series regular. So at just eighteen years old, and after a trip to Paris during which I was frustratingly not seduced by a debonair bohemian as I'd been promised by years of ingesting French cinema, I moved into a tiny Union Square apartment. I didn't know anyone, but I quickly began to make friends among the *Guiding Light* cast and other actors I'd routinely encounter on auditions. I also made friends in the city's music scene. I'd expanded my songwriting beyond ballads for Blue Eyes and put together a band that gigged around town, playing in legendary local spots like CBGB and the Bitter End. I booked a made-for-TV movie playing Mary Tyler Moore's daughter and got into a regular circuit of auditioning for Broadway. I was building a real life in New York, but where I developed my deepest friendships was in church.

An acquaintance introduced me to a small church that met in the apartment of a gentle-natured pastoral couple from South Africa. The Bible studies we had were similar to others I'd participated in throughout my life: intimate, casual, and filled with curiosity. Uniquely, our South African pastors actually encouraged us to visit other churches on occasion to diversify our spiritual diet. I started to frequent Redeemer Presbyterian, pastored by Reverend Dr. Timothy Keller, whose 2023 *New York Times* obituary described him as a "pioneering evangelist" who was widely respected for his intellect and engaging thoughtfully in contemporary culture. I didn't personally consider him an evangelist (which, to me, was a tan salesman with a southern accent on my TV, asking for money). Tim was a theologian and insisted on reason as the entry point for faith, which I loved because it reminded me of the way my dad would challenge me to think. Tim and his wife, Kathy, had started the Upper East Side church in 1989, and eventually, the congregation would number several thousand New Yorkers from all walks of life. There I met an auburn-haired Brit named Camille who was also an actress. We'd run into each other in enough casting rooms that once I saw her at Redeemer it sealed our bond. Having grown up Catholic, she had become curious about "all the other options." Since I was inquisitive, too, we had no shortage of conversation. Camille was the first actor friend I didn't feel competitive with, I just wanted to see her win. And so when she told me a few months into our friendship that she was moving to Los Angeles to try for more work, I was sad but also supportive.

I never imagined leaving New York City, especially having discovered such enriching communities in my spiritual and professional lives. I loved living there, loved the creative pulp that seemed to rush into my blood every time I stepped outside—the feeling of everyone piled on top of each other, in each other's way, holding each other up, and spurring each other on. I felt fearless there, and, most importantly, I felt like I was a part of something.

Things were even looking more promising with Blue Eyes! One weekend, he came to visit, and, after a long day of sightseeing and sexual tension, he finally stopped me by a streetlamp near Lincoln Center, leaned over, and kissed me. I was sure this would be the key that unlocked all the love we'd been holding back. Everything would follow now: marriage, house, kids, perfect life, forever together. But once he returned to school, we found ourselves back where we always were. So, predictably, I settled back into waiting for him to come around.

When my *Guiding Light* contract expired, I decided not to renew. I wanted to take the next step in my career. Staying in Manhattan for another year, I got tantalizingly close on dozens of big studio movies but never quite landed the job. It was rejection after rejection, but I was determined to make my dream happen. So, when my bank account started running dangerously low, I did what my parents had always done when money was tight: hit the road.

CHAPTER TWO

I had gotten a sense of LA's weird vibes on those high school trips, but the place was even more strange living there full-time. There was no sense of community. The city was all spread out, and I didn't know how to get anywhere. I wanted to enjoy the sunshine, so, idiotically, I bought a stick shift convertible Miata and suffered through traffic in four gears until my joints were swollen. I had a random job at a Beverly Hills florist where some misguided soul put me in charge of the register before I knew there was a name for dyslexia with numbers. (It's "dyscalculia," by the way.) I did quickly book guest spots on a few TV shows, but life in LA completely centered around ego and competition. Everything felt like a struggle, and I really felt alone, especially after leaving my community in New York. Things between my mom and me were still strained, so even though we now lived in the same state, we didn't see each other much and talked on the phone infrequently. I talked more with my dad, who was still back in New Jersey, but he was tied up with his new family.

The only friends I had were Camille and my new roommate, Mina, whom I'd been introduced to by an actor friend from New York. "She's an actress and a Christian, and you're both romantics," he said. Our first meeting was when she invited me to the TV studio where they filmed a network legal drama on which she was a series regular. Though I'd shot several pilots, I hadn't spent much time at a studio like this. Walking through the hallways looking for Mina's dressing room and seeing name after recognizable name lining the hallway inspired me. I heard, deep down, the echo of Grandma Doris's promise to me: that soon enough I'd see my name up on one of these doors, too.

The feeling didn't last long. When I reached Mina's dressing room the door was ajar, and I lost all confidence the moment I knocked and she turned her face to look at me. If this was the kind of beauty it took to make it in Hollywood, I didn't stand a chance. This woman should be warred over by Trojans and Greeks, and I was an alley cat, still cleaning dumpster lettuce out of my paws. According to our mutual friend, Mina was ten years older than me. No way this woman was a year away from thirty.

"You made it!" she said, and ran a hand that belonged holding cigarettes for magazine ads through her slightly limp, coffee-colored hair. I was glad at least my hair was thicker, because I had to take my wins where I could get them in drastic circumstances like these.

She opened her arms to give me a hug, but as she got closer, I noticed her makeup seemed streaked from tears. Then I noticed the cardboard box.

"It's kind of a weird day," she said. "I just found out I've been let go from my contract. I'm packing up my stuff."

"I'm so sorry," I said. "If it's a bad time, we can totally reschedule."

"No," she said, "I'm glad you're here. I'm glad to have the company. I feel like I've been banished from the kingdom. Everyone is avoiding me." An insecure laugh bubbled up through her pillow lips, and she wiped her eyes. Despite my outrage at God for giving her a face like that, I decided to forgive Him, all things considered.

Mina had also forgiven God for her current misfortune. As we spent the next half hour packing her boxes, she explained how, as disappointed as she was, she took comfort in the fact that this was clearly part of God's plan for her.

"I only became a Christian last year," she shared. "I grew up Catholic, but, you know . . ." She flicked both hands in front of her, like she was clearing the air. "I met this actor who's been on the studio lot filming a movie. His name is Harker Van Hewitt. Do you know him?"

I knew of Harker because he was a budding movie star, and his acting abilities were as singular as his name. Fellow actors usually get a sense of who among them is on the rise. "Yeah, he's fantastic!"

"Oh, Joy, he's just so smart and so humble. We started having these amazing discussions about Jesus and religious history and . . . I don't know, the Lord just kind of came alive to me."

"Are you dating him?" I asked.

"Oh, no," she said. "He's much younger than me. He's your age."

I wondered from the way she blushed, and how quickly she'd responded with their age difference, whether she'd at least thought about it.

"He's so talented. And his older brother, Abe, has a great band. It's like indie jazz rock. Like Dave Matthews."

"I love Dave Matthews!" I said, wincing a bit inside as I thought of Blue Eyes. "And I also play music."

"You should definitely meet them," Mina said as she pulled down an award that had decorated the now bare shelf by her mirror. "Actually, they host a Saturday night Bible study in their house. Did you find a church here yet?"

I shook my head. "I haven't even found a regular grocery store yet," I said.

"This Bible study has sort of taken the place of church for me,"

Mina said. "I just feel so close and connected to everyone. Coming from Catholic churches where it's very stiff and formal, this is just really different."

She paused, noticing the award in her hand that she was now wrapping in newspaper.

"I can't believe I have to start looking for another job all of a sudden," she said. Then she smirked. "Isn't it funny? I became a Christian and then my life started falling apart."

I remembered a conversation with my dad where he explained a core tenet of our faith: "Jesus never said life would be easy. In fact, His own life and death would prove that. But He did promise that He'd be with us through it all and give us peace."

I repeated this to Mina, and she smiled, closing up the cardboard.

"That is very true," she said. She took a deep breath.

A few weeks later, Mina invited me to move into the spare bedroom of her Beverly Hills apartment and help with the rent, now that she was out of work. Her auditions became fewer and fewer. She might've looked much younger than thirty, but casting directors could tell from her credits how long she'd been in the business. And Hollywood isn't kind to women once they leave their twenties. While her career was on a steady decline, I was starting to have more success, landing guest spots on shows like *Felicity* and *The Guardian*. I knew Mina was a good friend when, instead of showing any resentment toward me, she continued to be nothing but supportive and encouraging. It was the same kind of dynamic I had with Camille, whom I was still close to but didn't see very often, busy as we both were and torture as it was to deal with traffic.

Most nights we'd stay up late talking, and the only thing we talked about more than God was boys. Our mutual friend was right about Mina and me both being romantics. We went on and on about our unrequited loves. Blue Eyes was soon headed into law school (of course he was), so we didn't talk as much as we used to—though I remained his first call whenever he wanted dating advice. As I guessed, Mina's was Harker.

"Ten years isn't that big of a difference," I said. "I mean, it feels like it now, but it won't when he's thirty-five and you're forty-five."

"Well, technically I'd be forty-four."

"Yeah," I said. "It's not even a full decade."

"It's not just that," Mina said. "He just got engaged to a girl in Idaho. That's where he and his family are originally from."

Mina kept trying to push her feelings away. One evening, she announced that they were some kind of "transference"—that Harker leading her to a spiritual awakening made her feel closer to him than she actually was.

"I guess that makes sense," I said. "Still, it sucks when someone doesn't love you back. I'm sorry."

I lay in bed that night thinking about Blue Eyes, wondering if what I felt for him was similar. He had been a safe place for me for so long in the midst of trouble. Maybe it wasn't real love after all. Infatuation? For eight years? Was that possible? As I drifted off wondering what love even was, I imagined his big laugh, and it bounced around on the inside of my body. He was standing by the lake with a bare chest and wet, tan skin. He was wrapping a rope around his hand, pulling the boat into the dock. He was kissing me in Lincoln Center, awkwardly. Perfect, little white teeth bumping into mine. He was salt and oranges and family and memories in high school hallways and on Manhattan corners. He was everything I missed that gave me the feeling of home. What was I doing out here in LA? Where did I even belong?

I fell asleep to the sound of cars whooshing by on Olympic Boulevard, trying to trick my brain into thinking it was the ocean.

My cell phone kept ringing. The light was pushing through my linen curtains. I hadn't slept well, and now my phone would not stop going off. I stumbled over to it.

Mom.

"Hey, everything okay?"

"Turn on the TV," she said flatly.

"Why? What's—"

"Just turn on the TV."

Mina's small square television was in the middle of the living room in a giant oak armoire. I hit the remote and watched for a few seconds, my brain trying to make sense of the immediate chaos: Manhattan. Black smoke billowing. Sirens. People screaming. Ash everywhere. Just as I began to understand what I was seeing, an airplane flew right into the second tower.

For those next few September days I didn't leave the apartment, hardly even left my bed. Everyone I knew back in New York was safe, but I still felt incapacitating sorrow for the city I loved and the friends who'd lost loved ones. I didn't know how to move. I was stuck, unable to help, unable to connect, unsure how to grieve. New York felt like home, and I just wanted to go back.

At first, Mina gave me space. Then late that Saturday afternoon, she knocked and opened my bedroom door. I didn't realize how much I needed a breath of beauty until she leaned on my doorframe in a bedazzled blue velour Juicy Couture tracksuit while frosting her lips with something pink. Again: it was the early 2000s.

"I think it would be good for you to get out," she said.

I knew she was right. "Where?" I asked with a groan. I was in no mood to go to a club or a bar or even a movie. But that's not what Mina had in mind.

"Bible study," she said.

CHAPTER THREE

The front door of the Van Hewitt house in North Hollywood was always open on Saturday nights, though it wasn't a particularly safe neighborhood. The flat streets were easy terrain for the homeless to wander. The grocery stores and gas stations looked like they'd been plopped on bare corners, long forgotten by a kid who loved Monopoly, then grew up to be a city planner. Traffic whizzed by at all hours, and this boxy gray house was right on the main road, separated only by a small square of grass that passed for a yard in LA. I was surprised by how small the house was, considering the brothers' success. I knew Harker had an impressive list of screen credits, and Abe's band was popular enough that they were planning a small national tour, but I quickly came to appreciate its modesty. This house was the most the family could afford a decade prior when the two brothers decided to pursue acting and found enough success that their family relocated part-time from Idaho to LA. Though they'd certainly done well enough in the years since to upgrade, they were content with what they had and weren't interested in the flashiness that defined so many people in that town. And what the house lacked in size and fanciness it made up for with coziness.

This was thanks to the boys' mom, Pamela. She lived with them part-time and worked as an accountant for the boys' father and her husband, Ed. Ed was a doctor with a small private practice. He stayed in Idaho but would come down to LA on weekends or Pam would go up. Pam insisted on tidiness, so there was never a book out of place, never a rogue mug half full of tea, *always* a lit scented candle, and you absolutely had to take off your shoes before coming inside.

The family had been Seventh-day Adventists but grew disaffected with the church a couple years earlier and left. For the last year or so, they'd been hosting a Bible study group. Most of the members had met Harker and Abe through the entertainment industry. They weren't huge stars, but, like Mina, who every now and then got autograph requests on the street from tourists, they were recognizable enough that they might not feel comfortable being vulnerable in a normal church setting.

That first evening and the next couple months of Saturday meetings all unfolded the same way. It started with Pam hugging each person as they came through the door. She smelled the way I remembered the inside of my mother's lingerie drawer; like perfume and silk and sweat and those little bags of dried flowers, all resting neatly inside an oak chest. It was a drawer I secretly opened when Mom was at work, touching all the delicate fabrics, trying to understand more about being a woman. Or maybe I was trying to experience her warmth without the risk of her wrath. Now, tucked into Pam's neck, her unabashed maternal affection was a comfort I desperately needed.

This hug was followed by eight more with the rest of the people in the room, because nothing could begin until everyone had been hugged. By everyone. We hugged hello and goodbye and even for no reason at all. There was LOTS of hugging. Being an introvert, this was a hurdle for me, but what else was I gonna do? *Hi, one hug tonight is good enough for me. Pull straws on who gets to be the lucky winner. Or we can all just wave. Wanna wave?*

We'd mingle for a bit, then Abe started strumming his guitar, which was the signal for everyone to take a seat wherever they could find one. This cue I was familiar with. The evangelical Bible study format was the same everywhere, including at my South African pastors' small New York church and my anti–soap opera church in Jersey: arrive, sing, read, talk, pray, go home.

At the Van Hewitts' I usually snuggled into the L-shaped couch but ended up on the floor if I was late. We sang a few worship songs as a type of meditation: a way to focus on God and shut out the inner noise of distractions or stress. I didn't realize how much I'd missed singing until I sat down to worship with this group. Then Abe would open up his well-worn Bible to read.

His voice was calming. You know when you're in a room with harsh overhead lighting for hours on end and you can't figure out why you have a headache, then someone turns on a low lamp and your whole body relaxes? Abe was like the low lamp. You almost don't notice it's there, but when it shows up, you realize how much you needed it. I thought of Dad again and his bedtime story about how God is a light, which immediately endeared Abe to me in friendship. He had a sweet face that matched his inviting presence— his heavy brows perpetually raised over sympathetic green eyes— handsome, even, but often overshadowed by his brother.

Harker was born with the kind of symmetry and contours that could only ever have been destined to be plastered on billboards. Bafflingly, he also displayed a complete lack of vanity—the rare kind of person who walks by a storefront window and isn't tempted to glance at their reflection. Both brothers were pale like their father, only Ed was shorter. And neither Harker nor Abe put much effort into their wardrobe. I expected successful young artists to be buried in striped designer scarves and leather bracelets, but they were happy in Kmart t-shirts and thrift store denim. There was just no guile in the Van Hewitt boys. I trusted them implicitly.

Abe would finish reading, and then Harker might have some comments, and pretty soon we were all in a free-flowing conversation, challenging or encouraging each other. And when the discourse felt like it was coming to a natural end, usually Ed—when he was in town—would lead a closing prayer, his head involuntarily bobbing as he did. Then, after an hour or so, we'd leave—still with more hugging on the way out.

It was such a highlight in my week that I invited Camille, who'd also been missing the camaraderie we had in New York. Camille and Mina hadn't crossed paths yet, though they'd each been hearing me gush about the other for months. They got along just as I knew they would, quickly bonding over being raised Catholic. The three of us, along with the rest of the group—which was small, about fifteen people—were having such meaningful, close interactions during those Saturday evenings that it became very easy to fall in step with each other the rest of the week: lunches, running errands, movie nights, phone calls in which we'd pray with each other before a meeting or audition. It was a lot like life with my church friends in New York.

That's how it went the first six months or so. Until the night everything changed.

Mina and I were the last to arrive that Saturday. She opened the door ahead of me, and by the time I stepped inside she was already hugging Emily, a tall blonde shot of dopamine who had grown up with the Van Hewitts in Idaho. After her parents divorced she moved to LA with her mother and was now working as a newly promoted talent manager for a big agency. Emily had become one of those "ones to watch" in Hollywood. She hugged me next as my name soared over the chatter.

"Joy!"

This was always the greeting sent to me across the room by Pam, whose voice was in a permanent state of lilt. She came toward me with a little skip, then pounced with a squeezing hug. "We're *so* glad you're herrrre."

Camille hugged me next. Then Ed, who was in town for the weekend from Idaho. And then I smelled something coming from the kitchen, which was strange because the Van Hewitts never cooked. The fact that they had a stove was comical. For their entire lives they had subsisted on the strict Seventh-day Adventist vegan diet. Now that they were fumbling their way out of that, their parquet cupboards were stocked with Nutrisystem bars and "rehydrate me" boxes of TV dinners.

"Who's cooking?" I asked.

"Oh, gosh," Ed said, bouncing on his toes. "Our friends Les and Marti are here! Come on, I'll introduce you."

Whatever was cooking had a meaty base and a too-sweet scent that sat behind my nose where the leftover flavor hangs after you finish vomiting. We turned the corner into the kitchen, and I smashed into twin boys, I guessed thirteen, wrestling each other for a Nerf gun. The Barbarians kept running without an apology. I looked up to see several pans spitting on the stove and three new people in the room.

"Guys, this is Joy," Ed said. "She's another one of our precious daughters here."

"Precious daughter" had become a moniker for the young women in the group. I took it as a symbolic gesture of care. "Brothers and sisters in Christ" was a pretty normal phrase in the Christian community, so the idea of "spiritual parents" didn't seem like a stretch.

I was greeted with two identically sheepish smiles from a

slender middle-aged woman and an equally lanky boy of about seventeen. I guessed they were mother and son and that the two Barbarians were hers as well. They stood over the sink with impeccable posture above matching long legs, with twin heads of coarse brown hair and almond black eyes like mounted taxidermy doe heads. She washed the dishes and he dried. They both stood so close together it was almost as if their silhouettes were of a single person. But it didn't seem uncomfortable or unnatural. Only as if they always tried to take up as little space as possible. The woman opened her mouth. A sound resembling "hi" might have squeaked through, but it was drowned out by the room din and running water. The quiet boy waved.

Thank God, someone who waves.

I thought nothing else of them except that I should not like to have been born with those faces, since all the bones seemed to be ever so slightly in the wrong position, but they came off as nice enough people, and I instantly felt awful for having the thought.

Behind them, at the small breakfast table, stood a short red-faced man in his late forties with hair everywhere except the top of his head. His stomach ballooned forward under apish arms, which were hovering above a Pyrex dish as he massaged salt into a large flop of pink meat. There was something intimate and grotesque about watching his hairy fingers dig into the wet mass. I must have been staring.

"Gotta give it a little love before you beat it into submission!" He laughed jovially, wiping the back of his hand across a sweaty forehead. A steel meat mallet sat nearby, waiting its turn. "This barbecue recipe's been in my family for years. You're gonna love it."

"Great! Love barbecue!" I said, suddenly imagining every brisket I'd ever eaten having man hands all over it before it hit my mouth.

"I'd shake your hand, but . . ."

I laughed. "You're good."

"What was your name again?"

"Joy."

"Hi, Joy. I'm Les. This is my wife, Martine, and my sons . . ." He kept talking, but the stench of whatever was simmering on the stove was really starting to get to me. I heard the familiar strum of Abe's guitar begin and everyone quieting down in the living room behind me.

That night's Bible passage was Ephesians 2:8–9: "For it is by grace you have been saved, through faith—and this is not from yourselves, it is the gift of God—not by works, so that no one can boast."

When Abe finished reading, Harker said, "When Abe and I were praying about this passage, it felt like the Lord was reminding us how often we tie up our value in the things we do—even the things we do for God. Almost as if we're trying to impress Him." Harker spoke gently and naturally, as he always did. "But that's the whole point of grace. He's already done it all."

Abe chimed in. "I feel like . . . I think I'm being humble by making all these sacrifices and performing good deeds or whatever, but that's actually pride to think that I could ever *do* enough to earn God's love or favor."

As they continued on, Les made his way into the living room, walking on the carpet with his shoes. There wasn't an empty chair, so Ed scooted onto the floor and offered Les his wooden dining room chair, which Les gratefully accepted.

"Not to shift the topic," Harker said, "but I want to make sure you guys have all met Les and Marti and their boys. We know them from Idaho. They were able to come down and visit this week. They've been going through a lot of transition, and . . .

well, Les, do you wanna talk a bit about that? I don't mean to put you on the spot."

Harker smiled, and somewhere a slot machine hit WIN.

"Ah, sure!" Les chuckled uncomfortably. He shifted his weight in the chair that I feared might buckle underneath him. The Barbarians were tuned out at the kitchen table, drawing on a piece of paper. Quiet Boy was on another chair beside Les, and Martine was at Les's feet with her long legs tucked sideways like a pinup girl.

"Well, I've been the pastor of a small church in Washington for the last few years up near the Idaho border, where the Van Hewitts are from, and a few months ago Harker got ahold of a tape recording of one of my sermons, and the Lord just really spoke to him through it. So Pam and Ed came to visit our church and became more connected with the community we built there. And I've been talking with these guys a lot lately about transition because, ah . . ."

His voice grew sad.

"Unfortunately, we're just having to walk through some really tough stuff right now. We're seeing our beautiful church community get taken advantage of by the enemy." (Another Christianese term for Satan.) "We really started to see the Holy Spirit move in mighty ways, and there were just a lot of people in the congregation who weren't ready to grow. They didn't like the discomfort that comes from growing and healing. And it's just really unfortunate to watch it falling apart, but growth is hard for a lot of people. It takes an immense amount of courage to grow, and not everyone is cut out for that."

Martine was looking at the floor, eyebrows raised, lips tight, nodding in agreement. Quiet Boy stared straight ahead, motionless.

"So, sadly, we're in the process of moving out of our home—

the ministry home the church gave us where my kids have grown up. Well, since we left New York."

Sighs of empathetic disappointment echoed around the room. "You're from New York?" I asked, lighting up.

"Mm-hmm, right before we moved to Washington."

"No way, I just moved from there. I'm so heartbroken right now."

"Yeah, us too. Awful. I mean, honestly, between that and all the heaviness from leaving the church, we really needed a break. So, it was awesome when Ed suggested we come to California for a little sun and I could meet all you guys."

Ed interrupted: "Oh, that was Harker's idea, from his generous heart. We can't take credit."

"Okay, well, you'll have to let me give you credit for your *own* generosity," Les said, "because you guys have just blown us away." Then addressing the group: "Pam and Ed have offered their beautiful home in Idaho to me and my family for a year, to live there while we recalibrate and heal and just see what God has next for us."

"So, you'll be moving to LA full-time?" Camille asked Ed.

"No," Ed said. "I'll still be going back and forth, but Pam and I will move into the apartment above the garage and give Les and his family the house."

"Oh, wows" and "Amazings!" reverberated as everyone looked at Pam and Ed. Ed ignored the attention but turned up the corners of his mouth. Pam tucked her neck into her shoulders and grinned impishly.

"So, we're just so thankful and love hearing about the amazing things God is doing here with you guys in Hollywood," Les said, "and we look forward to praying for you and encouraging you however we can."

Les looked at me, briefly, with a smile of humble hope.

I felt awful for the way I'd misjudged him. Here was this sweet pastor, doing his best to get a congregation out of the rigid mindset of structure and religion, getting persecuted, having his family kicked out of their home, and I was wrinkling up my nose at him because of his appearance and whatever was in that pot on the stove. I felt so pretentious.

See, Joy. You never know what someone is going through. Thank God for people like him. I don't ever want to be too afraid to grow. The world is falling apart more and more every moment. I will not waste time in fear. I threw up a prayer: *God, don't ever let me be too afraid to grow.*

Despite that vow, though, I wasn't about to eat whatever Les had cooked. So, I made up an excuse to leave early. As I was putting on my shoes, Les approached me.

"So you're a New Yorker, huh? What are you doing out here?"

"I'm an actor. Like everyone else."

"Had any luck?"

"Well, I was on a soap opera for a couple years in New York, and I've been doing a few guest spots on some good shows out here."

"I'd say that counts as luck. That sounds like a huge blessing, too—you must've made enough money on the soap to come out here and just audition for a living!"

It was weird to talk about money with a stranger, but he was so friendly and unabashedly direct that it almost felt like a challenge. Like, *Are you mature enough to handle an adult conversation about money?*

"It wasn't bad," I said, keeping it vague. "But not as good as movies and prime-time television, which is why I moved out here."

"Where is your family?"

"Mom is in San Diego, Dad is in New Jersey."

"Ah. How old were you when they split? Or is it an Ed and Pam kind of situation?"

"No, they divorced when I was sixteen."

"Tough age."

Strangely, I felt a familiar feeling arise—the same refusal to be high-maintenance that Blue Eyes had always elicited.

"It was okay," I said. "I knew they were miserable, so it was honestly better."

"Did you grow up in church?"

"I did. Different ones depending on where we were."

"Oh, did you move a lot?"

"All the time. Probably always destined to be an actor or musician—or in the circus! You know, always on the road." I smiled.

"What church did you go to in New York?" he asked.

"A small home church—you wouldn't have heard of it. But I visited Redeemer Pres. a lot on the Upper East. Tim Keller is brilliant. I wish I'd have gone more regularly."

"No way! I used to pastor with him before we left New York."

"You did!?"

"I'm surprised our paths didn't cross!"

I couldn't believe it. He used to work alongside the man who had been instrumental in my growing faith. It was like God was sending me a confirmation that I was on the right track. I immediately thought this was someone I could trust.

"Well," I said, "I hope to see you again soon."

"Yes, Joy," Les said. "You definitely will."

CHAPTER FOUR

"Hand me the hoisin sauce," Les said over his shoulder to Camille, who was standing by the pantry when Mina and I walked into the Van Hewitt house. Les was in town again, and cooking again. "Peking duck was my favorite when I was in Japan."

"When did you go to Japan?" I asked while he leaned over to give me a half hug with his free hand.

"With the marines."

"Oorah!" Abe said playfully, pulling a naked, dried bird out of the fridge.

Les pulled the sleeve of his t-shirt up to reveal a terrible tattoo of a ship, an eagle, and a rifle all smashed together over SEMPER FI.

"How long did you serve?" Mina asked.

"Six years," Les said as he began painting sauce onto the wilted creature. "I was the best sniper in the unit. So good, in fact, that they asked me to train the whole platoon when I was only a private first class. Sergeants, too!"

Emily hugged me, then kept her face inches from mine, towering over me with her giant smile and happy, wide eyes. "How'd it go? Are you a cheerleader?"

Earlier that day I had a screen test for the cheerleading movie sequel *Bring It On Again*.

"I hope so!" I said. "I think it went well."

I'd been continuing to work steadily, picking up a Coke commercial, guest spots on various sitcoms, and screen-testing frequently. I even booked a few theatre gigs, which made me so happy because LA is not exactly known for its theatre. Nevertheless, I found myself in Arthur Allan Seidelman's new musical production of *The Outsiders*, alongside a group of talented actors including Allison Munn, who—in the familiar happenstance of Hollywood—had a recurring role on *That '70s Show*. (It wasn't the last time we'd work together.) And then, the coolest job of all—playing Pinky Tuscadero in *Happy Days: A New Musical* under the direction of Garry Marshall and the musical direction of Carole King and Paul Williams (who composed many songs for the Carpenters). It was an unbelievable opportunity and all this combined felt like confirmation that making the move to LA was the right thing to do. Plus, this new group of friends was further solidifying my place here with every week that passed. Even Les was starting to feel like a fixture in our midst. He still lived in Idaho, and while Marti, the Quiet Boy, and the Barbarians rarely visited, Les had been coming to the Van Hewitts' so often that he'd adopted the same high-back chair on every visit. Because he was older and was an actual pastor, we felt grateful for his presence there. We were honored that this church leader with such wisdom and experience chose to consort with a bunch of random young artists in LA. None of us noticed that he was gradually taking over Harker's and Abe's de facto roles as leaders of these meetings. Not even Harker or Abe seemed to notice. Or if they did, they didn't object when Les began reading the Scripture and kicking off the discussion.

Later that night, after preaching on Isaiah 43:25 and forgiveness, he leaned forward in his chair, fingertips steepled, his voice casual and inviting. "No one needs people pointing out where they're failing because they already know," he said. "You know what your problems are! Jesus already dealt with those things about us. Think about how you'd feel if you forgave someone you love for hurting you, but they could never let it go. Imagine if every time Marti hurt me she told herself that was part of her identity now. I've forgiven her! It's not even on my mind anymore! But every time she looks in the mirror she only sees all the ways she's failed. Would that make our relationship stronger or weaker?"

"Yeah," "mmm," and "wow" cascaded in various tones throughout the room.

"This is how it is with God," Les continued. "We have to let God's forgiveness change the way we see ourselves into seeing the truth of who we *really* are as loved and forgiven. This also means we get to speak that truth over each other."

"So, Les," Pam said, "how does that look on a practical basis in relationship? Because if the old has gone and the new has come"—quoting Scripture was part of Pam's casual vernacular—"how do we still address the rough edges in each other that need to be smoothed for the sake of authentic relationship?"

"Relationship" was another buzzword, like "precious daughter" and "enemy." Relationship was everything religion wasn't and everything we all wanted.

Les answered: "You choose to speak the positive truth of someone's identity, no matter how they're behaving."

Emily piped in. "Okay, so, like, my brother is always . . . pretty negative. Like, it's to the point where I can't really spend much time with him or even on the phone with him, because he just doesn't even want to be encouraged or feel better. So, wouldn't it be important for *the sake of our relationship* for me to tell him the truth? I mean, it's not a pleasant thing to hear, but I feel like if his sister can't tell him, I don't know who else will."

"Well." Les cleared his throat. "You just said 'tell him the truth,' but . . . what is the truth? That's a great example, Emily, because is the truth that he is a negative person? Or is that just how he behaves because of the stories he tells himself?"

Emily furrowed her brow, considering this.

Les continued: "What I would say is instead of pointing out to him what he already knows—"

"But does he?" Camille interrupted, looking at Emily.

Les flashed a smile with slight irritation in it. Camille didn't seem to notice.

"I know some people like this, too, and I'm not sure they actually are aware. I don't know if *I'm* aware of all my own flaws."

"Well, let me finish," Les said, then bypassed Camille and turned to Emily. "Instead of pointing out to him what he *most likely* already knows about himself, because he lives in that negative self-talk every day, you could say, 'Bro, I just want to let you know that I love talking with you. You're such a force of positivity in this world.'"

"I like that," Pam said. "It's so kind to be willing to look past the way a person is behaving and, instead, call them to rise up into the person God made them to be. And, Em, I watched you two grow up. I would say your brother knows what his own flaws are."

"But is it kind of—" I cut myself off. After seeing Les's irritated smile, I suddenly was more conscious of not interrupting, but now everyone was looking at me. "I mean, it feels a little condescending or passive aggressive, maybe . . . I don't know."

Les had gray eyes. That was the first time I noticed because, for the first time, they were focused solely on me. "It's only passive aggressive if you don't believe it to be true," he said. Then those gray eyes moved around the room and his voice rose slightly. His passion was inviting and rousing. "Don't let people get away with seeing themselves as anything less than utterly loved and adored by God. *That's* our job as believers: to sacrifice living our own fleshly reactions to someone's false self." He looked at me again. "We have to stop being selfish."

Is he . . . talking to me? No, he's just answering the question. Good Lord, the irony! I'm so focused on myself that I think I'm being singled out.

The rest of the room was silent, processing. I suddenly was aware that, aside from the Van Hewitt boys, Ed, and Les, the rest of us were women. Girls, really.

Harker began quoting Bible passages: "'Therefore each of you must put off falsehood and speak truthfully to your neighbor, for we are all members of one body.' That's Ephesians 4:25. Proverbs 12:17: 'Whoever speaks the truth gives honest evidence, but a false witness utters deceit.' Also Proverbs 4:25. And Zechariah 8:16. There are so many references in the Bible to using your physical voice to speak truth." Then he muttered to himself, "Tolstoy said something on this . . ." before standing up and going to the living room bookshelf.

As he searched, Les went on: "Sharing the truth takes courage and sometimes self-control, like in your case with your brother, Emily. Don't get mad at him; love the negativity out of him!" He was *so* engaging. He made this dialogue fun. "Now . . . I'll let you in on the real secret sauce—you ready for this?" Les smiled. "It works both ways."

He paused, waiting for some kind of acknowledgment, an "ohh" or "aha," but it didn't come.

Abe eventually spoke: "What does that mean?"

"It's not just about what *you* speak out. You can choose what you 'receive' being said to you! Don't allow someone to lie about *your* identity. If someone wants to label you against the loving truth of who you are, you are empowered to make the declaration

'I don't receive that.' It doesn't matter who they are—a stranger, a parent—don't accept it!"

"Okay, Dostoyevsky said, 'To love someone is to see them as God intended them,'" Harker added from across the room. "Exactly what you're saying, Les. But this is the quote I was thinking of, on truth." He flipped through Tolstoy's *Wise Thoughts for Every Day*. The pages were marked and highlighted. It reminded me of my dad's old Bible. Harker read aloud. "'Every lie is a poison; there are no harmless lies. Only the truth is safe. Only truth is so firm that I can rely on it. Only truth gives me consolation—it is the one unbreakable diamond.'"

"Love that, Harker."

I noticed Mina, beside me on the couch, becoming increasingly emotional. Her face was flushed, and she was breathing long and slow. I felt bad for her. After spending so much time with Harker these past few months, what had started out as an improbable infatuation had developed into a much more serious thing. "I think I'm falling in love with him," she confided to me on the night Harker announced that he and his fiancée had set a wedding date, and the girl was coming to visit soon. Mina spent the rest of that night with her head over the toilet. Since losing her job, acting work had continued to be nonexistent. She had no family here, and now this group that was her safe place was becoming her biggest pain point. Here she was, trying to focus on her relationship with God, but instead she was holding back tears because just the sound of Harker's voice ripped her open with longing.

I reached over and tucked my hand under her ankle to give her a little *you're not alone* squeeze. Her hand found mine, and it was nice to sit like that for a while. I wondered if that's what it felt like to have a sister.

Les's voice brought me back as I realized everyone was already praying.

"Father God," he said, "we just ask you this week to help us speak only the loving truth over the people in our lives. Our friends and family, the people we work with. Lord, that we just won't dwell on the negative and will, instead, see people the way you see them: already forgiven and free in Christ."

"Yes, Lord," we echoed in sincerity.

Les went on. "Guys, if you would just stretch your hands out to Joy."

Oh no, what did I do wrong?

"Joy," he said, "as we're talking about our true identities, I want to put this into practice—can I just share with you who I see you as?"

I felt unbearably awkward. "Sure, yeah," I said.

"I'm envisioning you in a pawn shop, and I just feel like you've been telling yourself for a long time that you're second best."

The room ricocheted with "mmms." A lump formed in my throat.

"God sees how hard you're trying to do the right things and grow into a good woman. But He wants you to love Him with abandon, like a little girl does, because the woman in you will be strengthened by the little girl. You are precious and beautiful to God. You are His little princess. You're gold! You're not *almost* there, you *are* there. You are not second place."

The air was thick. The lump in my throat burned. I felt like all my blood was in my face, pushing out an unstoppable stream of tears. I was so hungry for these words to be true. The Lenz family was broke, we struggled, things always went wrong, good things didn't happen to us. I was always playing catch-up, I was always *almost* getting the great job, I was always the runner-up, the best friend, the one who got left behind.

His words hit my core wound with surgical precision.

How did he know? *How did he know?*

I was overwhelmed. I'd never been told anything like this in all my church life.

"Joy, it's time for you to come out of agreement with the idea that you're runner-up and release the spirit of performance-for-love."

Les's nonchalant tone somehow made it all feel so normal. Like it was safe to believe because it wasn't a big deal. *Just readjusting my perspective. Easy. Relief!* "Yes" and "Thank you, Jesus" floated into the air around the room.

Les put his hand on my shoulder and it felt comforting. "You don't need to do anything to earn your place here. Not with God and not with us."

I broke. The sharp exhales and gasps of a choking sob over-took my body. *Ugh, this is humiliating to be so weak,* I thought. All these people were watching me cry. Not just cry. They were watching me need. Needy was the one thing I absolutely refused to be. Ever. I made sure of that with Blue Eyes. I would not be a burden to anyone. But then a colossal wave of relief hit. They saw me need . . . and still loved me.

Pam wiped away my tears with a tissue and the tenderness I'd always wished for and missed from my mom. "You're so precious, Joy. We love you."

Emily reached over to me and said, "Love you, sis."

"Yes, we love you, sis," said Mina.

That night I released a burden I'd been carrying forever, one that had compounded day after day, month after month, year after year. For the first time in my life, I didn't have to put on a show to have a place in the world. I cleaned myself up in the bathroom, and we all piled into the kitchen to eat. The food smelled just as gross as the first time, but I didn't care. I wasn't about to leave early. I wasn't about to miss a second of this unconditional love.

CHAPTER FIVE

"What do you mean you're asking God what you should wear before you get dressed in the morning?" Dad asked over the phone one evening.

"Dad, I think God cares about every single detail of our lives. I'm asking God for guidance on everything: what auditions to go on, what friends to hang out with at what times, what movie to go see, even my outfit choices. I just think if I'm going to be surrendered to Jesus, I need to fully surrender."

I shared this thinking he would be proud of me for my fearless abandon of selfish desires. His reaction was not as I expected.

"So . . . you think God wants to give you instruction on what clothes you wear? Didn't He give you the autonomy to make decisions like those yourself?"

"Well, think about it. Like, what if God told some stranger out there that they were going to see a girl in a purple shirt today, and that was the sign they needed? What if I'm supposed to be the girl in the purple shirt, but I never took the time to ask God what I should wear, so that person never gets to see the sign?"

Silence as he attempted to untangle that. Then he dropped his voice into a soothing tone I knew all too well. "And how long does it take you to hear from God about what you'll wear?" he asked.

This was the hostage-negotiator voice he'd learned during his post-Bible-college years as a mental health counselor. I was shaken, hearing him use this voice on me, as though I were one of those people who used to sit in his office. Intimidated. Angry. Hurt.

"I guess I get a feeling . . ."

"What kind of feeling?"

This was playing like an interrogation now.

"I don't know, like . . . something can just seem more right than something else."

"And you attribute that feeling to hearing from God?"

That phrase was so loaded for me. "Hearing from God." Every book of the Bible had people hearing from God. Every church I visited had pastors and congregants with a "word from the Lord." So, what was my problem? Just as Les had said, I already knew what my problem was. I wasn't dedicated enough. I didn't pray like I should. Not the way Abe and Harker did. They were always studying, discussing, learning, teaching. I just wanted to write and sing and sew and paint and do anything romantic and creative. No wonder I couldn't hear God. I could never sit still long enough for Him to talk to me!

Well, that was all going to change, I'd decided. I was serious, and now I had accountability and comrades to help, even if it meant standing up to my dad, whom I was terrified to disappoint.

"Joy, where are you getting this stuff?"

"What do you mean?"

"Who—" He stopped himself. Then: "Where did you say you were going to church again?"

"It's a home Bible study. Same as all the others we went to when I was a kid."

"But what church is it affiliated with?"

"It's not. It's just friends worshipping together."

"But who is leading it, what curriculum are you using?"

I was exasperated. "No one! I mean, there are two brothers

who are artists that started it. And there's an older pastor. But it's, like, just a group of friends. I mean, weren't Jesus's disciples just a group of friends?"

"That was a very specific time in history," Dad said. "And the leader—the rabbi of that group—was literally Jesus."

"Dad, I just want to do things the right way, and I'm seeking God's wisdom in everything I do."

He sighed. "Well, that's . . . good, honey. But I just think you should be careful that you're not over-spiritualizing things. Yes, God is mysterious, but I'm pretty sure He's more concerned about your character development than making sure you're in the right purple shirt."

I couldn't believe he didn't understand. I wasn't surprised that my mom was getting suspicious, because anything that took me away from visiting her more often *had* to be a threat. But it made me so sad that my father, who was so adventurous that his title at work was literally "adventure course director," couldn't be excited about the spiritual adventure I was on. I had made friends who loved the same God he taught me to love, and we were all seeking the kind of great, wild faith he experienced in his teens and twenties. Had his faith really fallen so far just because life got hard? Where was his endurance, his long-suffering, his fire? Where was *his* character development? This was the first time I felt like maybe I understood something about God better than my dad did.

That Saturday night, on the way to the Van Hewitt house, I watched LA fly by from the passenger seat of Mina's little black BMW, the last vestige of proof she had that she was once a success in this town.

"It's so crazy how every time I try to share with my parents what I'm learning and how I'm growing with the Lord right now, they're so resistant!"

"I agreeeee, Joie." Mina said nothing without passion. Even a mediocre espresso evoked animated apathy. "I want to start breaking these generational curses. This behavior that's been passed down over and over. I'm just *done* with it. I'm done with the enemy trying to sabotage our future."

"Right!?"

"Mm-hmm!"

"They just want to stay in their rut, in their safe zone!" I continued. "Even the boundaries I put up, like when my mom speaks something negative over me that isn't the truth of who I am, I say, 'Mom, I just don't receive that,' and she gets so offended. It's like she can't even grasp the concept of doing things differently for the sake of growing and being better."

Mina nodded. "I know. It just makes me so grateful that the Lord is revealing this stuff to us now, while we're young enough to change course. And I just want to be so, so aware of every choice I'm making so I don't fall back into *my* old family habits, too."

When we arrived at the house, Les was there, plus the Barbarians. His face lit up when he saw me, and he gave me the obligatory hug. Somehow he could tell I was a little melancholy. When he asked what was wrong, I explained to him the conversation that had transpired earlier with my dad. He put a sympathetic hand on my shoulder.

"Some people just don't have spiritual ears to hear," he said. "Especially people stuck in a certain religious routine with God. It's hard to see people you love resist the movements of the Holy Spirit. I'm proud of you, baby girl. It takes a lot of courage at your age to stick to your guns. I actually think it's pretty cool that you're willing to surrender your most basic choices to God's will. God's gonna honor that."

He added: "And we just get to pray for your dad."

I didn't notice that in all my protection over the "truth" of my identity, I wasn't practicing (nor was I encouraged to practice) speaking loving truth toward my own family. I guess it really *didn't* work both ways.

CHAPTER SIX

A couple weeks later, Dad came out to visit me in LA for a long weekend, claiming he had frequent flier miles he had to use before they expired. I had an audition at the time his flight landed, so Camille kindly volunteered to pick him up from the airport. "Knock, knock!" she said, coming into our apartment. "I have a delivery!" I turned the corner and saw my dad step in the front door behind Camille. Hair thinning and pulled back into a ponytail under his baseball cap, beaded cross necklace and sandals, duffel bag slung over his shoulder: he was still a hippie. We hugged. I was a hugger now.

Camille stayed for lunch, and Dad eventually directed the conversation to our Bible study. I suspected that was the real reason for the visit, not his refusal to squander a hard-earned freebie from Delta. I could tell he was concerned and fishing for information, only I didn't know what there was to be concerned about. "Dad, why don't you just come with me tomorrow night?"

"Yes, you should come!" Camille agreed.

"Oh, is it open to visitors?"

"Of course!" I said. "You're my dad! People bring visitors all the time." This wasn't entirely true. There used to be visitors, but the more emotionally intimate the evenings had become, the less at ease everyone seemed to be by the presence of an outsider. By now a new visitor was rare. Regardless, I was determined to prove to my dad that our little group was onto something good.

The weekend my dad visited the Bible study, Les was back in Idaho. Something about his presence had become so integral to the emotional highs we normally experienced on Saturday nights that it just wasn't quite the same without him there. The evening went on as planned: song, Bible reading, discussion, prayer, but nothing profound. From how much I'd hyped it up, I could tell Dad was a bit underwhelmed. "The music was nice" was all he said afterward. He also thought it was a bit strange how everyone ignored him.

"I can understand the kids your age," he said. "I guess it's awkward being around someone's parent when you're still a young adult. But the mom, what's her name?"

"Pam?"

"Right." Then the inhale and head tilt he'd been doing since I was a child. A gesture not only reserved for being pleased. "Is she always so standoffish?"

I had noticed her lack of engagement but gave her credit for being preoccupied. "She's just a neat freak," I said. "I hadn't told her you were coming ahead of time, and I'm sure she was just stressed out and self-conscious, wishing the house had been cleaner for you."

Overall, the evening seemed to allay Dad's concern about the group. He didn't bring it up anymore during the trip. Instead, he turned his focus on encouraging me to be in touch with my mom more regularly. They talked to each other once or twice a month—mostly, I knew, to compare notes on my life progress. I appreciated that they had found a way after the divorce to be friendly and stay connected. When I mentioned this to Dad, he wouldn't accept the credit.

"That's all your mother," he said. "She pushed to make that happen so you didn't feel like the family was so broken up. I'm glad she did. You know me"—he shook his head—"stubborn."

This information surprised me and made me consider that I might have gotten some things wrong about Mom. So, I decided to take my dad's advice and try to connect with her more—starting with an invitation to my twenty-first birthday party.

Having grown up feeling socially isolated, I loved any chance I got to bring people together and host. Hospitality was a skill I didn't realize I had until I was out on my own. I had a subscription to *Martha Stewart Living* and loved setting a mood or creating an environment where people could gather. For my party, held in our apartment's courtyard, I'd rented a long table for the guests, ordered catering from a favorite local French café, and even had a champagne fountain delivered.

As Mina helped me string up lights, she was uncharacteristically clumsy and distracted. She finally sat down in a folding chair at the rented table and collapsed her head into her hands, elbows on the white tablecloth.

"I think Harker is bringing his fiancée tonight," she said.

"Ohhh, that's right. I heard she was coming to visit. I'm sorry, Mina."

"I just keep praying God will take away these feelings! Nothing's ever gonna happen, so why can't I let it go? He's all I think about."

I didn't want to give her false hope, but I *was* a romantic, and I hated seeing her in pain. "Mina, I don't think it's that crazy to think something might happen between you guys. People break off engagements all the time."

She sniffed and swallowed, then gave a little laugh. "I guess that's true."

"Now, come on, let's fill this thing with champagne!"

An hour later, the bubbles were flowing, the food was hot, and my "dinner party" mix CD was playing. I'd included some Serge Gainsbourg and a song or two from Abe's band. I had thought about including some Dave Matthews, but I didn't want to be reminded of Blue Eyes. He hadn't called yet to wish me a happy birthday, and with him being two hours ahead, I was starting to give up hope. I'd been trying to distract myself over the last couple years since that Lincoln Center kiss—developing crushes on cute costars, dating a few guys here and there—but when it came to falling in love, I could never allow myself because of the unshakable belief I held that Blue Eyes was "the one." Not hearing from him was a glaring reminder of the truth: we had both been building new lives, and I wasn't his first call anymore.

The evidence of my new life began arriving through the courtyard gates. There was Camille and several other people I knew from New York who had also made the coastal move, a couple of LA soap actors and costars from recent acting gigs, and friends from my old florist job. And then there was the Bible study contingent: Pam and Ed, Emily, Abe and Harker (who was unaccompanied by his fiancée). This was the first time I'd brought together my Bible study friends with my non–Bible study friends. They all seemed to be getting along and mingling well, but having them all in one place made it easier to see the disparity between the two communities I had begun to cultivate. I could clearly distinguish how much more close, safe, and known I felt with my Bible study crew than with anyone else. I could also distinguish them because, except for Camille, none of them drank. I knew they weren't partiers, but not even a sip for my twenty-first birthday? *So much for the champagne fountain.*

At least my mom and stepdad enjoyed the bubbles. She was happy to have been invited, enjoying herself, not hanging off to the side or sitting by herself at the table but circulating through the crowd and smiling and laughing. That is, until she began talking to Pam. I was on the opposite side of the courtyard, but as their conversation unfolded, I watched Mom's smile fade and her eyes narrow into a look of skepticism and suspicion.

I made my way through the crowd so that I could defuse any hostility. As I did, I passed by my stepdad, who was talking to Harker.

"I hear you're engaged!" my stepdad said. "Congratulations, young man!"

"Ah . . . actually, that is not . . . currently . . . We decided to go our separate ways."

What? Had Mina heard yet? I would've rushed to find her, but she'd have to wait. Getting to my mom and Pam was the priority.

When I finally reached them, the look on my mother's face told me she was "tolerating" whatever Pam was saying to her. I arrived just in time to hear Pam finishing her thought.

". . . and sometimes as parents we get so wrapped up in our own problems we just lose the ability to tend to our kids' emotional needs." She smiled at me and pet my hair. "Hi, sweetheart. We were just talking about how amazingly resilient you are, considering how much your parents struggled."

Whatever my mom isn't, one thing she is, unarguably, is very smart. Her lips spread into a polite closed smile. Then I saw the blink that always happens before she inhales and says something brilliantly/devastatingly cutting. She opened her mouth.

"Wow, diving right in, huh?" I jumped in, trying to boost the levity.

"She's so impressive," Pam said to Mom. "So independent, so young! I'd never have been as brave when I was her age. You must be very proud!"

Independence was another topic Les had hit on recently, and specifically he told me mine had created an internal rebellion against God. "You probably felt neglected as a child, so I can see why you're always trying to control things rather than letting God take care of you," he said, and Pam had agreed. It was a harsh message, but so much of it felt accurate, and I didn't want to be too proud to accept good advice.

Listening to Pam now, I knew her comment to my mother carried those layers. And by the look on Mom's face, she knew it, too.

In a surprising act of self-control, Mom reached over and pulled me toward herself. Pam's hand fell off my back.

"Oh, I'm sooooo proud of my little girl," Mom said. "Well, not little girl. You're officially twenty-one!" She wrinkled her nose and squeezed me too tight—really laying it on for Pam. "I have your present. Are you ready?"

"Do I have to be *ready*?"

"Well, it's something all your friends will enjoy."

That scared me. "Okayyy."

She found a fork and tapped it against her champagne glass, causing people to quiet down. "All right, everyone," she called. "I have a special gift for Joy!"

The courtyard fell completely silent. Mom turned to me.

"I'm so proud of you," she said. "You've worked hard for so long to get to Hollywood, and I know there are big things in store for you. It's taken a long time, but I was finally able to assemble all of your great memories into one place."

She handed me a thick scrapbook with a pink ribbon around it. "Ta-da!"

I excitedly slid the ribbon off and opened it. My mom knew from my days at Grandma Doris's how much I loved a good scrapbook. It started off strong. Baby photos with a Crayola ocean and paper palm trees glued to the page stared back at me. Childhood photos of me singing were cut and pasted onto a flat cardboard stage. But then I turned the page, and there I was at age five, standing in the bathtub completely naked. I took a sharp breath, embarrassed. *I'm supposed to pass this around for my friends to see exactly how I'm . . . shaped?* It got worse. A playbill with photos of me in *To Kill a Mockingbird* and *Gypsy* was followed by a page that she had torn out of my seventh-grade diary, apparently after finding and reading it. I had journaled privately about my first kiss, and now it was plastered in a scrapbook and covered with paper hearts.

I was furious. I was mortified. I was enraged. I thought of what Les had said that one Saturday at Bible study: "If someone wants to label you against the loving truth of who you are, you are empowered to make the declaration 'I don't receive that.' It doesn't matter who they are—a stranger, a parent—don't accept it!" *Here you go, Joy. What better time to make this stand? All you have to do is say it. "I don't receive that." Just say it!*

But I couldn't. Not with the way everyone was "aww"-ing. I had no choice but to display these private moments for the whole crowd to see. My mother's face was brimming with delight and eager expectation of my gratitude for all the work she'd put into it. Telling myself to think of it as an audition for the role of appreciative daughter, I smiled, gave her a big hug, and said, "Thank you!" loud enough for everyone to hear.

As half the party pored over the scrapbook, that familiar floral lingerie-drawer scent arrived as I felt Pam's hand on my back.

She squinted at me and quietly said, "You okay?"

Tears immediately sprung up, but I shoved them down. Not

tonight. Not now. I nodded, and she sensed that I didn't want to discuss it. She smiled and presented me with a little gift bag, her shoulders dancing up to her ears.

"It's just a little sumthin' to remind you to live in the truth of who you are," she said. "A patient Beauty, not striving, but resting and waiting for the King."

I laughed. I knew *exactly* what was going to be in that bag.

Disney had just released a "Princess Personality Quiz" in the special features of one of their remastered DVDs. Pam had discovered this and, tying it in with Les's words about me being "God's little princess" a few weeks prior, she thought it would be a fun way for all of us "precious daughters" to engage with the idea of our true identity as "daughters of the king," so I joined all the young women in the group and took this ridiculous quiz. My biggest theatre dream for years was to play Belle in Broadway's *Beauty and the Beast.* I knew every note from the day that damn cartoon came out, and I auditioned for the Broadway musical several times while I was still living in New York, often making it to the exclusive producer sessions only to hear they were giving the role to Toni Braxton or Debbie Gibson. Still, I knew my day to play Belle was coming, so I should have known it was a crock when this DVD quiz told me I was Sleeping Beauty. Aurora was a stupid name that was hard to say, and she didn't even do anything the whole movie except twirl around the woods and shove a giant needle into her finger. *You had ONE job, Aurora.*

I reached into the bag from Pam and . . . I was right. Under the tissue paper was an enamel Sleeping Beauty key chain. Pam must have advised everyone because later, when the party was over and I opened the rest of my gifts, I found a variety of Aurora birthday cards penned with notes about "entering into a season of rest." I also got a NAP QUEEN sweatshirt, a pink mug with nighttime tea, and a sleep mask someone bought at Disneyland. Corny as it all was, I felt more seen by this collection of stupid Disney trinkets than by my own mother's loaded scrapbook.

Mina and I cleaned up after everyone left. I suggested we leave it for the morning, but she was so exhilarated by the news of Harker's broken engagement that she wanted some way to burn off the energy. We finished a little after midnight. I checked my phone one last time. Nope. He missed it. My twenty-first birthday, and Blue Eyes missed it. I was gutted. I wanted Mina's resolve and patience. She persistently managed to stay positive in the face of her adversity. "I know this is just a season," she'd say. "God's gonna come through with something amazing. I just have to trust Him."

I wasn't even sure what "trusting God" looked like. God seemed more like a friend who just walked with me through all the mud. At least I wasn't alone, but it wasn't exactly *rescue*. I was still dealing with the same insecurities, still fending for myself like Les and Pam said, and I still felt more like a trash panda than a princess. I was getting restless. Where was this extraordinary, miraculous God we served? I needed a sign that He still showed up to do impossible, unexpected things.

Then, a few weeks after my birthday party, I came home one night to find candles lit around the apartment. A vase of beautiful flowers sat on the coffee table in front of Mina, who was curled up on the couch and glowing.

"What's up?" I said.

"Harker was just here," she said. "Joy . . . he proposed."

CHAPTER SEVEN

Six weeks later, in the wooded backyard of the Van Hewitts' big house in Idaho—where Les, Martine, and their boys had taken up residence—Les married Mina and Harker. There had been no planning. They decided on a Sunday and were married seven days later. During the ceremony, Les held the rings in his hand between them and someone photographed it—a rainbow was captured, hovering over them. It was a sign from Heaven that God was blessing them. Blessing *us*. God was doing something radical and holy and outside the bounds of our understanding.

At least that's how Mina described it to me later, when she returned from her honeymoon to empty out her side of our apartment. I hadn't actually been invited to the wedding. None of us in LA had been, except Emily, because she'd grown up with Harker. This was, according to Les, "an intimate, holy event" that only a select few could be trusted to attend. Mina's parents barely got an invitation because they'd expressed concerns over how quickly the wedding occurred and the age difference. They made the cut only thanks to Harker, who felt strongly that her parents should be honored and shown grace. However, Pam was the one who took Mina dress shopping and arranged a small bridal shower for her, while Les gave the couple premarital counseling and planned the rehearsal dinner. Everything was paid for by Ed, the only person with a steady job.

I was hurt to not be included. It was a confirmation that I was still on the outside, somehow. The only reason I could think of was my continued devotion to Blue Eyes—a signal that I still had something taking the place of God in my heart. He had called me the day after my birthday to apologize. He had been consumed with studying for a big law school exam and completely forgot. His apology sounded sincere, but we were starting to fall back into our old pattern. This was what Les had meant when he'd said I was always trying to control things rather than letting God take care of me. This had to be the thing holding me back from taking the next step in my spiritual evolution. *If I'm going to see God do big things in my life,* I thought, *I have to prove how devoted I am. I have to be braver than I've ever been.*

So one afternoon in the now half-empty apartment, I made the call. There were voices behind him when he answered, laughing. "Dude, I did *not* take your Civil Procedures book. I finished my brief, like, a week ago."

"Sorry, is this a bad time?" I asked.

"No, J. These idiots are just leaving. Hang on." The noise settled, and I heard him closer now. He sounded like he was lying on his bed, sheets muffling the echoes. I could smell him.

"So, actually there's something I wanted to, um . . ." My breath was short and my heart was pounding. "What are we doing?"

"What are we doing?"

"Like, we've been friends for so long, and then we've been more than friends, and then back to just friends, and . . ." I didn't know how to arrive where I was trying to go. I could hear his breathing change. He didn't want to have this conversation. *I* didn't want to have this conversation. *What are you doing? Why are you doing this? Say "never mind," Joy. "Never mind"!* But I was resolved. God was calling me into a wild faith, and there wasn't room for doubt or, like Les said, living like I was in second place. I was ready to throw away anything that would hinder me.

"If we're not going to get married, then I don't know what we're doing."

He didn't say anything for a long pause. I lay down on my bed, too. We were side by side in my mind.

"Married? I mean, Joy, I'm . . . I'm still in school. I'm not ready to marry *anyone*." The word stuck in his mouth like he'd never said "marry" out loud in his life.

"I don't mean right now," I said. "I'm not asking you to say you wanna get married right now. But I need to know if that's where you see us going. I'm just . . ." *Spit it out, Joy.* "I'm in love with you. I've been in love with you for eight years. I can't keep doing this. It's bad for me. It's hurting me."

He exhaled forever. I barreled on.

"If you can't tell me that you're at least thinking this is a possibility that we should explore, then I . . . I have to let you go."

He was quiet. *Say something. Fight for me. Love me! SAY something!*

Eventually he did. "I don't know what to say. I'm just . . . I'm not in a place to make that decision right now."

For the next week, I was miserable. The depression and lethargy was the worst I'd ever experienced. Each day was the same: I read my Bible, slept, wrote in my journal, slept, ate if I felt like passing out, took an occasional shower and screamed the entire time, read my Bible, slept. When I missed the Saturday night meeting, Pam came to check on me.

"I'm so proud of you, Joie," she said after I explained what happened. "You have let go of the idol you had put in place of God. I'm so inspired by your faith."

Seeing her words weren't helping, she suggested I come to Idaho for a while.

"It's becoming like a little God spa up there," she said. "I think it would do you good to just be a kid in a house full of family. Would you like that?"

I would like that. That's what I needed. I needed to be surrounded by family.

After Pam left the apartment, I booked a ticket for the very next day. Because I'd been shooting pilots, movies, and TV episodes since I was a preteen, I had grown accustomed to boarding planes, arriving at strange airports, and being driven to random locations to get to know a group of strangers. So, nothing about this made me nervous—it was just another trip to another place.

Like Pam said, their big house in Idaho had become a refuge to more than a few people in need of a peaceful retreat. Even Emily's best friend from college was currently staying in a guest room there, and she had been sent to pick me up from the airport. Jasmine was short, had a tiny smile between cute bubble cheeks, and wore violet contacts over her brown eyes.

"Welcome to the God Spa!" she said, parroting Pam's line as she met me curbside at the terminal. She hugged me. The hugging apparently extended across state lines. "I'm Jasmine."

"I'm Joy. Thank you for making the trek to the airport." I choked back a cough that had been developing for a few days.

"Easy. Happy to help. Ah, sorry! Lemme move those to the back." She reached her manicured hands toward a small stack of books on the passenger seat. I picked up the last one and handed it to her: *French 3.*

"Tu parles français!" I exclaimed, happy to know someone else who was a Francophile like me.

"Oui! Je me remets à niveau. Es-tu fluent?" *Yes, I'm brushing up. Are you fluent?*

"Je comprends . . . more than I speak." I laughed. "I visited Paris a couple years ago after graduation, but I haven't practiced since then."

"I'll get over there someday."

Before long we were swapping life stories. Contrary to what I expected from her studiousness, Jasmine had climbed out of a Las Vegas trailer park, leaving behind two vaguely disinterested parents and a wandering older brother. She graduated summa cum laude with a BS in philosophy and a minor in literature. But while she had extracted herself from her family, she hadn't entirely escaped dysfunction. One night she answered a distress call from her boyfriend.

"He'd been acting weird," she said. "I found him in a parking lot with a stash of crystal meth." Two days later she stumbled into the emergency room for a broken jaw, severe bruising around her neck and wrists, and a rape kit. Emily knew the Van Hewitts had this big house, so she called and asked if her old college friend Jasmine could spend the summer in their home. Wander the field behind it. Just rest and heal. "They wanted to help, but Les and his family were moving in. And then Les said he was happy to have me stay, since he wants to really make it a ministry home anyway."

"Oh, he does?"

"Yeah, I think typically pastors are given a home to live in by whatever church they're working for. But he doesn't want it to just be his place—he's got a vision for a ministry home and a new church . . . I'm not sure about details or timeline, but I can say it's been a huge blessing to me already."

Les said Jasmine could stay as long as she wanted until she felt she was ready for the next phase, whatever that might be. As of that moment, she had been there six months.

I looked out the window. I'd always associated Idaho with potatoes, but clearly that was in a different part of the state. The woods we were passing at 75 mph already made me feel like I was in a fairy tale. The forest stretched up higher than I'd ever seen. There was lush foliage in New Jersey, but the trees didn't tower and loom the way these evergreens did.

"I've never been to the Pacific Northwest," I said.

"Oh, I love it here." Jasmine took a deep breath. "It's so quiet."

It looked warm outside because the sun was shining, but rain pattered down on the windshield and I pulled my sweater around me from the chill. I coughed again.

Jasmine handed me her bottle of water. "I drank out of it already, if that's okay."

"I don't want to get you sick with whatever this cough is," I said.

"Just have the rest," she said.

We drove along miles and miles of highway until finally there was a clearing in the wall of green, a little town appeared, and the *Beauty and the Beast* soundtrack played in my brain. *Little town, it's a quiet village . . .*

The magic moment didn't last long. The farther into town we drove, the less charming it all became. Mina and Pam had talked about this place as if it were an idyllic hideaway, but between the fast-food joints, strip malls, and chain stores, the only thing not lined with concrete was a quaint brick-faced restaurant, ground-breakingly called the Bistro, on a corner by defunct railroad tracks.

After a few more twists and turns, we slowed onto a gravel road scattered with several midcentury homes. It was the kind of country path where kids' bikes lay on unkempt front lawns and you didn't know if they'd been there for an afternoon or a year. Jasmine slowed the car and rolled her eyes.

"This gravel road is the worst. If you're not going five miles an hour, the rocks kick up and scratch your paint."

The road dead-ended at what had to be a ten-acre field and we arrived at the Van Hewitts': last house on the left. Or this *was* the Van Hewitts'. Now it was Les's.

It was an odd addition on this street of humble homes. White-painted brick unapologetically rising up, up, up out of the ground. A horseshoe-shaped driveway paved with brown pebbles. Bushes spaced out exactly five feet apart on both sides of the path with small silver lights poised, ready for evening. To take it in at a distance, the house was instantly impressive and bore a striking resemblance to something I'd seen before. *What was it?* It wasn't just the immense amount of detail that felt familiar. It was something else, too. The sky was big over this plot of land. All the trees had been cleared away, presenting the home almost as a theatrical set piece. It didn't belong here.

"Ed built this house, you know," Jasmine said as we turned onto the pebble path. "I guess he modeled it after George Washington's house in Mount Vernon."

That was it. Ninth-grade field-trip-to-DC memories flooded back. Blue Eyes sleeping next to me in the back of the bus with his headphones on. My head on his shoulder. *No,* I told myself, and yanked my brain back into the present moment.

Unlike the first president's impeccably attended manor, the closer we got to the Big House, the more I noticed its disrepair. It wasn't falling apart by any means, but knowing how meticulous

Pam was, I expected the home to be pristine, glowing. Instead, wear and tear shone through. The white paint on the house had a thin layer of grime. Everything had a layer of grime, really, including the cars parked out front.

These were what my stepdad called "A to B cars"— unimpressive, but they got you where you needed to go. An old black Camry with bumper damage and an old Mitsubishi Delica that badly needed a wash. Someone had written in the window dirt FOR A GOOD TIME CALL xxx-xxx-xxxx. We both noticed it at the same time, and Jasmine scoffed, shaking her head.

"That's Dontay. He's always messing around." She smiled playfully. "I promise we love Jesus here."

"Hey, Jesus is a good time. I'm down!"

"Can you imagine, you call that number and it's someone just sharing the Gospel?"

I tried on my best 900-number voice: "Hey, handsome, I can't wait to tell you about Romans 8:38." Jasmine put the car in park, laughing, and we went inside.

When she opened the front door, a tangled gray cat escaped past our feet. Jasmine reached down and swooped it up before it got too far.

"This is Salome." She held the cat up toward me. I tried to smile. Nobody mentioned a cat. "I call her Salami because the boys are always making sandwiches and petting her so—"

"So she smells like salami," I finished for her.

Jasmine chuckled, and closed the front door behind us.

I was hit with that rank sickly-sweet scent I remembered from meeting Les when he was cooking at the Van Hewitts'. Inside, the home itself was beautifully designed, though outdated by a few decades: marble-floored entryway, expensive linen wallpaper bearing smudge marks from grubby hands, a rounded cherrywood banister with white-carpeted stairs that were browning in the middle from foot traffic. Dining room to the right, living room to the left, and, straight ahead, a large kitchen with a massive bay window. *Better Homes & Gardens* would have done a feature here in 1985.

In the living room, Les's twins, the Barbarians, played a video game. They didn't glance at us. We entered the kitchen, where a couple in their midforties sat at a table. The man was playing solitaire. The woman was using soda water to try to remove spaghetti sauce from the top of her pink uniform. Jasmine introduced me.

"We've heard so much about you!" the woman said with a southern twang, her platinum hair falling in her eyes as she stood up to hug me. "I'm Lucy!"

"Hi, sweetheart, I'm Kurt." Kurt stayed put, but the up-and-down look he gave me felt more invasive than a hug. He had a bony face and cold blue eyes that quickly scanned my body. I immediately disliked him but then felt guilty for passing judgment without even knowing him.

"Kurt and Lucy are living in the basement," Jasmine explained.

"Temporarily," Lucy added. "We were a part of Les's old church, so we're staying here awhile as we sort out next moves for the new ministry."

"I don't know what you're talking about, I'm just here for the free food," Kurt joked, and Lucy swatted him playfully.

"Les, Marti, and the boys are upstairs," Jasmine said. "Pam and Ed live in the garage apartment, and I'll show you where we're staying." She waved for me to follow her.

As I tailed Jasmine down another hallway, she whispered over her shoulder, "Lucy's the only person I've ever met who sells Mary Kay in real life."

"Oh, is that why she's wearing that vintage waitress uniform?"

"Yes! Isn't it funny? She thinks it's glamorous."

"I guess it sort of is . . . especially with the blonde hair!"

We turned into the only downstairs bedroom.

Floor-to-ceiling windows. Navy velvet curtains. Same pearly-striped white linen wallpaper as the rest of the house. An unmade full-sized bed with an empty Cheetos bag on it, and twin bunk beds that were tucked in perfectly. Jasmine threw her purse on the top bunk.

"You can take the bottom."

I put my bag down and looked around. "How many of us are in here?"

"Just you, me, and Gretchen."

"Gretchen? I haven't met her. And you said Dontay, too? How am I gonna keep track of everyone?" I laughed.

"Ha, I know, it took me a minute, too. Well, you know all the Van Hewitts, obviously. Pam, Ed, Harker, and Abe."

"Yes. And Mina."

"Oh gosh, I wish you'd been here for the wedding. It was so amazing."

"That's what I hear," I said, trying to be gracious.

She continued. "And now you know me, Jasmine. Hi! I'll be the tiny brunette helping you remember your French."

I smiled. She was fun.

"And you just met Kurt and Lucy."

"Skeleton-looking guy and Mary Kay lady."

"He does look like a skeleton. I'm glad it's not just me. They have a son who is thirteen. Brandon."

I took a breath. "Brandon. Thirteen. Son of Skeleton Kurt and Pink Lady Lucy."

"That one won't be hard because there's only four teenagers, Brandon plus Les and Marti's boys."

"Oh yeah," I said, "Quiet Boy and the Barbarians. That's what I've nicknamed them."

Jasmine laughed. "He *is* so quiet, and the twins are wild! I'll call them that, too, between us."

My eyes drifted to the unmade bed. "And Cheetos? What'd you say her name was?"

"Gretchen. She arrived a couple months after me. She's kind of . . . aimless. It's not meant to be a judgment. I just have always been a very driven person, so it's a bit of a challenge for me to connect with her. Her family has problems similar to mine—addictions, super poor—I guess that just affected us differently. But she's kindhearted. Pam met her in LA last year and hired her as an assistant for all the accounting work she does for Ed's office."

"Gretchen's from LA? I'm surprised she didn't come to Bible study."

"I think she moved up here, like, right before you and Camille started going."

"So you've met Camille? I didn't think she'd visited here yet."

"No, I've just heard about the 'gorgeous, redheaded British actress' that Les keeps ribbing Dontay about meeting one day."

I thought it was a little odd that Jasmine knew when Camille and I started attending Bible study. What else did she know about us? Come to think of it, when I told her my story in the car, there were a couple times when she replied as if she already knew. I hadn't thought anything of it then because I was so distracted by the majesty of the passing trees. But why would Les or Pam be sharing things we talked about in LA with the group here in Idaho? Those conversations at Bible study were supposed to be private. I told myself it meant they were invested in all of us and looked forward to bringing everyone together. I was sure neither of them would share anything about me with someone unless they were trustworthy.

Les and Pam hadn't given us much backstory on the Idaho group, however, so Jasmine explained that Dontay played college football on a scholarship and was expected to get drafted, but he tore his ACL. He was so depressed after his injury that he dropped out of school and hiked awhile around the Pacific Northwest. Then one weekend he landed at Les's old church.

"Les has been mentoring him ever since," Jasmine said. "He came along with Les and Marti when they moved here."

"His family doesn't mind that he just moved in with another family?"

"Single mom. Dontay says she's happy that he's experiencing a family environment that she couldn't provide. Les calls him his 'adopted son.'"

"Aww. Okay. Dontay. Football. Call him for a good time. Got it."

"Haha, exactly. And that's everyone in the house! You'll meet a few more people on Wednesday night, but don't worry about that now."

I'd been hearing about the Wednesday night Bible study from some of the LA crew who had visited before me. It sounded basically the same as our Saturday night group, but somehow more profound. No one was ever able to identify exactly what the "magic" was, but there was a reason "God Spa" was the affectionate nickname given to this big house. Every time someone would return from a visit here, they reported astounding personal growth and seemed even more committed in their faith. People here were clearly taking life and faith seriously.

"So," I said, "what do we do now?"

"That's kind of the great thing about being here," Jasmine

said. "Everyone will give you your space to do whatever you need to. You can go explore. There's a beautiful trail through the field in the back. You can lie in bed and journal, go play the piano, hang out at the kitchen table. Just take time to connect with the Lord in whatever way you need. There's no expectation. Just *be*."

No expectations. That seemed impossible. There were always expectations. To prepare, to perform, to deliver, to speak up, to be quiet, to relax, to behave, to be intelligent. There were expectations to pay attention, be on time, be professional, be original but don't be weird, be creative but don't make anyone uncomfortable. Be collaborative but trust your instincts. Be tough. Be sweet. Smile. *Sing out, Louise!* My life had been like one of my dad's adventure courses, balancing and dodging. What would it be like to just be 100 percent myself?

My phone dinged. Mom texted something about wanting to come up to LA for lunch that weekend. I hadn't told her or Dad that I was headed to Idaho because I was looking for ways to further enact my independence from them. The more I folded into Les and Pam's world, the more misunderstood by my parents I felt and the less I trusted them.

I ignored her message and took Jasmine's first suggestion: a walk alone in the field behind the Big House. As a rule, I was generally more comfortable alone than with others precisely because of the expectations I often felt accompanied company. I knew it was a weird thing to do—to show up as a guest in someone's home and promptly disappear to be on my own, wandering through their green acres—but it was what I wanted. That was fully *me* in that moment. I figured what better way to test out being totally myself than with a group of virtual strangers?

So, I wandered. I daydreamed. I opened up the journal I'd brought along and wrote a song, I picked flowers and made a bouquet and finally returned to the house just as dinner was finished cooking. Les and Marti were so happy to see me. Pam and Ed, too. They were in town that weekend. It was a full house, and the laughter and loud voices over the meal were refreshing after being in my apartment by myself for the last week. Dontay was the loudest, most boisterous of the bunch. He was twenty-one but acted like he was still a teenager. He arrived to dinner straight from his shift at the Mobil station, dressed in coveralls that fit snug around his massive football player body. He never stopped talking, fidgeting, or moving around. He was pure comedy. He even got a chuckle every now and then from Quiet Boy, whom I'd caught glancing at me a couple times, his eyes darting away when I noticed. It was a different kind of look from the leering one Kurt had given me. Way more innocent. He wasn't my type—not a chance—but after Blue Eyes's rejection, I was happy to take the confidence boost.

I hated to go to bed straight after eating, but my cough was getting worse and I thought it best to get some rest. Amid all the banter and bustle as plates were cleared, someone handed me a red glass bottle of cough syrup. I took a spoonful, then retired to my room, changed into sleep clothes, and crawled into the bottom bunk with my journal. As I lay there thinking back over the day, one thing occurred to me: unlike at the Van Hewitt house, here Les wasn't wearing shoes indoors.

CHAPTER EIGHT

My face hurt. My mouth was stale. *Why was I so tired?* I lifted my head and felt the flannel pillowcase peel off my face where crusted saliva bound us together. The corner of a book was under my pillow at just the right angle to put a throbbing dent in my jaw. My journal. I was in a dark room—tall windows covered in blackout curtains. I heard voices outside, and the sound oriented me. The door was behind my head.

Right. I'm in Idaho.

I pushed myself up and breathed deeply, blood coming back into my extremities. My Coldplay *Parachutes* t-shirt and red French-cut briefs untucked from their crevices as my feet hit grimy carpet. A crack of light came from under one of the curtains. I stumbled toward it over whatever wrappers or garbage was on the floor by Gretchen's bed and pulled back the tall blue curtain.

Light filled the room, and I pressed my face against the cold glass. Heat blew from the floor vent. *Why is the heat on in the summer?* I fumbled with the window lock. A beautiful breeze swept in, and my head started to clear. I'd never had to pee more in my life. I found my sweatpants in a pile at the bottom of the bed I'd been asleep in, grabbed my glasses, and headed to the nearest bathroom, which was in the kitchen.

"She lives!" someone said. I hadn't yet put on my glasses, so it was hard to make out who was in the room. I smiled through chapped lips and raised my hand hello.

"You really are a sleeping beauty." This voice I recognized as Pam's.

"I guess so!" I said. I closed the bathroom door behind me and peed for a minute straight. I cupped some water into my mouth, splashed my face, put on my glasses, and went back into the kitchen.

Just as the night before, the room buzzed with happy chitchat, a sound I had craved in my quiet and tense childhood homes. Martine was washing dishes. Kurt and Lucy were in their same chairs. Pam was playing checkers at the kitchen table with Gretchen, who had started on a new bag of Cheetos.

Jasmine was on the floor in the corner by the table, painting her toenails. She smiled up at me. I looked at the microwave clock: 4:07 p.m. *Wow, I slept for almost twenty-four hours.*

"Every time I went in the room yesterday, you were out," Jasmine said.

"What do you mean 'yesterday'?" I said. "What day is it?"

"Monday."

"Monday?" I asked, still rubbing sleep out of my eyes. "What, did I sleep for two days?"

"Almost!" she said. "I guess you needed the rest."

It seemed to have helped my cough, which was gone.

The Barbarians were still playing video games on the living room couch, now with Kurt and Lucy's son, Brandon. Someone was clumsily repeating the same four bars of a song on the piano. I craned my neck to see Quiet Boy hunched over the keys and instantly longed to hear the strum of Abe's guitar instead.

Kurt was talking about *The Matrix*, which he'd only just seen for the first time: "I loved the 'unplugging' parallel to real life as not just being what we can see. I felt like God was reminding me to question the illusions and distractions in this world and see the deeper layer of what's really going on."

Oh, you noticed that, did you? The entire message of the whole movie?

Why was I being snarky? *This isn't LA, Joy. Most people don't study film for a living. Stop being so judgmental.* I was tired. And hungry.

"It's like that Pierre Chardin quote," Jasmine said, focusing on getting the dark purple shellac just right. "'Nous ne sommes pas des êtres humains vivant une expérience spirituelle. Nous sommes des êtres spirituels vivant une expérience humaine.'"

Everyone looked at her with confusion.

"Allow me to translate," Jasmine continued, laughing. "'We are not human beings having a spiritual experience. We are spiritual beings having a human experience.'"

"Who is Pierre Shar-don?" Lucy whispered to Pam in a southern affront to French. Pam shrugged.

"Oh, you're so fancy," Kurt said with an edge to his voice. He was smiling, but in the way a psychotic kid smiles before he skins a cat.

The front door banged opened.

"Boys," Les called, "come help with the groceries!" The piano stopped immediately, and Quiet Boy passed through the kitchen and out the front door. The Barbarians hopped to.

Realizing I hadn't checked my phone in two days, I grabbed it from the bedroom where I'd plugged it in before going to sleep.

Twenty-six missed calls. Mom was nineteen of them, Dad was five, and Camille was two. *What in the world?* I called Mom back first, returning to the kitchen with the phone to my ear.

"Oh, thank God!" she exclaimed.

Bethany Joy Lenz

"Is everything okay?" I asked.

"Joy, where *are* you? We've been worried sick! Your father and I have been trying to find you."

"Why, what happened?"

"What happened? You disappeared!"

"I didn't disappear. I came to Idaho to visit my friends. What do you mean you've been trying to find me? I've only been away from my phone for two days."

"When you didn't return my texts and calls since Friday, I started to get worried. I don't know where you are, where these people live, if you're okay . . ."

I remembered what Les and Pam had been telling us about setting boundaries with the people in our life who want to keep us stuck in the same lies about our identity. I was not going to let my mother's issues with control force me into feeling obligated.

"Mom," I said, "I'm an adult. If I want to get on a plane and visit some friends, I can do that, and I don't need to tell you about it."

The kitchen started getting quiet as everyone heard what was happening.

"I know you can, Joy. But if someone is worried about you and calling you repeatedly and texting, it's just kind to let them know that you're all right."

"But why is it my responsibility to make you feel better when you're being unreasonable, Mom? Just because you're demanding something doesn't mean I have to give it to you."

"Joy, we don't know these people!" She raised her voice and then contained it again. "It's okay for parents to be concerned about their child if they don't hear from her in days."

"But I'm not a child."

Les and Quiet Boy came through the front door loudly. QB

was laughing at Les, who was in the middle of telling a story. ". . . my God, the waitress's eyes went as big as your mother's nipples when you boys were still suckin' on 'em!"

Pam flapped a hand to shush them. I walked into the hallway.

"I didn't say you were," Mom said. "I said you were *our* child. Honey, you'll always be my daughter no matter how old you get. And I just think it's the right thing to do to let someone who's worried about you know that you're okay. All you had to do was send a text. Your father even called Camille, and she said you didn't respond to her, either!"

"What? Why does he even have Camille's number?"

"I don't know. I guess she picked him up from the airport once, and he wanted to be able to get ahold of you if he has to, since you never call us back!"

I was done. "Okay, Mom, I don't know what you want me to say. I'm fine. I'm in Idaho for a couple weeks. Everything's fine. You don't need to worry."

She sighed and paused. "When are you coming back?"

"I don't know, after the Fourth of July."

"Okay. Will you please respond if I text you?"

"I'll respond when it feels appropriate."

"What does *that* mean?"

"We're about to eat dinner, Mom. I'll have to talk to you later."

She sighed again. "Okay. Please call your dad and tell him you're all right."

I hung up. Everyone in the kitchen was talking again, giving me privacy. Pam appeared in the hallway and put her arm around me. I started to cry.

"Oh, there now." She petted my head. "I'm proud of you. It's hard to set boundaries. Yes, ma'am, it hurts to grow sometimes."

I nodded, wiping my eyes. Pam handed me a small, folded tissue. She always had a little plastic envelope of tissues in her purse or pocket, ready for anyone who might begin to cry—because crying meant growing. In addition to hugs, we also were highly encouraged to cry.

I texted my dad while she kept an arm around me.

Hey, I'm fine. Just got sick and took some cough medicine that knocked me out. Love you.

I walked back into the kitchen to more pedantic observations about Neo and Morpheus.

"I'm gonna go take a shower and get ready for dinner," I said. I went back into the guest room to gather my toiletries and a towel. Us girls staying in the guest room had been asked to shower in the basement, which was Kurt and Lucy's bathroom. The upstairs shower was for Les's boys and, we were told, "it wouldn't be appropriate." I'd have rather gone into the garage apartment to use Ed and Pam's shower since I knew them better and it felt odd to be naked in a stranger's bathroom. But I was a guest and I didn't want to be fussy.

As I was walking out of the bedroom, I saw the tall red bottle of medicine I had taken sitting on the dresser. It seemed larger than I remembered—too large for a bottle of over-the-counter cough suppressant. This was prescription stuff. The label was worn and the expiration date was old by a couple years. I turned it over in my hand, the milky syrup coating the inside of the half-empty bottle. I read the label.

KURT B—

HYDROCODONE

Strange, I thought. *Strange that someone would just hand over a bottle of expired codeine. Didn't I only take a spoonful? Why had it knocked me out for so unreasonably long?*

I carried the bottle out and handed it back to Kurt in the kitchen. "Here's your medicine back. That stuff is strong!"

Lucy stopped short, midsentence, and stared at the bottle. "What is that?"

"That medicine I took for my cough."

Kurt swiped it from me before Lucy could free up a hand to inspect it. "Thanks for bringing it back. I'm glad it helped."

Lucy seemed bothered. She looked at Les, who had been un-bagging groceries but now was stopped and also staring at Kurt. Lucy looked back at me. "How much of this did you take?"

I felt like I was in trouble but couldn't figure out why. "Umm, I don't remember taking more than a spoonful."

"Well, you must've taken more than that to sleep for thirty-six hours," she said in a challenging, almost accusatory tone, but her eyes started to water.

I looked between her and Kurt, who was looking at the floor as if he was the one in trouble. I didn't understand.

"Well, we're glad you're back to life!" Les called out. "This is gonna be a fun couple of weeks!"

CHAPTER NINE

Later, I would come to see those two weeks in Idaho as the turning point. Had I just stayed in LA depressed and mopey over Blue Eyes, would I have avoided it all? Possibly. But then I wouldn't have had Rosie. I think about that every time I tell my story. It was all worth it for her.

My first couple days at the house were spent just like my first afternoon: wandering the surrounding acres, writing songs, bird-watching. But soon I tired of being by myself and spent more time with the group. We played softball at a nearby field. Despite my abysmal lack of team sports skills and inability to hit a ball into fair territory, everyone was encouraging and cheered me on. We cooked together—helping Les prepare his meat-heavy feasts but also contributing our own dishes. For the Fourth of July, I made strawberry shortcake cupcakes and printed miniature Declaration of Independence papers to serve them on. I even burned the edges to make the paper look old, and it was nice to be appreciated for my hospitality skills. I cut flowers from the garden, arranging bouquets to set on the kitchen table or in the bathrooms. I also joined Jasmine in her and Marti's effort to give the house a long-overdue vacuuming and thorough deodorizing. The place was an indoor playground for Les's boys and was starting to smell like a locker room.

Mostly, though, we talked. In the kitchen, in the living room, in Ed and Pam's garage apartment, on the front porch, over the occasional dinner in town at the Bistro (or whatever chain restaurant the gang was in the mood to be bloated from)—raw, vulnerable conversations sprouted up anytime.

The deepest conversations happened Wednesday nights. Though I'd heard these meetings were more intense than our Saturday Bible studies, I still wasn't prepared for how much more.

"The Jezebel spirit is attacking this body of believers," Les said to the group gathered in the living room that Wednesday following the Fourth. He sat on the redbrick hearth and held up a stack of thin, fold-over booklets and passed them around the room. Everyone took one. This included Emily, who had come to visit and, even though her father still lived in her childhood home a short drive away, was staying on the sleeper couch in Ed and Pam's garage apartment. Also, there was a young couple named Juana and Miguel whom I'd only met that night. They were introduced to the group through Juana's job at a bank. A couple months earlier, Pam had gone in to do some banking, she and Juana had got to talking, the subject of religion came up—as it always quickly did among members of the group—and Pam invited her and Miguel to the Wednesday night meetings.

"Manipulation is happening all around us," Les continued. "In culture, in our homes, in Hollywood where a lot of our California Family is ministering. Pressing into relationship and community is how we thrive and keep each other in check when there are so many things trying to keep our focus off the Lord. The enemy hates relationship." "Relationship" was Les's new buzzword obsession. "The more we thrive, the more attacks the enemy is going to launch on us. The presence of outside resistance is proof that we're on the right track."

The stack arrived to me. *Revealing Jezebel: Manipulation, Seduction, and Rebellion Against Authority.* I took one and passed the rest on.

"In case you're not refreshed or familiar with the story, Queen Jezebel was the worst example of manipulation and control in the Bible, and King Ahab was her husband who abdicated his own authority to her. She walked all over him, worshipped idols of Baal, had hundreds of God's prophets murdered, and Ahab stood by because she was so seductive. Just like the snake in the garden."

This was new to me. They didn't talk about Ahab and Jezebel in Sunday school. My dad never taught me about Old Testament characters still existing in the world today as oppressive spiritual powers that I *still* needed to be on guard from. Listening to Les talk, I felt so naive. I was a sponge.

"Eve wanted to do things her own way in the garden. She didn't want God to be in control, *she* wanted to be in control, so she rebelled. Now, the first thing this spirit does? Creates doubt." Les held up his thumb. "We have to guard our hearts against anything and anyone that makes us doubt what we already know is true." He extended his index finger. "The second thing it does is control and create rebellion."

"Uh, technically that's two things, Pop," Dontay said with a smile. The energy in the room loosened up a bit with a few chuckles.

Oh, he calls him "Pop," I thought. *Like he's really adopted. That's so sweet.* I'd known Dontay only a week, but I was starting to develop a crush. The way his muscles flexed and rippled as he ran around the softball bases or even just leaned over to rustle through a pile of bottle rockets. The way his bright smile was so infectious. The way he smelled faintly of gasoline even after he'd changed out of his coveralls. I felt safe around him. I knew I was all screwed up from Blue Eyes. I wondered if this was what romance was supposed to be—a feeling of safety, an almost familial love. Aside from his generally immature behavior, which I argued to myself that he'd grow out of, I really enjoyed his company. Especially how he seemed to be able to poke fun at Les in a way no one else could. Well—usually.

Les didn't laugh or smile now. He just looked at Dontay flatly. "No. It *is* the same thing, because rebellion is seeking independent control. The best way to protect against the seduction of being self-willed is to press into relationship. Trust each other to see blind spots, and be ruthless with our own thoughts when they are leading us into doubt."

"Doubting what, specifically?" Emily asked.

"Doubting what God has already told us is true."

"So, like, questioning what we already believe?"

Les cocked his head. "Do you believe the truth?"

Emily blinked. "Yes."

"Then it's not a belief. It's true."

I raised my hand, and Les smiled at me. Mimicking a schoolteacher, he said, "Yes, Joy!"

Everyone chuckled, and I read off the cover of the booklet. "What does *Rebellion Against Authority* mean in this context?"

"Well, who is your spiritual authority, Joy?"

"I mean . . . God."

Les laughed. "Yes, obviously God. But how about here on earth? Is there anyone you allow to have spiritual authority over you?"

It felt like a trick question. *My parents?* I thought. *Not anymore. The pope? If I were Catholic!* My answer was: *No. No human has spiritual authority over me.* But that somehow felt like the wrong answer.

"Can you tell me what you mean? Like, I understand the concept of authority. We have a boss at work who has authority over us at our job and we have to do what they say. Or, like, a parent has authority over a child. But, spiritually—"

"The Bible is full of relationships where someone is given a role of spiritual authority over another person. Saul and David, Elisha and Elijah, Moses and Jethro. God assigns other people to help us when we need guidance or we're making bad decisions because of our own blind spots. So if you were trying to control things, for example, and someone with spiritual authority in your life cautioned you against that but you ignored them—that's rebelling against the authority of God in your life."

Lucy interjected: "You're not married, but, if you were, your husband would be your spiritual authority." She rubbed Kurt's leg.

My chest instantly tightened. In spite of hearing this statement my whole life in church, gender roles in American Christianity never sat right with me, or my mother, or either of my grandmothers. But in the context of this Jezebel conversation, it occurred to me that perhaps that was exactly the point. I came from a long line of independent, dominant women, and just maybe the Jezebel spirit had already infiltrated my family, my mind. Maybe that was why I could never get on board with the whole "submissive wife" idea. Was I being attacked by an ancient spirit of control? Was being a woman in submission the key I had been missing all along—the reason Blue Eyes couldn't see a future with me?

"It's not just a question for the single people," Pam said, looking at Miguel and Juana. "Who is helping to guide you and keep you on the right track?"

"To me that's you, Pop and Mama," Dontay said to Les and Marti. "You're not my biological family, but you're my spiritual Family. And you guys, too, Ed and Pam."

"Oh, yeah, in that case, me too," Jasmine said. "Kurt and Lucy, you guys as well. You are all older than us and have more wisdom and experience. There's a natural order in any church group. You know, pastors, deacons, elders, et cetera. Within the context of *this* group of believers, you three older couples would be who I say have spiritual authority in my life. I mean, you're basically our spiritual parents."

"I agree," Gretchen said, nodding.

"Definitely," said Emily.

Juana and Miguel exchanged an uncertain look. After a moment of hesitation, Juana said, "Well, I mean, yes, following that logic I suppose it does make sense."

Quiet Boy, as usual, stayed quiet.

Les looked at me expectantly.

I wish it had occurred to me in that moment to ask him one question: *Who has spiritual authority over you?* Such a simple and vital question to ask any leader—spiritual or otherwise. I didn't ask, though. Instead, I thought sincerely about who had invested the most in my life recently. Pam was becoming the warm, sweet mom I never had. Les was becoming the emotionally available father figure I always wanted. This whole group felt like the loud, fun, real family I had dreamed of. If anyone was going to help me figure out the right way to live, it would be them.

"Joy?" Les asked. "Does that resonate with you?"

"Oh man," I said with a smile. "Absolutely."

CHAPTER TEN

With Mina having moved in with Harker, I couldn't afford the rent on our place. It was a large two-bedroom in Beverly Hills, and I needed a more long-term solution. I had gotten the cheerleader part in *Bring It On Again*, but while I had some savings built up from other recent work, who knew how long it would be before my next job came in. I found a listing for a studio apartment in the Valley. It had a window that overlooked more apartments and was on a loud main road, but the reason I chose it, even more than its affordability, was it was close to the Van Hewitts'. No more sitting in fifty-five minutes of Coldwater Canyon traffic or, God forbid, the 405. Soon, though, people would be driving to me, as my apartment became a secondary hub for the group.

That summer, Mina announced she was pregnant. What she had with Harker was everything I wanted to have when I got married—which didn't look like it would be anytime soon. The dating scene in LA was not for me. I had gone on a few dates, but I always felt hopelessly inelegant and bumbling. Since I'd cut out Blue Eyes, Dontay was the closest boy to me who I could imagine dating, and, after those two weeks in Idaho, I imagined it plenty. In reality, the distance made it impractical.

I was convinced that the reason I hadn't found a partner yet was because I still hadn't surrendered enough for God to reward me. Mina was willing to sacrifice acting, and look how she'd been rewarded! I didn't feel like I was supposed to give up my acting career, but I decided I needed to make *some* kind of active sacrifice that would benefit others. One Saturday night I told the group that I was going to open up my new apartment to anyone who wanted to come pray at any hour. I wanted my home to be a sanctuary. Any hour of the day or night. No need to call or check in. The door would always be unlocked. I had no fear about it whatsoever and wholeheartedly believed the Lord would honor my sacrifice by protecting me from strangers robbing or attacking me.

Emily was the first person to visit. One morning she came in quietly at 6:30 a.m. and pushed play on the stereo I'd set out with a worship CD ready to go. I saw my small reading light go on and could hear the whoosh and flip of her Bible pages as she hummed along with the music. Lying on the canopy bed, which I'd inherited from Mina, I imagined God in Heaven was also turning the pages in His book of single men, deciding which one I'd soon crash shopping carts with in a grocery store meet-cute.

Other members would drop in every now and then, once or twice a week. There were only nine of us now, several attendees having waned off over the year since Les's entrance. For these drop-ins we didn't need to talk; it was just understood that my home was a safe place to come rest, and I loved being able to provide something I had spent my life seeking to have.

Then one night around midnight I got a call from Camille. She was whispering. I could barely hear what she was saying, but the panic in her voice was obvious.

"Are you okay?" I asked.

"Some really intense things have been happening in my apartment lately."

"Like what?" I asked.

"Um . . . God, this sounds so crazy." She paused. "Can I just come over and stay on your couch tonight?"

"Of course, come over!"

"I just . . . I think I'm seeing things."

"What are you seeing?"

She took a long breath. "Demons."

This wasn't the first time Camille had called me with stories about miraculous things happening in her life. Every Saturday night I noticed how closely she paid attention and even took notes. She was listening to sermons on tape from various ministers, and visiting different churches. She really took her exploration of faith seriously.

It seemed the more she invited Jesus into her day-to-day life, the more He was showing up for her. She'd have a dream about a high school friend she hadn't connected with in years. She decided to pray and fast for them, and two days later that person called her. She'd also been dealing for almost a year with a ton of drama from an ex-boyfriend who was suicidal and obsessed with her. She prayed for God to intervene, and within a week the guy had left town and moved on. I actually was a little jealous of how quickly and how much God was showing up in her life. I mean, what was *she* sacrificing that I wasn't? But more than that, I was excited and inspired to watch someone's faith blossom from rote religious activity to friendship with God.

"Well, apparently whatever spiritual door I've opened is letting in more than just God," she told me as we sat on my couch. I'd made some tea before she arrived, but she was too nervous to drink it. "The last few nights I've been waking up in the middle of the night totally paralyzed. Tonight I was lying there, unable to move, and this awful black—I mean, I don't want to be overdramatic, but I don't know what else to call it—*demonic* figure was hovering over me in my bed. Basically, holding me down. Then more showed up, and they were all, like, swarming around my bedroom. And all I could think of was to say 'Jesus,' but it was like they were choking me and I couldn't say it."

"And you weren't dreaming?"

"*No*. Absolutely not. I wish I had been."

"What did you do?"

"I just prayed. In my mind." She let out an incredulous laugh. "It was the craziest thing. I just called to Jesus in my mind until I could get it out of my throat, and as soon as I said it *they left*. Like, shrieking."

"Oh, wow, Cam." I shook my head. "Wow."

"Yeah." She looked at me and anxiously fiddled with the strings of her hoodie. "You don't seem freaked out. Have you ever had, like, supernatural stuff happen?"

I had.

Only once, but it was an encounter with God that I couldn't explain, and never told anyone about. One overcast late morning in Union Square when I was still living in New York City, I left my apartment to take a "thinking walk": a favorite activity to generate inspiration or help me problem-solve or practice lines for an audition. As the light drizzle turned into a heavy rain, I ducked into a small café that was totally empty, besides the staff. I was embraced by the smell of bacon and coffee. They let me take the largest booth there, a horseshoe-shaped bench against a wide window. I sat near the edge so I could people-watch through the glass, and I ordered a fresh-squeezed orange juice.

Life was good. I was nineteen. My job on *Guiding Light* was satisfying for the time being. My church life felt full; my friendships were lively. Sitting in the café, casually thinking about Blue Eyes and our weird little merry-go-round, I started talking to God in my mind like I often did. Then a thought occurred to me that I'd never had before.

For a brief moment, the drizzly city street I was watching became . . . plain. Sort of dull and real. All the romantic icing I used to put onto everything in my mind melted away (don't tempt me, I WILL sing "MacArthur Park"), and the thought I had was: *What if all this Jesus stuff is just nonsense? Made up.*

The "Jesus stuff" was working for me and I was content overall. I figured, worst-case scenario, we all convinced ourselves of different things to make life go by a little easier, so I'd keep on believing. *I guess I'll find out when I die,* I thought.

And then everything went warm.

My heart slowed. My skin suddenly hit a perfect temperature, as though all the cells in my body were moving in tandem with the sun and my blood was a lazy river. In the empty café, in my empty booth, someone sat beside me. There was no flesh. No body to touch. There was only the deep and familiar presence of someone who leaned in and spoke tenderly into my ear. The voice was gentle and masculine, joyful, weighty, and . . . did I feel breath?

"Never doubt that I am real," I heard.

Tears filled my eyes involuntarily, and I was so, so still. The voice spoke and then it was gone. I wasn't paralyzed or shocked; I only became motionless in the desperate, *desperate* hope I might feel that presence again. Or to hear that voice again. Even to recall it in my mind. But it was just out of reach. The only thing that lingered was a feeling of pure love encircling every molecule and cocooning me in an ocean of it, right there where I sat on sticky red vinyl, on a pissing-rain day, in the greatest city in the world. I could have stayed there forever.

"I think supernatural things happen all over the world all the time," I said. "Just less so in Western culture maybe, because we're so quick to dismiss it. Well, we dismiss the good spiritual things anyway. Everyone loves ghost stories, but angels and Jesus are too far-fetched, I guess. But there's plenty of other cultures that live with spiritual interactions in daily life."

"Well, I really don't know what to do with this," she said. "I'm just trying to get a good night's sleep. I don't need *dementors* in my bedroom!"

I laughed. "On the bright side," I said, "now you know what to do to make them leave! Who needs a priest?"

I smiled. She smiled back, but she was still very unsettled.

"Look, I'm not an expert in this stuff," I said, "but I definitely believe there's an ongoing war between good and evil in the world. Your relationship with God is deepening, so it wouldn't surprise me if there was something spiritually dark that wanted to scare you away from that. You know? Keep you from experiencing God's love and becoming more of who you really are."

Camille nodded her head. "That makes sense."

"Can I pray for you?" I asked.

She again nodded her head. I took her hand and a deep breath. I closed my eyes and imagined the creator of the universe shrinking down into human form and sitting in the room beside us. I didn't like to pray aloud—I felt ill-equipped. I couldn't quote Scripture like Harker or Les could and I didn't always know what to ask for, but as I prayed I could feel the tension in Camille begin to fall away. I could feel the comfort that was coming to her through my prayer.

In that moment, with my eyes closed, I thought of Les and of what a huge responsibility it must be for him to constantly bear the weight of *people*. People asking for help, for wisdom, for prayer.

The thought made me grateful that I was being shepherded by someone who was so strong and unselfish, because even though it felt good to be a conduit for peace in Camille, I felt something else, too, something that in the wrong hands could be used to manipulate and abuse: I felt power.

CHAPTER ELEVEN

That Christmas, instead of going to either of my parents' houses and—to use Les's phrase—"pressing into" the family I'd inherited through their new spouses, I opted to go to Idaho. Everyone had been invited by Les and Pam to enact our right to "break away from the expectations other people put on us." Everyone except Camille, that is. I didn't find out until later that she'd been excluded. I thought she'd opted to spend Christmas with her family. Looking back, I wish I had seen her exclusion as the sign it was: that Les sensed Camille was not someone with the vulnerabilities he needed in a victim. Her family was intact, she had a strong base of love and support in her life outside of the group, and even with all her supernatural experiences, faith was something she approached more with logic than emotion. Camille was too much of a wild card, whereas I was a sure thing.

My parents were upset, as expected. I had been shuffling back and forth between them on holidays since they split to make it fair for each of them, but it didn't feel fair to me. I was tired of extended family gatherings with the new spouses' second cousins while suffering through incessant questions about being an actor. I wanted to enjoy Christmas and be somewhere I actually fit in.

They weren't the only parents who were unhappy. Dontay told me how confused and disappointed his mom was that she hadn't been invited to spend the holiday with him. Same with Emily's father. He still lived in the house where she'd grown up, not far from the Big House. He didn't understand why she would come back into town and stay there rather than stay with her family, and why she would come over only on Christmas Eve, and why he wasn't allowed to at least come to the Big House on Christmas Day. They'd spent so many holidays with the Van Hewitts before!

Emily just told her father there wasn't any room, now that Les and his family lived there and with everyone visiting from out of town. The real reason was what Pam had told all of us: "This is a precious time for us with Jesus and each other. We don't want to risk the flow of the Holy Spirit being interrupted by someone who isn't part of the circle of trust and vulnerability we've established."

Les concurred: "Not everyone belongs in the war room, you know? We need to honor the calling God has put on us as a community and protect that."

None of us disputed this. It made perfect sense to us.

On Christmas Eve, while Emily was at her father's house, the rest of us gathered in the living room. Everyone was there, including Juana and Miguel. Piled onto the couches, filling up the floor space, dining room chairs lugged in so everyone had a space to sit. To see the Los Angeles and Idaho groups together in one room felt important. We weren't just friends, we belonged with each other—*to* each other. *This has to be what family is supposed to feel like*, I thought.

Les had a new book to share. He had found a Welsh "prophet" gaining attention in the charismatic community by authoring a book titled *Designing Community Prayer*. As before, copies of the book were passed around.

"I feel so much of Heaven's heart in this book, friends," Les said. Salami jumped onto his lap and he stroked her, in his own little production of *The Godfather*. "I had a vision from the Lord that we are all on a ship together. The sea got rocky, and some of us were scared and wanted to jump ship, but we all had the same prayer, and we prayed it over and over until the waters were calm. Then I saw this book and I knew it was for us. God is giving us the tools to withstand anything together, if we stay in the boat. We need to apply all the things the Lord's been revealing to us and create crafted prayers that we can recite anytime."

"So, this is how crafted prayers work," Pam explained. She had an open notebook in her lap and a pen in her hand. "Abe's gonna play some music on the piano, and you just call out whatever God brings to your mind: the name of a person you want to pray for, a relationship you want to see restored. I'll write it all down, and afterward we'll use these things to create a prayer that we can all pray every day until we see our prayers answered."

Harker got up to dim the lights and light some candles, then sat back down next to Mina, her beautiful swollen belly a testament to how much God was blessing her for being an example of a surrendered, submissive wife. The atmosphere softened, and Abe started playing a worship song. It felt peaceful and safe. QB took hold of a small djembe, and the music swelled. People began singing. I closed my eyes and joined along in harmony, my voice lifting slightly above the rest.

As QB slapped out a steady rhythm on the drum, Les read from the book of Matthew. By now, all the meetings were run by Les and I wondered how Harker and Abe felt about it. It seemed natural for Les, a pastor, to be leading meetings in his own house— except it wasn't *really* his house. I glanced at Harker, considering what it might feel like having Les move into their childhood home, become best friends with their mother, and take over the leadership role in the Bible study. *Maybe it's a relief. They're so young to be discipling such a large group anyway.* I decided to see it that way and appreciated the brothers' humility.

"'Let the little children come to me, and do not hinder them, for the kingdom of God belongs to such as these. Truly I tell you, anyone who will not receive the kingdom of God like a little child will never enter it.' Mmm," said Les. "We're over here trying to be independent and do things on our own, but He's given us to each other as a physical representation of His presence. To lift each other up, hold each other accountable. You wanna see the kingdom of Heaven? The way is living surrendered like little children."

I didn't want to be hard and tough and do things on my own anymore. Feeling more confident and comfortable, I was the first to offer a crafted prayer.

"That the Lord would show me how to be innocent and reliant on Him again, like a kid," I called out as piano and drumbeat continued. Ed, bobbing his head as usual, reached over to pat me on the back. I looked at him, and he smiled with sweet eyes.

After everyone had called out their crafted prayers, the music stopped and we took a short break for Pam to go through and organize all her notes. I grabbed some water from the kitchen, where Les caught up with me.

"That was sweet, baby," he said. "I'm proud of you. I think that's gonna be really important for you in this next chapter of life. Relying on God like a child. Relying on the spiritual parents He's put in your life to represent Himself here. You're gonna see a lot of healing in those places in your heart where you get to be parented."

"Thanks, Les. I feel grateful to have you guys stepping into the role for me," I said.

"You have such a pretty singing voice," Les said.

"Aw, thank you," I said.

"But sometimes you overpower everyone and it can be a little distracting."

I suddenly felt terrible. *Of course* I was in the way. "Sorry . . . Shoot, I'm sorry."

"I just know honesty is important to you, and we've got to live in a space where we can say uncomfortable things to each other and let it be okay."

"No, I'm glad you told me!" I kept trying to make my voice quieter, basically mouthing the words. "I'd rather know!"

"I figured you would." He winked and walked back into the living room. I was disappointed in myself but grateful someone cared about me enough to tell me the truth and trust that I could handle it. In a way, it reminded me of how respected I used to feel by my own dad—he had always assumed I was capable. But there was an element of trust between us that had been missing for a long time, and now it felt like Les was picking up the slack.

Though everyone had called out all sorts of prayers—such as Emily wanting to see others and herself the way God saw her— the final crafted prayer was edited into something that could fit everyone. Before the end of the stay, we were each given a little card that Pam even had laminated, on which was typed out:

> I am a child in need of help, Lord. Teach me how to be dis-
> cerning and not cast pearls before swine. Release me from
> the need to fulfill others' expectations of me. Familial pat-
> terns no longer dictate who I am.

It was, of course, a methodical plan to isolate us from our loved ones. The more we functioned like a family, the easier it was for Les to manipulate us. He didn't even need to be subtle about it anymore. One afternoon over that holiday visit he started casually using a term I'd never heard before: "bio-family." This was meant to describe the family we were born into but wasn't necessarily the family we were *called* into.

"We can honor our bio-families without betraying who God's called us to be," Les explained with passion. His right hand always fell into a salute posture, thumb tucked under straight fingers. The more passionate he got, the more he'd emphasize with it. "He's brought us together for a purpose. We're on this ship, and we commit to never letting each other go. And that's gonna ruffle some feathers"—he laughed—"'cause it's not the way the world does it! But we're not here to please man. We're here to please God."

On Christmas morning, a flurry of people moved around one another in the house, cooking and trading plates, pouring juice and coffee; someone wanted plain pancakes and someone else wanted blueberry. Les fried up a good pile of bacon, half of which was eaten by the Barbarians. Ed, Pam, and Harker were the only ones who didn't eat meat, so Pam made a cornflake and cottage cheese casserole (shockingly, still intact by the end of the night). Miguel and Juana brought their four-year-old daughter, and the three of them went outside with Emily, Lucy, and Brandon to build a snowman. Harker read his Bible on the living room floor, Mina and Jasmine read the Welsh prophet's book on the couch, QB played a video game, and Dontay hopelessly worked on a Rubik's Cube. It was everything I wanted in a family holiday.

"Who'd you get for Secret Santa?" Dontay asked me. These were the only gifts we would be exchanging, and Les's idea was that they should all be bespoke. Custom-made for the person whose name you chose.

"Don't answer that!" Jasmine said, swatting him. "You're not supposed to ask people that. What if it's you!?"

"It's not me," Dontay said, assuring. "She's been walking around with pink paint on her hands! Joie, did you make me something pink?"

I looked up at Dontay from the beanbag chair I had flopped into and picked at the pink-paint evidence from the mixed-media collage I'd just finished making for Emily. "Nope." I smiled. "Not for you."

He stuck out his tongue at Jasmine, who rolled her eyes.

I enjoyed their sibling-like behavior. They'd both been living in the house for a year or so. Unlike those of us in LA, they were part of Les's real inner circle. Some nights, Jasmine and Dontay would even disappear into the master bedroom, invited to watch TV with Les, Marti, and the boys, where *The Sopranos* made a steady appearance. It was Les's favorite show. He really related to Tony—the way Tony was always under attack from outside forces and did whatever he had to do to keep his family together. I wasn't a fan of the show then—too much "tough Jersey" that I didn't want to revisit, and I was fine to sit and journal anyway. But I did wish sometimes that I was invited.

Suddenly, the supersized beanbag I was sitting on folded in around me and I was lifted off the ground. I could hear Les and Quiet Boy chuckling as I was wrapped tighter and tighter. So tight that I couldn't move. I felt extreme, visceral panic. And then I had a rapid succession of flashbacks: Three nurses putting me into a straitjacket so the doctor could stitch up a cut under my eyebrow from a living-room acrobatics incident. The man who played Boo

Radley to my Scout in that regional production of *To Kill a Mockingbird* throwing me up into the air in an outdoor pool in Texas. It was the summer my parents separated. Was he trying to date my mom? He later gave me a gold ID bracelet with his name on it. A boy in seventh grade shoving me against a chain-link fence and holding a metal bat to my throat because he was mad at me for ignoring him. An 11:00 p.m. meeting with director James Toback in his editing bay, naively thinking I was helping him out by meeting him late since he was on a long shoot, only to be paralyzed for an hour listening to him verbally undress me, saying things like "Every woman likes to be licked a different way." A young man in New York who was a part of my church violently lifting and holding me against a wall on the street while our friends watched. He pressed his body into mine and said with hot breath, "You'd better not talk like that unless you're ready to do something about it." I have no idea what I had said, but I remember our whole group of friends doing nothing but waiting for it to be over.

Les and QB were laughing. Everyone was laughing.

"One, two . . . three!" QB said, and I was in the air, free for a moment, only to land back on the bag they were holding. They wrapped me up again, getting a good grip on the bag.

"One, two . . . three!"

Oh, it's a game! I realized. *They're playing with me. They're not trying to hurt me. They're playing. Like family. There's no reason to be scared.*

The fear I was holding broke off, the flashbacks dissolved, and I started to laugh. I laughed so hard my eyes watered. When I landed on the ground again with a plop, safe and sound, I looked up. QB was smiling. Les and Dontay were chuckling.

I always wanted brothers.

Les tousled my hair. "You looked like you could use some shaking up," he said.

I stood and threw my arms around him in sobs.

"Oh no, I'm sorry, baby, did we hurt you? We were just playing."

"No, it's not that." I pawed at my face. "I just feel so loved. The only thing I've ever wanted was a big family like this."

Les hugged me back. "You *are* Family, Joy. You belong here." And if those weren't the magic words, that Christmas felt more meaningful than any I'd ever experienced—due in large part to the Secret Santa. Instead of being shuffled around to extended bio-family, suffering through the obligatory fawning over impersonal gifts like socks or a new Costco blender, this Family was exchanging gifts that had been painstakingly crafted for each person: a knitted sweater, a painting of someone's favorite childhood memory, custom jewelry. The generosity of time and thought put into these was extravagant.

That night in my bunk, I examined my own Secret Santa gift. It was from QB. He had built me a small wooden box, burnt my name and a rose into the top of it, and screwed in a lock; inside was a hand-bound journal with flower-adorned paper he'd molded and pressed from pulp. It must have taken months. It didn't strike me as romantic at the time because I saw him as a brother, but I felt seen and cared for. I fell asleep thinking about the next time I could come back to Idaho. I would have stayed longer, but January in LA was pilot season.

PART TWO

CHAPTER TWELVE

"I really think you should reconsider," my manager said from behind the desk of her Los Feliz office. "This pilot has a lot of buzz."

A couple days before, she had sent me a script for a Warner Bros. teen drama pilot called *Ravens*. I flipped through it without really reading.

High school, basketball, dumb jokes about sticky magazine pages, angsty girl, boring best friend, teenagers having sex . . . eh.

"I don't want to be stuck on a teen soap," I told her. "Especially not after two years on *Guiding Light*. I want to do film. I'm a good actress, and I want to tell meaningful stories and work with the best of the best."

"You will. You're consistently getting down to the last handful of actresses on huge studio movies. I think a job like this can only help push you over the line."

I'd started working with my manager while I was on *Guiding Light*. She believed in me so much she would—and had—personally walk into any casting office that wouldn't give me a chance.

"But no one on TV does film," I said. Which was true. It was an era before streaming, when movie stars wouldn't appear on an American TV show unless it was a cameo on *Friends*, and really talented TV stars couldn't pick up a role in a movie for fear their "little-box fame" would tarnish the grandiosity of the film.

"There are actors starting to cross over from TV to film," my manager said.

"Who?"

"Jennifer Aniston."

"She's the most famous woman in the world."

"Katie Holmes, Michelle Williams, Keri Russell . . ."

"Katie, okay. But Michelle is just doing indie movies. I haven't seen Keri in a film at all."

"Keri was just in *We Were Soldiers*, the Mel Gibson one."

I sighed. "She got that? Damn it. I liked that role."

"See."

"But they were all leads on their shows," I said. "This *Ravens* part is just a side character."

"I think it's gonna be a real ensemble show," she said.

Historically, I jumped at the chance to do any kind of work. But now, as I was trying to "come out of agreement" with the old narrative of me being second best, settling for a side role in what I thought was a teen soap felt like a spiritual test. *Do I really believe that God has better things for me, or am I going to keep believing a lie?*

"Listen," I said. "Since I was twelve years old I've been sitting in New York casting offices with Anne and Scarlett and Kirsten and Natalie and I *still* sometimes see their names on the sign-in sheet for screen tests I'm at. I mean, Julia Stiles can't be available for *everything*. Let's just wait. It's gonna happen."

"Okay," my manager said. "You know what you want. The WB loves you. There will be others."

And there soon was. I booked the female lead in a superhero pilot by *Mr. & Mrs. Smith* screenwriter Simon Kinberg for megaproducer Jerry Bruckheimer. Ironically, Camille had been cast in this role first, and I was next in line when she had to decline due to scheduling conflicts. Sure, technically this was violating my "no settling for second best" vow, but I saw it as an exception since it was Camille I was stepping in for and so it seemed more ordained by God. Also, a girl's gotta eat. It was a huge TV show with a huge budget and lots of buzz because no one was doing superheroes yet. After the pilot was shot, the word on the street was that this show was absolutely getting picked up. Then, just like so many before, it didn't.

With the discouragement of this, I pressed in even harder to the Family in LA—though we were experiencing a few changes. Now that Mina had her baby, she and Harker were preparing to move to Idaho full-time; Abe was focusing more and more on his band; and Les wasn't visiting LA as much as before. He called regularly to check on me and others in the group, but since he had started to develop a formal "ministry" vision for the Idaho "Big House Family," as we'd all playfully started referring to it, he didn't have as much time to visit. Naturally, Pam stepped into the leader/mother role to everyone in the LA group, including a few new girls who had found their way to us, like Emily's little sister and Gretchen's twin cousins.

Everyone started booking regular visits up north since Les couldn't come down to LA, but the one person who never came was Camille. In fact, we had all been seeing her less and less. She was a popular working actress, often on location for jobs, so I thought that was why. But one day we went to lunch, and the truth came out.

The week before, her parents had been in town, and they met up with a bunch of us at the Whisky a Go Go for a concert by Abe's band. Halfway through the set the band took a break, and I caught a brief glimpse of Pam exchanging some words with Camille's mother that didn't seem pleasant. But unlike the birthday conversation between Pam and my mom, the confrontation lasted only a moment, and Pam was soon smiling and talking to Emily, so I thought nothing more of it.

"Honestly, it was pretty weird, Joie," Camille said, moving the salad around her plate. "My mom was just asking her about what her role was in the church—"

"Wait, does she know that it's not . . . like, we don't have a church?"

"Yeah, but I think that's also what is confusing. Who's in charge?"

"No one," I said, just as I'd told my dad on the phone before. *Why did people keep asking about this?* "We're just friends meeting and doing life together."

"But there *are* leaders."

"Well, yeah, I guess. Harker and Abe sort of lead it, and I would say Ed and Pam are spiritual parents for us down here. And Les and Marti for the group up in Idaho."

She scrunched her face sideways and pinched her lips together. "Well, it definitely started with Harker and Abe just opening their home for people who were curious about God and wanted to pray and stuff. But . . . I mean, Joie, it hasn't been like that for a long time. Les and Pam have clearly taken over. And what are 'spiritual parents' anyway?"

"I don't see it as taking over. I see them as being really selfless and willing to step up into those natural parental roles for all of us. Spiritual parents basically step into the places where our bio-parents failed, and they help parent and guide us."

"'Bio-parents'?"

Because Camille hadn't been in Idaho for Christmas, she hadn't heard this term.

"Yeah, you know, biological parents, biological families. We've been adopted into God's kingdom, so the families that we were born into aren't always the families that are meant to have authority in our lives. In a lot of ways, Pam and Les function more like parents to me than my own do."

Camille considered this. "I guess I understand how—since there's so much drama with your parents—how maybe it's really helpful to have older figures who will care about you in that way."

"Yes, it's a huge blessing!"

"But I've got a good relationship with my parents. My family's not perfect, but I don't really need spiritual parents. I have parents."

"But if your parents don't know Jesus, how can they . . . I mean, spiritual things are spiritually discerned. If they don't have a relationship with God, then they can't give you wise counsel."

"Well, I don't know if you have to be a person of faith in order to have wisdom—"

I cut her off: "It says in the Bible that wisdom comes from God."

"But they *do* have a relationship with God."

"They do?"

"I was raised Catholic."

"Yeah, but that's religion. That's not moving with the Holy Spirit."

She shook her head and sighed. "Look, all I know is my mother was just trying to ask Pam for more details about the Bible study, like who's in charge, what authors they're teaching, who Les is and what his credentials are. Like, did he go to seminary? My mother was curious, and Pam got really closed off and started talking to her like she was an *enemy* or something. It was so weird."

"That doesn't sound like Pam."

"Well, Mom tried to assure her that she's only trying to understand because I'm her daughter and she loves me. And Pam said, 'She's our daughter, too, and *we* love her.'" Camille paused and her eyes went wide. "Like, come on, that's kinda creepy—telling someone's mother that she's actually your child instead?"

"I . . ." I didn't know what to say. "Are you sure your mom heard her right? We were in a club."

"She said Pam was very clear."

". . . I don't know, Cam. Honestly? I just . . . I don't believe Pam said that." I shrugged apologetically. "I've known her for almost two years now. She's always been really sweet and consistent and—"

"My mom wouldn't randomly lie about that."

"She must have misunderstood, then," I concluded.

We sat in silence at the table, neither of our meals being properly disturbed.

She shook her head and looked down. "I think I'm just gonna take a break from Bible study."

I couldn't believe we were here, God having brought us both so far and she was going to bail.

"Doesn't this seem like the enemy is just getting exactly what he wants?" I said. "You've come so far, your prayer life is thriving, all these amazing little miracles are happening all the time. You're really gonna give that up because of a misunderstanding?"

Camille looked at me with tremendous sadness and pity. At the time, I thought it was for herself—for not being strong and courageous enough to fully surrender her life to God. Now I realize it was for me.

"Anytime you wanna talk or hang out, you know I love you and we're good . . . That's just not the right place for me right now."

We ended lunch with one last hug and went our separate ways. I wouldn't see her again for two years.

CHAPTER THIRTEEN

In June, I received another phone call from my manager about *Ravens*, the TV series I'd turned down. It had been picked up and now had a new title: *One Tree Hill*. They were recasting a role and were specifically asking for me.

"It starts shooting in ten days in North Carolina, and I think she'd be perfect for this part," the casting director told my manager. "Can you please ask her to reconsider and come read for us?"

I still wanted a film career. I knew I had a thousand different characters inside me and a hundred ways to play them. I wanted the chance to learn and play in the majors, and this TV job still felt like Little League. But I also wanted to *work*. Where was the line between being grateful for every opportunity and not compromising my own vision? I didn't know. I prayed for wisdom, decided to let God make the choice for me, and told my manager I'd take the audition.

I sat in the waiting room with a *really* pretty brunette who was listening to this cool new iPod thing everybody was talking about and had laser focus on her script pages. She smiled politely at me and then went back to her work. I was called into a bright room with the show's creator and a couple of other people. I read my scenes for the girl-next-door part they had originally called me about, and it went very well. The script was fun and easy, the dialogue was natural, and I felt comfortable in this Haley James character's skin. Just as I was about to leave, the casting director surprised me by asking if I would read for a different part they were writing: a "vixen next door." Instantly, all my internal Christian-purity-culture alarms went off. I was trying to be the best version of myself now. Innocent. Childlike.

Oh, no. The enemy is trying to trap me. How can I be a good Christian if I play the sexpot?

I read it for them but gave a subpar performance on purpose in hopes that they'd only consider me for the first role. I didn't need to worry. I never had a real shot at that vixen character. The casting director was probably trying to use a good actress to prove to the showrunner that no one would be better for that dynamite part than the pretty, headphoned brunette I had just met.

The next step was the screen test two days later. Things were moving so fast because filming for season one would begin within the week. In most cases, the screen test is the last stop after a series of callbacks before you get the job. Your contract is negotiated before you arrive, and your episodic fee is always based on your past paychecks on other shows. Every job drives up an actor's "quote," which is a weird conundrum for actors who, like me, were still considered unknown but had higher quotes because of all the grounded TV pilots we'd shot. Do we take the lower paycheck to make ourselves more appealing to the studio's budget? Or do we hold the salary we've earned and hope the studio values us? It's a gamble on yourself, knowing that if they can hire a different actor for cheaper, they will—so if you stick to your quote (like I did), you'd better bring something really special to the screen test.

This particular screen test also served as a "chemistry read," which means they put you in a room with ten executives in chairs and an actor who's already been cast. The Suits are trying to assess if you look good together on camera and if you have that elusive, non-manufacturable *something* that makes everyone want to keep watching their show.

One of those executives (whom, to this day, I've never actually seen wear a suit) called my manager the night before the screen test. He had also been in charge of another project I'd been invited to test for a year before: the Amanda Bynes show *What I Like About You*. I had turned down that invitation. The show was marketed toward tween girls, and I was concerned that the big-sister role I was testing for—which eventually went to the lovely Jennie Garth—was a woman living with her boyfriend. I didn't want to normalize "living in sin" for young girls.

After my manager got off the phone with this executive, she called me.

"I have a direct quote that I've been asked to relay to you," she said, "to make sure you know exactly what you're getting into before you sign this contract."

"Okayyy," I said cautiously.

"He said, 'You tell her this show is about fucking and sucking, and if she's gonna have a problem with that, she shouldn't come in tomorrow.'"

My manager paused. I didn't know what to say. She didn't, either.

"So," she finally asked, "what do you think?"

I had seen the pilot. It was clearly influenced by *8 Mile*, the recent Eminem–Brittany Murphy movie, which was graphic and raunchy, but which I actually loved because of how real the pain felt. In spite of my childhood stint as a singing songbook sidekick, I loathed "Christian" movies. They dealt with tragedy and pain in a way that was too pat and lacked the complexity and nuance of real life. I believed it was imperative that stories portray relatable darkness and struggle because, to me, this is where redemption can come alive. So, grit didn't scare me, and the *One Tree Hill* pilot had grit.

The show was about two half brothers attending high school

in the small town of Tree Hill. One brother was the son of a single mom. Though they lived paycheck to paycheck, they were happy. This brother was a reader and poet, but secretly a basketball whiz, a skill he inherited from his father. His father still lived in the town, but in the wealthy area with his wife and second son by a minute. This brother was also a basketball star and the most popular kid in town. The brothers fought over a beautiful moody girl. Her best friend was the sexy comic relief. I would be the awkward girl next door.

In the pages I'd read, the characters had significant depth. I knew my character was the most wholesome of all, so I didn't feel too at risk of being objectified. One thing I was sure of: I wasn't in Hollywood to make Christian movies. I wanted to tell real stories. *One Tree Hill* felt different from most bubble-gum TV with subliminal agendas. I believed in this show and its ability to send meaningful, uplifting messages to the audience.

"Just tell him I understand what he's saying," I said to my manager. "I'm not gonna try and stop them from writing about real teenagers. I believe in this show and I want to be a part of it."

The screen test took place at the Warner Bros. Ranch in North Hollywood. I'd been screen-testing there since I was in high school. One time, Selma Blair went in after me to screen-test for *Zoe, Duncan, Jack & Jane*. Her water bottle started leaking all over her hands just before she walked into the testing room, and I remember thinking, *Damn. That is _perfect_ for this character. She's totally gonna get this*. And she did.

The ranch was more informal than the enormous, gated WB studio lot a few blocks away. Little casting and production bungalows peppered manicured paths of flowers and shaped topiaries.

It always felt magical going there and knowing I was creating art, even for a moment, in the same place where some of my favorite childhood shows like *Bewitched* and *I Dream of Jeannie* were filmed. When I had time after tests or auditions, I would usually drive around and look at the sets from those bygone days, preserved like monuments, as well as the new ones under construction. This time, though, I didn't dawdle. I parked toward the far edge of the lot to give myself time for a thinking walk, running lines as I slowly headed toward the screen-test building I had been walking into for years.

I signed in and soon was escorted into the testing room by a casting assistant. I waved at everyone, as was customary. No hugs here.

"Everyone, this is Joie Lenz. She's reading for Haley. Joie, this is Chad Michael Murray. He'll be reading with you."

This guy Chad was apparently pretty famous already, with recurring roles on *Gilmore Girls* and *Dawson's Creek*, but I didn't watch a lot of TV then, so I wasn't at the disadvantage of being impressed by him except for his compelling performance in the pilot as Lucas Scott, the bookish-secret-sports-star-from-the-wrong-side-of-the-tracks. He was tall but stood hunched and bashful. Then he shook my hand with both of his and smoldered at me. *Was he doing Brando?* Funny how I'd have jumped out of a moving cab in New York to get a guy this hot to notice me, but here in a work context, I just thought he had something in his eyes. I could see why he was becoming a star. He had all the right elements for taping up on a bedroom wall.

"Hi, Joie, thank you *so much* for coming in today."

I smiled back and said the thing you're supposed to say: "Oh my gosh, of course, thank you for having me!"

This was a dance of niceties everyone in LA seemed to do. I

preferred the pragmatism of New York casting directors and actors who might thank you for coming in as a measure of professional courtesy, but only in the way one might thank their mailman for dropping off a package. Questions and answers and kind exchanges were sincere. New Yorkers are time-savers and primarily interested in a job well done. If you do a good job, *then* they thank you profusely. If you're a cool person who works hard, they keep bringing you back. It was very straightforward.

Los Angeles social cues confused me. The way people interacted had so many time-wasting layers. *Hi, unemployed, unknown actor who has been invited into one of the most elite rooms where everyone here has the power to give you the life you've always wanted. Let me show you how humble I am by thanking you for sacrificing your time, even though we both know this is literally the only place in the world you want to be. I just want to make sure you leave this experience knowing that I'm amazing.*

Oh, but no! Allow <u>me</u> to show you how humble <u>I am</u> by expressing how lucky I feel to be invited into your presence. It is I who am grateful. And you are too kind to even imagine I would rather be somewhere else. Also, if I don't get this job, I just want to make sure you know that I know you're amazing, so maybe you'll give me a different job some other time. Then we can talk more about how amazing we both are!

After all this sucralose, the rejection of not getting a job in LA always hurt worse than it did in New York, because I am a person who believes people.

To be fair, Chad's sweetness was actually sincere, as I would come to learn. I just always hated how in Hollywood auditions you had to perform a scene before the scene had started.

There was a cafeteria lunch table and two chairs by our marks that we could sit at or not. They rolled the camera, and as I looked at this sandy-blond-haired guy I was supposed to be high school best friends with, Blue Eyes was the obvious emotional reference. Any nerves I had dissipated when I realized all I had to do right then was relive one of any number of summer days with him, our feet hanging off the lake dock.

I moved the chairs out of the way and jumped up to sit on top of the table like a bench. This caused a slight but clearly discernible change in the room's energy. There was the faint sound of people leaning forward in their seats. I thought I even heard a chuckle. Clearly no one who had auditioned had pulled this move. Chad smiled, excited that I wanted to play and have fun. That's what acting is supposed to be. That's why most of us started doing it. Because nothing is more fun than make-believe. But once you start doing it professionally, the trick is to not get lost in your ego and forget how. Trying to become more childlike in my spiritual life, however, was allowing me to be more childlike in my acting life. Chad eagerly joined me on the table, and we started the scene.

HALEY: Did you ever figure out your porn name?

LUCAS: What are you talking about?

HALEY: Your porn name. Um, you know, you take the name of your first pet and your mother's maiden name and you put them together. What was the name of your first pet?

LUCAS: You know that. I had a dog named Rocket.

HALEY: Oh, Rocket! Ah! I loved Rocket. *[Pause]* So your mother's maiden name is Roe. Rocket Roe! *[Laughs]* Nice.

LUCAS: What's yours?

HALEY: Uh, oh, I had a bunny, named Bunny.

LUCAS: You had a bunny named Bunny?

HALEY: Yes, I did. And my mother's maiden name is Beaugard. So . . .

LUCAS: Bunny Beaugard.

HALEY: *Dawson's Freak*. Starring Rocket Roe and Bunny Beaugard.

LUCAS: Nice.

HALEY: Shut up!

At this line, I kicked Chad sideways with my foot. *Boom.* The energy of the room shifted even more. I think because Chad was kinda famous, all the other girls reading with him were perhaps intimidated or afraid to touch him. These executives had been watching this scene over and over again, but the moment our bodies physically connected, they all woke up. Sometimes that's all it takes to get a job: doing something that wakes up the room. So, I leaned into that, and for the rest of the scene I treated Chad like a little brother.

HALEY: Hey, um, this game tonight. You're not playing anymore?

LUCAS: No. *[Pause]* You know I've never walked away from anything before, Haley?

HALEY: Yeah.

LUCAS: But I can't do it. And even worse, I don't know why I can't do it. You know, it's like, no matter how confusing or screwed up life got, the game always made

sense. It was mine, you know. And in a lot of ways it's
who I am. But I can't be that person in their gym, or in
their uniforms, or . . . in their world.

I had read these lines over a dozen times, but only there in the
room did I recognize the parallel between what Lucas was going
through and my own life. It was as if I were talking to myself.
And having Chad there as a physical manifestation of my inner
turmoil, I was moved to offer myself comfort in a way I hadn't
been able to in all these months. I reached out and put my arm
around him.

HALEY: I hear you, Luke. But I know you. And I know
that no matter what happens you're still going to be the
same guy you always were. No uniform, no . . . whatever,
is gonna ruin that, you know?

Chad smiled at me. But Chad was no longer Chad. This was no
longer make-believe. We had reached that rare but always sought-
after moment in acting where the performance becomes reality.
A kind of transubstantiation. For those brief moments, on that
altar of a cafeteria table, Joy and Chad became Haley and Lucas. I
paused, jumped up off the table, and ruffled his hair.

HALEY: Call me later. We'll go get some pizza.

He laughed and pushed my hand away, and we made faces at
each other and I walked out of the scene.
I knew something special had just taken place, but if the Suits
did too, they didn't let on as we said the usual thank-yous and
goodbyes and other gag-inducing politesse.

As I walked back to my car I heard someone shouting, "Joie!" I turned and saw Chad jogging across the parking lot toward me. Now that our work was done, I could better appreciate his attractiveness, though the sight of him jogging mainly reminded me of Dontay running the softball bases and made me long for the next chance I'd get to see him in Idaho—my crush had been steadily intensifying over the last few months.

"Hey!" I said. "Did I leave something in there?"

"No," Chad said. "I just wanted to congratulate you and say welcome to the show! You knocked it out of the park in there."

He came in for a hug. I didn't know what to say. I'd never had an actor come out from a screen test right away and tell me I got the job. That was reserved for producers, managers, and lawyers to haggle about before someone won the prize of calling the actor with the great news. The star of the show was personally telling me *on the spot* that I got the job. I felt bubbling excitement, but I also had been in this business long enough to know nothing is real until you're filming. And even then you could end up on the cutting-room floor or the whole project might get shelved. I knew better than to get excited, but I thanked Chad and said I hoped it worked out.

The phone call from my manager came the following morning: I would leave for Wilmington, North Carolina, in five days.

Over that next week, I was riddled with anxiety about leaving my new spiritual Family. It was a series pickup, which meant twenty-two episodes, eight days per episode—essentially the next nine months of my life were committed to this new assignment.

I'm not ready for this! I'm just relearning how to be a kid. I'm trying to heal. Why did I put myself in this position? Why did I even say

*yes in the first place? I've been on my own for so long and now I finally
have a Family, and I don't want to go out on my own again!*

Les and Marti called me together to say congratulations: "We
heard the news! Sounds like a fun job, and we just wanted you to
know we're cheering you on!"

My car would be picked up for shipping the morning of my
flight. I gave my apartment key to Emily in case anyone wanted to
continue to use it for a prayer retreat, packed a couple of bags, and
prepared my mind and heart to leave.

The Bible study group gathered for a farewell meal at Coco's,
a chain restaurant, on LA's outskirts. Since the Van Hewitts in
their former life as Seventh-day Adventists had long viewed food
as fuel and nothing more, they had less than discerning taste buds,
and Coco's—one step up from a diner—was their favorite go-to
spot. I knew better than to complain. I'd once tried to reroute us to
sushi when Les was in town with the Barbarians. He joked about
how high-maintenance I was.

In the parking lot after passing over most of my country fried
steak, sweet Ed asked if he could pray for me. I appreciated Ed's
prayers because they always seemed reluctant. I could relate to the
feeling of awkwardness that accompanied talking to God out loud
in front of other people. I appreciate that quality even more now
that I know what a red flag it is when someone is reaaaally comfortable improvising elaborate prayers. That wasn't Ed. He lived
in Pam's shadow, quiet and often solitary. So whenever he offered
to pray, I knew he meant it.

"Lord, we are humbled to be here to encourage your daughter
Joy—"

"Your precious daughter," Pam interjected.

Ed paused and then continued. "We thank you for caring about
us and listening. We thank you for giving Joy this opportunity to

get to know you better in a new environment. Please keep her safe. Give her safe travels . . ." My eyes were closed, but we were holding hands, and I could feel him bouncing on his toes as he thought. ". . . give her permission to be excited."

The group echoed their "yeses" and "amens." Everyone else prayed, too, an awkward tradition in many charismatic crowds where all are expected to pray because it's a bad look if you don't want to talk to God. For this reason it took about thirty-five minutes to break the late-night hand-holding circle and leave the parking lot of this mediocre chain restaurant in the central valley. Emily sent me off with a journal that had Bible verses written on various pages, Pam gave me a card that said something overly sappy, and I climbed into my car, finally alone.

Driving back to my apartment, I thought about the last line of Ed's prayer, and my anxiety turned to excitement.

Who is this Haley James? Does she have a southern accent? How does she walk? Is she a fast talker or slow talker? Do her ears stick out? I could put some bobby pins behind my ears to make them poke out— that would be cute! Does she have blonde hair like mine? Or should it be brown? The other actress from the pilot is blonde, maybe I should change to brunette. Where is she insecure and where is she confident? What kind of family did she grow up in? Is she clumsy? Is she goofy? Is she studious and quiet?

I had so many questions. So many ideas.

I spent the next day of flying—including a connection and layover—furiously writing as many things as I could think to ask about or create for the character. At last, I landed in Wilmington.

CHAPTER FOURTEEN

August in a southern beach town is only one thing. Hot. Like some stressful Hitchcock film where the sun has moved closer to the earth and Vera Miles is dragging herself on the ground to reach the city's last working water fountain. Stepping out of the airport, I was ambushed by a steamy mass from the Atlantic burrowing into my bones. I breathed as deeply as I could, with the weight of water and salt on my chest taking me right back to my childhood in Florida. Gloriously, my skin was wet in under ten seconds. In the car, I asked the driver if we could turn off the air-conditioning and roll down the windows. He looked at me in the rearview mirror and smiled at what he thought was a joke. When he realized it wasn't, his smile disappeared, and he dutifully rolled down the windows. En route to the studio, where I was due for a wardrobe fitting, he drove well over the speed limit, trying to generate more of a breeze (and get me out of his car quicker).

We turned into the EUE/Screen Gems Studios in downtown Wilmington. These were legendary stages owned by Frank Capra Jr., whose father was the famous 1930s and 1940s film director of *It's a Wonderful Life*, *Arsenic & Old Lace*, and Hollywood's first rom-com, *It Happened One Night*. Capra Jr. wanted to build a Hollywood East with lower production costs and to take advantage of the historic small town and beach scenery. *One Tree Hill* would take over the filming stages from *Dawson's Creek*, but before that show Screen Gems was the filming place for movies such as *Em-*

pire Records, Crimes of the Heart, Blue Velvet, 28 Days, A Walk to Remember, and Drew Barrymore's *Firestarter.* Eerily, it was also the place where Brandon Lee died during an on-set accident while filming *The Crow.*

I was used to the LA studios that towered over everything and whose manicured garden paths were tread on by executives headed to important meetings in buildings with beautifully framed movie posters and cappuccino machines. This was far humbler, with six low-ceilinged stages on blacktop, a gravel lot for trailers, and no roses. Staff and crew all knew one another from filming the pilot and being in preproduction for a month already. In the production office—its walls covered in mood boards and actors' headshots— I was greeted with smiles and sweet tea and then looks of surprise when I told them to call me "Joy" even though the production sheet said "Bethany."

Prior to my arrival, I had decided as part of my commitment to "becoming who God made me to be," I would not volunteer at a soup kitchen or build houses with Habitat for Humanity, but go back to my birth name. "Joie"—the nickname I'd adopted at thirteen and that everyone knew me by professionally—yes, *that's* what was standing in my way! A false self I'd created to try to make myself special. In an act of defiance against acting as an idol in my life, I would throw away all the professional credits I'd amassed for ten years and would henceforth be known by my full name: "Bethany Joy Lenz." At least, that's how I wanted it to appear in the show's credits. But on set I still wanted people to call me "Joy."

A production assistant showed me to my trailer, the front half of a double banger, which I would waste no time in decorating with obscene amounts of *stuff* from Target. On my way to meet hair and makeup, I passed a tall boy with dark hair whom I'd seen in the pilot. Teen shows like this one were famous for casting actors way older than their characters. Gabrielle Carteris had been twenty-nine when she started playing sixteen-year-old Andrea Zuckerman on *Beverly Hills, 90210*. From what my manager told me, the age gap of our cast wasn't so egregious. Most of the actors were in their early twenties. But this kid had to be an actual teenager.

"Oh, hey, I'm James Lafferty," he said, stopping to shake my hand. James played Nathan Scott, the privileged half brother.

"Hi, I'm Joy, I'm playing Haley," I clarified. "You were great in the pilot."

"Nice to meet you! You said Julie?"

"Joy. Bethany. But"—now reciting this for the seventy-third time and regretting my decision—"Joy-is-my-middle-name-everyone-calls-me-Joy."

"Oh, got it. Well, welcome to the show, Joy! Hopefully we'll get some scenes together!"

Oh, we would have plenty. Neither of us knew it at the time, but our characters would get married in high school and become one of the most popular TV couples in pop-culture history.

For now, we were just strangers in the heat. The PA who was showing me around heard something on her radio earpiece and clicked the little black box microphone attached to her shirt. "Copy that." She looked up at James. "New basketball coordinator is here to meet you."

"Okay, see you soon!" James said, and hurried off.

I waved bye and stepped up into a cool blast of air from the hair and makeup trailer.

As with many productions, this trailer was the nerve center of the whole operation, since it's the one place every actor has to visit before they walk on set. Hair and makeup is a constantly evolving organism. The mood of the room changes depending on the content of the scene that's about to be filmed. There were mornings

I'd walk in and Motown would be blasting and three people would be waiting because the six chairs were already full of actors, some half-dressed, and everyone chattering. Other times I'd step in and find silence, save for the dull drone of a single blow dryer as a lone actor prepared to shoot an emotional scene and needed no distractions. This was the sacred space where all secret conversations were held. No microphones inside, and whispers could easily be tucked under all the other sounds. This was where we would see the raw, real versions of one another before the makeup went on, before the hangover cleared, after the breakup, after the on-set argument—all of these more likely given how young we were. Because of their eagerness to listen, their ability to keep secrets, and the wisdom they dispensed—along with plenty of dirty jokes and the occasional hidden bottle of tequila—to me, the women who ran this trailer were the Mama Bears.

I extended my hand to the peppy, freckled hair department key but was pulled into a big hug.

"Welcome to the showwww!!!" she said with a cute, tight voice.

The rest of the Mama Bears followed suit. The ritual of hugs reminded me of the Big House and made me a bit sad, but there was no time for melancholy as I was whisked into a chair and brushed, examined, color matched, and questioned.

"Oh, your hair is curly. We'll have to straighten it. Are you against going brunette? Split ends. Let's trim you up."

"What's your skin type? You've got an olive tone, so maybe you're combination but lean oily. How does your skin hold makeup in humidity?"

The wardrobe designer also dropped by to fuss over me.

"Do you feel like Haley wears more vintage or, like, the Gap? Hourglass figure. Are you sure you're a twenty-six in jeans?"

I watched them buzz around me. *Pat, pat here, pat, pat there, and a couple of brand-new straws. That's how we keep you young and fair in the merry old land of Oz.* I was happy to go along with all of it. We were building a character. Creating something out of nothing. It was magic in the making.

The next day we had a table read with the whole cast over lunch. I sat beside two 1990s heartthrobs: Paul Johansson and Craig Sheffer. Paul had been a big deal on TV in the '90s and was playing Dan Scott, the father of the half brothers at the center of the story. He also reminded me a bit of Dontay: he had the same imposing size—though more Canadian lumberjack than college football player. Craig had appeared in films such as *Some Kind of Wonderful* and alongside Brad Pitt in *A River Runs Through It* and was now playing Dan Scott's brother, Uncle Keith. Like Paul, he had a rugged vibe, only covered in denim, which worked for him *very* well. I developed a crush on him, too, which Paul would later taunt me about endlessly. The first thing Craig said to me, after doing a double take under the room's harsh fluorescent lights, was "Whoa, you look like a monster!" Which is always nice for a young woman to hear. We laughed about it, and then I met more producers, hugged Chad, waved at James, and shook hands with Hilarie Burton. Hilarie's career had started as an on-air personality for MTV. This was her first dramatic role. She was playing Peyton Sawyer, the girl the two brothers were fighting over. Though she was much more jovial and self-assured than her character, Hilarie had a similarly magnetic aura that drew everyone in: she was already everyone's sister; one of the boys with no competitive vibes toward the girls. I liked her right away.

The only person at the table whom I avoided was one of my

acting heroes, Moira Kelly, who I'd watched more times than I could count in the rom-com classic *The Cutting Edge*. She'd starred opposite Robert Downey Jr. in *Chaplin*, then went on to *The West Wing*. Now she was playing the mother of Lucas Scott. Since childhood, I had experienced a kind of paralysis in desire. The more I wanted something, the more terrified I became. There was the possibility that I would get what I wanted, only to fail and find out I'm not worthy of it. There was also the possibility I would *not* get what I wanted, also proving I'm not worthy of it. Knowing that she was in the show was what confirmed for me it had substance. I wanted Moira to be my mentor, to learn everything she had to teach about the craft of acting, but I was so scared she'd say no, or she'd say yes and I'd disappoint her, that I simply shook her hand, said hello, and watched her from a distance for the next ten years.

As the weeks went on, the cast and crew spent time getting to know one another, finding ways to bond, figuring out who got along and who didn't, anthropologically sorting ourselves into categories: nerdy, jock-y, foodie, debaucherous, old, whimsical, religious (guess who). We fell in stride with whoever matched our sensibilities.

Hilarie and I were a cross section of nerdy-whimsical, but definitely most heavy on the whimsy. We talked on a loop about our childhood love for Shelley Duvall's '80s TV show *Faerie Tale Theatre*, quoted Sondheim, shared poetry, and drove all over Wilmington antiquing. We both collected odd things, like taxidermy and Victorian grieving lockets with human hair inside. She also loved to craft and was always making something new out of something old. Once, I entered my trailer and discovered a gift from her: a Macallan 10 whisky box she'd painted in bronze acrylic, adorned with a glued-on flea-market photo, and covered in an original poem written with metallic marker. She grew around my heart like a honeysuckle vine and I was happy for the feeling of sisterhood.

Late as I was to the production, I wasn't the last cast member to arrive. At the table read for the third episode, in walked the pretty iPod girl from my audition. This was Sophia Bush, who was playing Peyton's funny BFF, Brooke Davis. Sophia herself was also hilarious and a bit mischievous, always down for an impulsive adventure. Shortly after she arrived in Wilmington, she asked me to go with her to pick up a pit bull puppy that someone was selling. We drove two hours across North Carolina. On the return trip, we had in the car not only the pit bull puppy but a golden Lab puppy I bought, caught up in the moment. That night I slept over at her apartment, and the four of us creatures piled into her brand-new pristine white bed. The next morning we woke up with the bright sun pouring onto us and puppy shit all over the comforter. We were in fits of laughter.

"I thought you raised a bunch of dogs growing up!" I said.

"Well, my *parents* did!" she cackled with that throaty husk she'd soon become so famous for, and we stripped her bed while the dogs wrestled on the floor.

A few weeks later, I realized I wasn't equipped to raise a hyper puppy while working long hours, and I found a nice family with a farm for her to live on. I also soon realized I wasn't equipped to get too close to Sophia. As bubbly and compassionate as she was, she was even more intelligent. She had the kind of brain that logged daily activities on a mental spreadsheet, or could read Carl Sagan's *Cosmos* and tell you "We make our world significant by the courage of our questions and by the depth of our answers" was on page 120 at the end of the fourth paragraph. Her mind could've been put to good use by NASA—except, of course, she's so beautiful the astronauts would never want to leave Earth. She reminded me of the way I felt around Blue Eyes's family and his cheerleader. Sophia was a Nantucket girl, and I was trying so hard not to feel the sting of that comparison again.

I failed to notice that she was also trying hard. Frequently favored and constantly underestimated in life because of her beauty, Sophia worked obsessively at proving her value—a character trait that made her perfect to play Brooke Davis but clashed with my own insecurities and militant beliefs about *how* one should go about proving their value. I missed the irony that I was doing exactly the same thing, only I was using religion as my benchmark. My budding friendship with sweet Sophia became a casualty of this and, instead of sitting shiva for my ego, I really fucking wish I could turn back time, walk into her trailer, and give her a long, hard hug.

The only people on set who I knew for sure were Christians were two wardrobe girls and the driver who picked me up from the airport and would shuttle me to and from the set each day. Once he knew I was a Christian and liked to talk about God, he didn't mind so much keeping the car windows down. I made a few visits to the church that he and his wife went to, but the more I hung out with them, the more I was reminded that they weren't my new Family. When I brought up strategies for deflecting demonic attacks from Jezebel and dismantling religious structures, they just looked at me strangely.

If Christians in a small southern town weren't ready to dive in that deep, there was no way my costars would. Aside from that, I'd been a professional actress long enough to know that, though it's a creative space, a Hollywood studio is still a workplace. In those days, politics and religion were topics of conversation people still avoided at work and dinner tables, because the thing we were creating was more important than everyone agreeing with us.

I did talk freely about leaving town to go back to Idaho on occasion to visit family. Until, that is, enough friendly small talk starting with "Where are you from, Joy?" led to a perplexed expression and the dawning realization that whoever was in Idaho was not, in fact, my actual family at all.

"So, you live in LA near your mom, and your dad is in New Jersey . . . but you have a *group* in Idaho where you spend all your free time?"

I never knew how to respond. The answer was yes, but the way they said it made it sound strange. *How do I explain years' worth of bonding and spiritual growth and friendship to someone who has never experienced it?* I decided early on the less I said about my spiritual life, the better off I'd be.

Keeping my inner life a secret only added to my loneliness. I *wanted* to join in with the cast and crew in all their bonding adventures, but I was afraid of being what Les had called "double-minded." How could I bond with them and keep my deepest inner self a secret? I'd be lying to everyone just to get a false feeling of belonging. I feared my lifelong desire for approval would take over and I'd lose all the spiritual ground I'd gained.

During my last trip to the Big House before leaving for Wilmington, Les told me over a late-night chat on the front porch, "What happens is we become addicted to the high. The dopamine hit you get from the attention of people you think are impressive—that's addictive. There's a part of you that wants something from those people you work with. So, you have to treat yourself like an addict. Just remove yourself from situations where you'll be tempted."

To accomplish this, I rented a house on Wrightsville Beach,

isolated from all the activity. Instead of going out for drinks with the cast and crew, I stayed in and wrote songs on my piano, learned my lines, and waited for visitors from my new Family.

Emily was the first. She stayed for a week, visiting the set and meeting everyone. She was friendly and easily integrated into the environment since, in her job as a talent manager, she was already so familiar with Hollywood.

With the weather finally cooling as the winter months approached, Emily and I took long beach walks with tea and sweaters. On our last stroll before she left, she told me about a major life change.

"Soooo, I have some fun news! I'm moving to Idaho!"

"Whoa, bury the lede!"

"I know—I didn't want to take away from celebrating you here, but I'm so excited."

"Did you get an apartment?"

"No, I'm gonna room with Jas for a few months until I find a place."

"Wait, are you quitting your job?"

"I am!"

"Why? You've worked so hard to get where you are!"

"I've been talking a lot with Les and Pam, and the thing is I really want to be a wife and a mom, and staying in LA is only advancing my career. I want to take the leap of faith to show God that I'm ready for the next step—you know, create space in my life for what's important to me! I can always go back to a career, but I only have a short window to be a mom. And I really don't think I'm gonna meet anyone in LA."

"Wow, I can't believe you're leaving the industry. That's wild. I bet your bio-mom will be super upset."

"Oh, yeah." She rolled her eyes and sighed. "That Jezebel

spirit is coming out strong. She literally tried to ship me off to some relatives in Sweden. The closer I get to the Lord, the more she freaks out because she can't control me anymore. She's mad at Pam because she feels betrayed. She was like, 'I've known Pam for twenty years and I trusted her to look after you, and now she's got some sick bent on making you her own daughter!' Like, she can't handle the fact that God is providing me with a mom figure to fill in all the gaps that she couldn't fill herself."

I shook my head, knowing my own mom felt the same way. The coastal breeze blew over us. "This stuff is not easy," I said. "I think about Camille and how she couldn't make space for the gift God was giving her in having Pam as a spiritual mother. The enemy is always gonna try and keep us from God's gifts, and you're not letting him. I'm proud of you."

"I'm so proud of *you*!" she said. "This is hard, to be all the way across the country from your whole community. And to stand your ground and not give in to living life the way everyone else here is? You're inspiring!"

"Where are you gonna work?" I asked her.

"Oh! I totally forgot to tell you. Les is buying a hotel to turn into a ministry center, and I'm gonna manage it!"

"What?" I was thrown. How was Les going to afford a hotel? Everything about his and the Big House Family's life was meager. He didn't have a job and was only just starting to build his new ministry. I wasn't sure how they afforded *anything*.

"Howww . . . I mean . . ." I laughed nervously. "How?"

Emily clearly understood. She shrugged her shoulders and turned up her hands. "He says he has a plan!"

CHAPTER FIFTEEN

Since that conversation about "spiritual authority" the summer before, the group had begun to more clearly delineate who were the "children" and who were the "parents." Les and Martine, Pam and Ed, and Kurt and Lucy had settled into clear roles as parents. In fact, they made it official, forming a Leadership council they were calling the Hamoatzah, which they explained was Hebrew for "council."

The official nature of the group meant they were required to have more meetings among the six of them. This was the reason Les gave for why he and Kurt were flying to see me but could stay for only one night. I believed them, though now I suspect they knew that if they stayed longer than one night, I would insist they come visit the set, and they didn't want to raise any suspicions being introduced to my coworkers. Also, one night was all they needed to ask me for money for the hotel—the real reason for their visit. That evening we grabbed a burger at the local Irish pub downtown. Everyone else in the place was drinking Guinness. We stuck to sodas. They sat across from me looking more put together than usual. Collared shirts, combed hair. This was their way of dressing up for a business meeting. Kurt handed me a foldout pamphlet they'd designed and printed at Kinko's. On the front was a photo of a Quality Inn and Conference Center and the words "A DREAM COME TRUE. A PROPHECY FULFILLED."

"Ohhh, it's a *motel*!" I said. "Emily said it was a hotel." A motel still seemed costly but made a little more sense

"Really?" Kurt said. "We just flew all the way out here and you're gonna start this meeting off by devaluing us? Okay, Hollywood."

My face flushed. I was terrified of being misunderstood by the people I loved the most. Not that I loved Kurt, but I didn't know how to handle men being mad at me—well, anyone, really, with the exception of my parents, but men especially. Kurt's temper seemed always on the cusp of exploding.

I shook my head. "Sorry! That's *really* not what I meant to do."

Les smiled. "No, it's okay," he said. "You've been put up in so many nice places all over the world with your acting jobs, I understand that hotels might look different to you than most people who haven't had that extreme privilege."

He was right that I'd stayed in many nice places, but I knew there was a difference between a hotel and a motel. I wasn't a *complete* idiot. A hotel is where you stay with your family on vacation, and a motel is where you stay when you pick up a hooker or drive a Mountain Dew truck across the country. Nevertheless, I didn't want to argue. They could call it whatever they wanted, what difference did it make to me? It was their dream.

It's not a woman's job to counsel or correct a man. I read that in the Jezebel book we had all studied.

Kurt let out a sharp exhale-laugh and moved past his irritation. "We've been praying about this vision that kept coming up in the Hamoatzah meetings. God's been able to provide so much healing at the Big House, and we want to bring that to a larger platform."

"We see the massive potential for God to shake up this area by bringing our Family into one place where we can just love on people," Les said.

Love on. The way he said it was odd. *Let people know they're loved*, I assumed he meant, which is a kind and normal thing for anyone to want to do. Right?

"We know how much you enjoy hospitality. I mean, it's one of my and Marti's favorite things about you—how you're always leaving little notes for people or folding up the bathroom washcloths just *so*, making fresh flower bouquets. You have such a heart to make people feel seen and feel special, and we just see this as a perfect fit for you."

"We have several investors so far," Kurt said. "Dontay's mom is giving sixty-five—"

"Seventy-five," Les corrected him.

"Right, seventy-five. And Ed and Pam, of course, are in for fifty."

"Thousand?" I said with some surprise.

"Yes," Kurt said, unable to conceal his annoyance for very long. "And that's dollars, not pesos."

"It's a real family business," Les said. "And especially with you here, so far away from everyone, this would be a great way for you to stay involved. You know, you can help us decorate the rooms and plan out the hospitality rollout for when guests arrive. I think you'd have a lot of fun."

"Yeah, it does sound fun," I said. It didn't really. The main reason I liked hospitality was showing affection to my loved ones. Doing it for complete strangers at a Quality Inn in Idaho wasn't my idea of fun, but I didn't say that because I knew that one way I could show affection to my loved ones was supporting their dreams.

"So, you're making what per episode on this show?" Les asked.

Money wasn't something we ever talked about in my family. Probably because there never was any of it. And, as an actor, you *especially* never told someone what your salary was. Contract negotiations were shrouded in secrecy. I don't recall anyone other than my manager and the New York firm that handled my financial advising ever asking me that question. But the silence was getting awkward, and I figured if this was real Family, we should be able to share everything with each other.

"Um, forty-five, I think? Yeah, something like that."

"Okay," Les said, "for you, maybe coming in at ten is a safe bet, because you're doing, what, twenty-two episodes?"

"If we don't get canceled," I said. "Which the producers always tell us we're about to be." We knew the show had been gaining a steady audience, but being in Wilmington in those days before social media, we were so far removed from pop culture, we didn't know how well we were actually doing. I now believe this was strategic on the part of our show creator and network execs—an effort to keep us from getting inflated egos, becoming too assertive, or, most crucially, banding together to renegotiate our contracts as a group. They would tell us for the next eight seasons, "We're about to be canceled."

"But you have a guarantee of a certain amount of episodes in your contract, right?" Kurt asked. "I mean, we don't know anything about Hollywood, but Emily and Harker said that's kind of how it works."

"I can't remember what they landed on," I said. "Math and legal stuff scare me, so I just let my manager make the deals."

Les smiled. "Well, ten is a good number. That's basically nothing for you. The best part for you is that, because it's a ministry project, it's a tax write-off. And, honestly, it's a risk-free investment."

"We could easily do this with the bank," Kurt said, "but we just wanted to give you a chance to invest in and benefit from what God is doing."

Les tilted his head and looked at me with arched eyebrows. "Wanna come in at ten?"

I felt so grown up, making deals.

"Yeah!" I said. "That sounds amazing! Only, why is it for sale? Is there something wrong with it?"

Kurt was irritated yet again. "No, there's nothing *wrong* with it. You think we just came in here with no research and we're gonna try to sell you on something that's a lemon?"

"No, I don't think that," I said. "I'm just wondering why they're selling it."

"Do you not understand how loved you are?" Kurt said. "How protective we are over you? No one wants to see you fail. We're on your side! Do you not get that?"

"Yeah, baby," Les said. "There's nothing wrong with the hotel. Companies that own lots of properties like this—this really is what they do. They flip them all the time. It's actually a great property. It's right off the highway. There's a conference center attached to it, as you can see here."

He flipped over the brochure and pointed to a glossy photo of a low gray stucco box in the middle of a parking lot.

"Think about all the ministries we could help out of this space," Les said. "We could have church services there, do homeless outreach, host women's retreats and guest speakers."

His Welsh prophet friend was already on board to be the first. It did sound like a wonderful way to participate in the community, and I believed in wonderful, magical things—such as people with zero hospitality industry experience successfully running a multimillion-dollar business overnight.

Later that night in bed, I looked through the pamphlet more closely. Inside, there was more information about Les and his first ministry. It read:

The Journey began when a church full of Christians began crying out in prayer for the Holy Spirit to come and dwell.

The Holy Spirit revealed himself, and things began to happen. Miracles began to become more commonplace. One man, was healed from a documanted case of congenital heart disease that ended the life of his father, and brother. His clean bill of health sent ripples of praise followed by tremors of fear. The religious leaders grew more, and more concerned, until it became nessesary for them to ask us to leave, despite our desire to stay.

I was fascinated. First by the fact that I had never heard this story before, and second because I couldn't imagine someone printing up a business pamphlet without using spell-check. He was throwing commas around like confetti, too. What a disaster.

Don't be a snob, Joy. Everyone is good at different things.

I thought instead how humble Les was that this amazing thing happened and he didn't brag about it to any of us. He was only sharing it now as a testimony to God's goodness. This guy spent six years in the marines teaching snipers, raised three boys, pastored a church in New York, then moved across the country and led a charismatic movement of miracles in an Oregon church, suffered through getting kicked out because of it, and now he was starting over again!

What an amazing person, I thought. *I would love to help make his dream come true.* The possibility of being an owner of a hotel wasn't my dream, but facilitating a ministry that would help people was.

I called my financial advisory firm in New York and told them I wanted to invest. They said they thought it was a bad idea, but I knew they just couldn't see things with spiritual eyes the way I could. God was going to do something amazing and shock us all!

I instructed them to cut the $10,000 check.

CHAPTER SIXTEEN

Over the next couple months, I stayed informed of developments back in Idaho through calls with Jasmine or Emily and through the Family's group email chain. Like this one from Les:

Dear Family,

Update from this Wednesday Family meeting: What a privilege it was, for us to welcome Harker & Mina's precious little girl into our Family. Now as she is pregnant again we have the extrordinary honor to flood Mina with prayers during this time when the enemy would seek to discourage her with lies about her identity because post-pardum is not from God.

Dontay, is also asking for your prayers in his new role in Maintenance at the Hotel! We give glory to God for the miraculous way our Savior has turned Dontay's life around and now, he is able to do his own ministry through serving our guests. We're just blown away by this man of God who walked away from the worldly temptations he was offered in sports, in order to serve behind the scenes. He is making himself lowly, like Jesus, and I'm humbled that he calls me "Papa." I'm proud of you, my boy. You are famous in heaven!

Please also continue to pray for our beautiful Joy, braving the beasts of Hollywood in North Carolina. Joy, you are not alone! We are all here behind you holding you up, in prayer.

We Are a Ship!

Les

I was glad for the emails and phone calls, but the truth was we were living different daily lives. My hours were long, and when I wasn't working on the show, I was writing songs or painting, sewing, doing anything creative. I was still the kid who played in Grandma Doris's attic, and I still enjoyed my own company. By the time winter arrived, I just didn't feel as close to everyone as I used to. I was feeling really on my own again, like I did before the group.

I loved the early-morning call times; loved unfurling myself onto the hair chair and cackling with the Mama Bears; loved stepping onto set, running lines in an oversized puffy coat with half my makeup done and my hair in giant Velcro rollers; loved how much creative input I got to have. That was the biggest difference between being one of the stars of a show and being a guest star on someone else's show. As a guest star, I always deferred to the director's ideas. Now, I felt allowed and encouraged to contribute my own.

Unfortunately, having ADHD and OCD that wouldn't be diagnosed until years later, I occasionally got carried away. I'd fixate on something insignificant to everyone else—a freshly baked pie on the counter in my character's kitchen, perhaps. Set dressing to everyone else, but I didn't know how to authentically move forward in a scene unless I understood *why* the pie was there.

"I'd love to have you start over by the window and end the phone call over here by the kitchen counter," the director would suggest.

"Okay, no prob. Although, are you seeing this pie on the counter?"

"The pie? Um, yeah, it's in the shot."

"I'm just wondering when Haley would have had the time to bake a pie today if she's been running all over town."

"Uh, right. Well . . . she brought it home from Karen's Café."

"Okay. But who's it for? I'm just alone on a phone call in this scene, and I don't have any scenes eating pie later, *and* the rest of the episode I'm not home."

Confused, the director would offer: "Haven't you ever just brought home a dessert for yourself?"

"Yes, but this one is uncovered on the counter, steaming."

"I just want some movement in the background. The steam looks pretty in the light."

"Totally. Except . . . never mind."

"What?"

"Well, the steam implies either I just baked it, which we know I didn't, or that I just heated it up because I plan to eat it right now, which we also know isn't happening because Haley is about to leave again."

The director would call out, exasperated, "Set Dec? Can we lose the pie?"

"Unless you want to *cut* the pie and I can eat a slice *during* the phone call," I'd say. "I think I could make that make sense."

"Do you *want* to eat pie during the phone call?"

"I mean, I don't think it's really a pie-eating kind of call, but if you need it for the shot . . ."

"We only have one pie," the set decorator would call out, "so we can't reset it."

"Okay, no pie," the director would say. "Just lose the pie."

"Sorry, I just want it to make sense. I'm sorry."

What I didn't realize at the time was that I had been doing so much compromising of myself in microscopic increments with Les that, subconsciously, I was grasping for control in any way I could get it, like haggling over pie.

I tried to keep these spirals to a minimum, especially after re ceiving feedback from the producers through my manager: "Joy's so talented, but . . . difficult." My manager told me not to worry about it because she didn't much care for the producers and creator of the show. Us girls were in our early twenties, and none of us had been series regulars on a network TV show before, so we didn't have a frame of reference for how things were supposed to be. Several times I walked into wardrobe to find ten bras laid out for me to try on, be photographed in, and have the photos sent back to the producers for them to choose one.

"Oh, I don't really want to be in a bra on TV," I would say. "I don't think it suits my character much, it's not in the script, and it has nothing to do with the scene, anyway."

"This is what the creator wants you to wear in the scene," the wardrobe designer would say apologetically.

When I stood my ground as a matter of religious modesty, my manager would get a call from him: "She's being difficult again. We told you what this show was about!"

And, in fairness, they did. The "fucking and sucking" executive had been very clear about that. I guess I just looked at my character and figured that would be other people's storylines. There was no nudity clause in my contract that said I was required to strip down to my underwear on TV. But my manager was in LA and three hours behind North Carolina, so every time I tried to get ahold of her to explain the situation and ask her to intervene, it slowed down production, which just made me look even more "difficult" to everyone else. Now I see the similarity between the creator's strategy and Les's strategy. In hindsight, it became clear that they both used geography to isolate us young and trusting people from our support systems and pressure us into doing what they wanted.

But whereas the creator's only leverage was fame, Les's leverage was my eternal salvation. The choice was easy. And Les had been teaching us that worldly opposition was a sign from God, using verses like 2 Timothy 3:12: "Everyone who wants to live a godly life in Christ Jesus will be persecuted." The more my personal beliefs and preferences interfered with the creator's demands, the more he started writing things into the storylines that I assume were an attempt to humiliate or antagonize me. Like making other characters call Haley "fat." Or having Haley "overreact" to her high school boyfriend watching porn. That one was a *big* battle. I saw the dialogue that was written for Haley as degrading and doing a disservice to the young women who looked up to me. I tried talking with the creator about it, but by the day of filming not much had changed, so I rewrote a lot of my own lines in that episode. It caused confusion and aggravation for the director, the other actors, the script supervisor, and the producers, and I felt awful. But I didn't know what else to do. It repeatedly came down to either honoring myself and my beliefs or giving in and saying, *Ugh, it's not worth the fight.* And I had been conditioning myself to hold fast to my beliefs, no matter the cost.

Even though both Les and Pam stressed that no one in Wilmington was "spiritually safe" for me to trust, I started to enjoy the company of my costars.

I spent more and more time out of the isolation of my trailer, often watching Chad and James and some of the other cast and crew play basketball in between setups. James's work with the basketball coordinator had really paid off. He was already a gifted athlete but learning from a true professional had given him an edge that made filming the basketball scenes easier, and they were more thrilling to watch since we knew it was actually James and not a stunt actor making most of these incredible plays. James kept to himself on set a lot, too. In between setups, his nose was usually buried in impressive literature like *Moby Dick* or Kerouac while I was in my cast chair knitting or writing a script on my laptop. We didn't socialize much in the off-hours but on-screen we were building a heavy-hitting love story, which felt funny considering my personal dating life was stagnant. The two men who safely filled the void of male companionship were Paul Johansson and Craig Sheffer, with whom I could be found often over dinner ordering expensive wine and debating on religion or discussing art and philosophy for hours.

Tired of the loneliness of my beach house rental, I moved downtown to be nearer to all the action and become more a part of this new community. I found a creaky—or what the listing described as "historic"—home on Orange Street. I decorated it with large velvet curtains and antique treasures like ornate side tables, a pink brocade fainting couch, and a mannequin dress form.

For the first time since I'd left New York, I was starting to feel like myself. And then one night Les called. He always seemed to sense when any of us were starting to grow distant or curious about life outside the Family. Somehow, he could tell what I was feeling even from over two thousand miles away. Learning that I'd moved from the beach house, he became annoyed.

"Did you tell anyone before you did that?" he asked.

"I didn't realize I needed to ask anyone before I moved," I said. "It just seemed like a good idea. I was feeling too lonely out there."

He paused and sighed. "That's the whole point, baby. It's not good for you to do things alone. That's just an old way of living for you. It's okay to ask people for help. Lean on your Family, we're here for you."

"Yeah, I get that. And thank you! I just didn't think where I lived made a difference to anyone."

"Everything you do makes a difference. We care about you!" He paused again while I sat in feelings of disappointment with myself. "You know, it might be worth having a meeting about this when you're back here for Christmas."

I had already sent an email to the group letting them know I would be spending another Christmas with them, despite my mom's best efforts to convince me to spend it with her.

"What do you mean 'a meeting'?" I asked.

"Well, you've been trying to do all this on your own. I mean, really, for your whole life. Your parents had so much of their own stuff to worry about, and you've just been raising yourself all these years."

There was truth to that, I knew. But when he brought them up, I realized how much I was starting to *miss* my parents. My dad was still in New Jersey, but in a new house with his wife and my little brother—who, sadly, I hardly knew. Early in my LA days, I had started to build good relationships with my stepdad and his two children, but now we hadn't spoken in almost a year. Maybe it wasn't *them* that I missed but the life I had once. Grandma and the attic, Blue Eyes and the lake—a life that didn't exist anymore. I felt all upside-down, and the one place I felt for sure that I belonged was in Idaho.

"Joy, tell you what, let's do a Family meeting, and you can share what you're struggling through. Everyone can listen and speak truth into you in the areas where you're feeling discouraged."

"Like a meeting with the entire Family, and everyone just has to sit there and listen to my problems?"

"Not 'has to.' We *get* to. It's a privilege to press into each other, and you are actually giving us the opportunity to grow in our ability to hear from God, to understand real sacrifice, and to love you. That's what families do. I know you didn't have that growing up, but family meetings are a pretty normal thing."

I was quiet. I hadn't thought of it that way before.

"You obviously don't have to if you're not comfortable or don't trust everyone here."

"Oh, no, I totally trust everybody," I said. "I guess it feels selfish to ask an entire group of people to sit around and listen to me complain. I have a great life. My problems are nothing compared to so many people's."

"But don't you feel blessed when one of your sisters here calls you to ask for advice or prayer?"

"Yeah."

"How is this any different? Don't withhold a blessing for other people because of your pride. Pride goes before the fall, right? Proverbs 16:18. You have an opportunity to be a huge blessing in everyone's life here by just sharing your heart."

I listened. I desired nothing more than to have a purpose. If all it took for me to make a difference in the lives of the people I had come to love the most was letting go of my ego and embarrassment and sharing my heart, then that's what I would do.

"Yeah, that makes sense," I said.

"Good," Les said. "I'll set it up."

CHAPTER SEVENTEEN

As soon as the motel purchase was finalized, Les started hosting twice-a-month church services in the conference center. Unlike the Wednesday night meetings at the Big House, these were open to the public. Dontay was the Family member most familiar with computers, so he set up a website. But these were hardly ever updated with dates and times, so the people who attended were the members of the Big House Family, plus friends and extended bio-family: Emily's father, who visited on occasion at Emily's invitation and was always happy to see Ed and Pam, but was clearly not a fan of Les and always avoided him; cousins of Miguel and Juana; some of Lucy's Mary Kay friends; Kurt's brother, who was even weirder than him. Since meeting times were ambiguous, people relied on Les to announce the dates (usually last minute) to Big House Family members, and we were responsible for telling whomever we wished to invite. It was just a way of controlling everyone's plans. *You never know when the next service will be, so drop everything when it's happening!*

The motel was experiencing similar chaos.

"There's so much renovating that needs to be done," Dontay told me. He was in charge of maintenance, even though he'd only ever used his hands for catching a football. "Things break every day. But I'm learning a lot! I just figured out how to fix a hotel ice machine. Never knew how to do *that* before!"

As the motel's manager—a job she was given because her previous job also had "manager" in the title—Emily was facing even bigger challenges.

"Honestly, every time I make a decision about anything it seems to be wrong," she told me. "If I don't run everything by Les or Kurt, then there's always a problem afterward. There was a problem yesterday about how the *towels* should be folded. I had asked the staff to do this double foldover thing—I did some research—and they were doing it well, but then Les thought they shouldn't hang longways, they should be folded to look puffier and more square. They called me in for a, like, hour-long meeting about functioning too independently. And Kurt gave me a speech on presentation and hospitality and how the staff should and shouldn't be spending their time. Apparently, my way of folding towels takes twice as long, which I don't think is true. But they're asking me to consult them on *literally everything* right now. So, it's just hard to actually get anything done. Even though it's annoying, the truth is that I *don't* want to just run around independently, making a bunch of decisions that are outside of God's vision for this place. So, it's probably good for me anyway."

That was how well Les and Pam and the other leaders had trained us . . . conditioned us . . . groomed us. As soon as we started complaining, no matter how justifiably, we caught ourselves, chastised ourselves for being so negative and spoiled and ungrateful, and turned it into a blessing—an opportunity for learning and growth.

Even so, it was hard to put that positive spin on the motel when I finally got to see it in person over Christmas. What a piece of shit. Old carpet. Bad fluorescent lighting. The fact that it was so close to the highway meant never-dissipating smog and a just as constant stream of shady drifters loitering in the parking lot.

The Big House wasn't in much better shape. When I walked in, I noticed several piles of dried cat shit in the formal dining room. Maybe it was vomit. Whatever it was, it had been there a very long time, along with scattered yellow stains. The whole entryway smelled like Salami's litter box. When I pointed it out to Dontay, he said, "Oh man, Pop keeps telling me to clean that up and I keep forgetting. Ugh, I'm just so tired from the motel every day."

"Isn't she . . . his cat?"

"Yeah, but I told him I would do it, so he's just waiting until I follow through."

"Geez, what does Pam think about all this? I mean, her beautiful house is just getting torn up."

"I know. I feel bad about it. But I think Jas actually asked her about it the other day, and she said we need to have grace for Les and the boys. You know, nobody's perfect, so we just should speak the truth about them and let the Lord help them change their habits."

"The truth being . . . ?" I asked.

"You know, 'You're so good at keeping the house clean,' 'You're great stewards of this house,' like that."

It was the same advice Les had given Emily years ago in LA about her brother with a negative attitude—a tactic we had all been trying to implement in various ways. As I looked at the piles of cat shit, it didn't seem like it was working.

Walking into the back bedroom, I noticed Gretchen's bed was worse than before: tissues, hair ties, crumpled clothes and balled-up dirty socks, wrappers, an empty soda can. Jasmine's side was still clean and tidy. It was like the episode of *I Love Lucy* where Lucy partitions off the living room because she's tired of Ricky making a mess.

Even more troubling was a large hole in QB's bedroom door. Apparently, one of the Barbarians had made him mad, and QB punched right through the door. He was now walking around with a heavy brace on his wrist and torn-up knuckles. This kind of aggression wasn't really surprising, given how Les so often talked about war and warriors. He claimed the enemy was attacking our Family and lamented how men had become so weak and allowed women to walk all over them. "Men were built for war!" he often said, before regaling us with stories from his time in the marines. This also seemed to be expressed in a couple of new decorations in the house: in the living room, there was now a large oil painting print of a man-of-war at sea. He was running with the nautical theme of his vision—under a magnet on the fridge was a paper with WE ARE A SHIP printed in big letters. I was relieved there were no typos like in the motel brochure.

Les thought QB's assault on the door was funny, joking about it in an email to the group, so I tried to laugh it off, too. I didn't grow up with brothers. *Maybe this is just what boys do.* I did wonder how Pam and Ed felt about seeing their stately home dilapidate. We weren't in Grey Gardens territory yet, but they couldn't have been happy about it. Not hand-sanitizer-ready, eat-off-the-bathroom-floor Pam. How was she okay with this?

Again, reflexively, I quickly blamed myself for being so judgmental about the condition of the house. *You're so snobby from living in your big, beautiful, old southern palace with its gorgeous curtains and antique furniture doing some silly TV show while these people here are devoting their lives to God and aren't concerned with material things. It's none of your business how Pam is dealing with it. That's between her and God. Maybe it's good for her to not be so neurotic!*

One person who was not brainwashed was Dontay's mother, who had come to spend Christmas with her son and his "new family"—and also to check on her investment in the motel as the largest backer. Esther John Valentine was her name, which was satisfying to learn because she had such a bright presence it would have been a severe disappointment to hear her say something like "Hello, I'm Janet." Meeting her, I thought of bumblebees. The defiance of physics they enjoy by flying while having a carriage too large for their wings was not dissimilar to Esther's bafflingly large breasts hovering, waistless, over bamboo-thin legs. I spent much of the holiday trying to figure out what muscles in her body worked the hardest to keep her from falling over.

Esther wasn't suspicious of the group the way my parents and Emily's parents were. She and Les had never met but exchanged friendly emails regularly, and he sent her links to his weekly sermons. With church happening in the conference center twice a month—or at a moment's notice whenever he felt like preaching—Les recorded his sermons and had Dontay post them on YouTube.

Esther was excited to learn how much Dontay was contributing to the ministry. She was also excited to learn he had gotten engaged. That was another reason she'd come for the holiday: to meet her soon-to-be daughter-in-law, Jasmine.

Jasmine had called to tell me a couple weeks before the holiday. Of course I was happy for her. But I was also a little disappointed. Not because I really had feelings for Dontay—my crush on him had waned. I realized I loved him more like a brother and I knew, whenever I got married, I wanted wild attraction, sparks, and chemistry. It's just that I was running out of options. Most of the guys on *One Tree Hill* were in relationships, plus they weren't Christians, which meant they were off-limits anyway. But I hated being a vibrant young woman in her twenties and watching everyone around me pair off. Sophia and Hilarie were in relationships, Paul was always tied up with someone, even recurring actors were coming into town and starting little "locationships." Now that Mina was with Harker and Jasmine was with Dontay, the only single guys left in the Family were Abe and QB. Which really meant just Abe, because I was not remotely interested in QB—even before the door destruction.

Esther was overjoyed upon meeting Jasmine. They hit it off right away. And yet a few hours later her whole demeanor changed. Because in that span of time she'd gone to visit the motel with Les. Afterward, when she walked back through the front door, everything about her seemed different. Her energy was subdued, and she seemed to be looking around the house suspiciously. Dontay had put her bag in Ed and Pam's garage apartment, where she was meant to spend the night. She disappeared into their space for about ten minutes, then emerged with her bag, passing the guest room where Emily and I were hunched over, crafting on the floor.

"Where are you going, Esther?" I asked. "I thought you were staying here."

"Well, I did, too, but I guess there was a mix-up, so I'll be staying at a hotel instead."

"Our hotel?"

Esther gave a derisive snort. "It's a motel," she said. "And it's barely even that. No, I'll be staying someplace else." Then she took a long look at me. "Where is *your* family, dear?"

"Um, my mom's in California and my dad's in New Jersey."

Given Esther's mood, and not wanting to offend her as a parent, I refrained from saying "bio-mom" and "bio-dad."

"Are you close with them?"

"Not really. I mean, I love them, they're good people. But I just feel more at home here. Feels more like family to me."

She nodded her head, staring at me for slightly longer than felt comfortable.

"Well, I'm glad you got to see the motel. It was a big investment for me, too. I'm excited about the ministry vision."

"You invested?"

I nodded.

"How much, if you don't mind me asking?"

"Um, ten."

All the muscles in her forehead went up. "Really?"

"It's okay," I said, sensing her concern. "I have a weird job that pays me well."

"Well, I'm sure you have good financial advisers then and you know what you're doing."

I thought about my financial advisers and how they were 100 percent against this investment.

Esther nodded to herself and continued on toward the door.

"See you tomorrow at Christmas," I said.

She looked back at me. "Goodbye, dear."

Christmas morning, jet-lagged and still on East Coast time, I woke up early to a dark house. I moved lightly toward the kitchen to make coffee, but heard low voices in the living room. I stopped and listened.

"He just contradicts everything that I say," Les said softly. "It's like he's actively trying to create division in our Family."

That would have been the moment for me to announce my presence in some way. A cough or flipping on a light or even just moving normally through the kitchen. Except I reaaaaalllly wanted to know what was going on.

I heard Kurt's voice next. "Everyone's only loyal to him because he's so impressive. He's smart and good-looking—"

"And he knows it."

"And he *knows* it. Right. And they both were friends with a lot of these guys first, so . . ."

"So his ideas will carry weight because people trust him. And Mina."

"And *Mina*. Right. But she's not very credible right now with the whole postpartum stuff," Kurt said. "I'm not too worried about her."

"I know we're calling it postpartum," Les said. "But honestly? I think she's bipolar."

"Might be."

"The hard part is, we're just at the beginning stages right now, you know? So, someone like Harker can derail . . . what God is doing here."

"Yeah, that kind of independence can open up a door to give the enemy a foothold. If he starts talking openly about his thoughts that are in direct conflict with the Hamoatzah . . ."

There was a silence. I breathed as quietly as possible. My body was starting to itch from being frozen in position, lest a creaking floorboard give away my trespass.

"Where's Pam with it all?" Kurt asked.

"I think she's with us," Les said. "Obviously she loves her son, but she doesn't want to create confusion. And, you know, all the girls look up to her."

"Well, that's why I asked."

They paused again, and I could hear them adjusting their positions on the furniture. It really was so dark. *Why are they just sitting in the dark?*

"Well, I'm glad we're on the same page," Kurt said. "It's important that we present a unified, you know, *presence* as Leadership. So let's just talk with him and make it clear—"

"*I'll* talk with him," Les interrupted.

"All right, well, sooner than later."

"I'll do it when the time is right," Les said sternly. "Don't forget there's only *one* reason you're here."

What does that mean? I wondered.

Then they were moving off the furniture, footsteps starting to make their way somewhere. Every room in this house seemed connected to two others, so anyone could appear suddenly from any direction. I started slowly walking backward, praying the floor wouldn't creak, but didn't get far before I heard Kurt open and close the basement door.

Okay, he's gone. One down.

But Les's footsteps were still moving. I didn't know in which direction. He could be headed right toward me or he could be going back to his room.

You're an actress. Act! I started humming. *Better to get caught on my own terms.* I strode confidently into the kitchen and he was there, turning the corner at the same time as me.

"Oh!" I said, pretending to be startled. "Morning!" I'm a terrible liar. Good actress, bad liar.

"Hey, baby." His voice went up two decibels. "You're up early."

"The time change . . ."

"Well, Merry Christmas." He pulled me into a hug.

"Merry Christmas!" I was usually comforted by Les's hugs,

but after overhearing that conversation and lying to him just then, I felt uneasy.

"You been up for a while?" he asked.

"Just rolled out of bed. Coffee."

"I came down to make some, too."

It was the slowest coffee I'd ever waited for. I wasn't often alone with Les—always too many people around, always too much commotion—and under normal circumstances I would have been excited to have one-on-one time with him. These weren't normal circumstances. I did my best to sound chipper as we talked about Christmas presents and plans for the day. Finally, the coffee was ready. I took mine back into the dark bedroom and turned on a book light. I tried to read my Bible while waiting for Jasmine or Gretchen to wake up, but I couldn't let go of what I'd heard. Could Mina really be bipolar? What exactly was Harker trying to "derail," and why? I hate that my suspicion automatically landed on them rather than on the obvious, devious scheming of Les and Kurt.

A few hours later we gathered in the living room for the home-made Secret Santa exchange. This year I'd gotten Martine. I decided to make her a silk robe and hired a private sewing tutor in Wilmington to teach me how. It turned out beautifully and I couldn't wait to give it to her.

Les kicked off the gift exchange with a prayer, followed by one of his usual monologues. "Wow, look at us, we managed to get everyone together in one room for Christmas again!"

I looked around but didn't see Esther. I mouthed to Dontay across the room, *Where's your mom?*

He shook his head. *Not coming,* he mouthed back.

Why?

He was about to reply, but Les was still talking, so Dontay waved me off: *Tell you later.*

"Thank you, everyone, for the sacrifice you're making by choosing to celebrate with your spiritual Family instead of your bio-families this year," Les continued. "I know that's not always an easy thing to do, especially with expectations that so many families have of each other. It takes courage to do things God's way in the face of people telling you it doesn't make sense. Jesus did things all the time that confounded the Pharisees and even his own disciples. The way of the Lord looks like foolishness to the world, but everyone in this room chose to—well, to look foolish! All for the sake of doing what you knew God was calling you to do. So, just give yourselves a hand!"

Everyone clapped, though I noticed Harker was slow to join and early to stop, which seemed like a confirmation of the conflict I'd heard Les and Kurt whispering about. In Harker's refusal to clap more vigorously, I saw him as the underminer rather than the undermined.

"I am so proud of the safe space we've created for each other," Les continued. He then gestured to Dontay. "I know that was hard for you, son, so I appreciate you setting that boundary and making that sacrifice. The vulnerability God is calling us into today might be uncomfortable if there was someone in the room who wasn't a part of this spiritual Family."

"I gotchu, Pop," Dontay said. "It's totally worth it. We have to have that kind of safety."

Well, that answers that, I thought. And it did feel safe. We had a short worship time, then we exchanged gifts. Afterward, as everybody got up to get a snack or refill their drink, Les came up to me. His chubby fingers were wedged inside the small handle of a coffee mug that read I LIKE IT WHEN THEY CALL ME BIG POPPA.

"Hey, would you just pray for Dontay?" he said quietly. "He's having a hard time navigating things with his mom. Esther is used to controlling everything about Dontay's life, and now he's choosing his own Family, and so, you know . . . that Jezebel spirit of control is just rising up in her. You know what that's like. I know your mom is having a hard time with you being a part of this Family, too."

"Oof, yes. Talk about control."

"It's common for so many women. Was your grandmother pretty controlling?"

"My mom's mom, yeah!" I said. Unlike Doris, Nanny Marge was an Irish spark plug. If you offended her, she'd put it in her pocket for a rainy day. She'd had a wealthy childhood until Black Tuesday, 1929, then worked her way back into financial stability and had four kids with a sweet soldier who possessed a talent for betting on all the wrong horses. After losing everything to the track (and throwing a few cast-iron pans across the house at him), she rebuilt *again* and eventually moved to Papua New Guinea as a missionary. By the time I was a kid, she was back in the USA and—because she felt her hardships had damn well earned her the right—she had something to say about everything in everyone's life. I loved her, appreciating the storyteller and armchair theologian that she was. However, several family members found her insufferable and cut her off altogether.

"Jezebel is a generational spirit," he said. "I'm proud of you for breaking the cycle and standing up to her."

Les took a sip of his coffee.

"She sent me an email," he said. "Did I tell you?"

"Who? My mom?"

"Yeah, she was asking questions about our theology as a church."

"She's always digging around in my life."

"Well, she was nice about it. I like your mom. I think she's just having a hard time adjusting to you choosing spiritual Family over bio-family. Do you want to read it?"

"I don't think so, actually. It's just gonna piss me off."

He laughed. "Well, I don't mind talking with her. So, if she's ever bugging you about stuff, feel free to pass her over to me. Your dad, too. He's been a little more aggressive than your mom, so I'd be honored to protect you in all that."

"My dad? What did *he* do?"

"Oh, I thought you knew. He's been contacting members from my old church, trying to find out more information about me."

"So annoying. I'm sorry."

"Like I said, it's really common for bio-families to feel threatened when they realize they can't provide something that someone else can."

Why couldn't my parents just let me be happy?

"Thanks so much for fielding all that, Les," I said apologetically.

"No prob, kiddo." He smiled and patted the side of my face with his hand. "We can get into more of your personal stuff in your meeting with the group tomorrow!"

"Looking forward to it!" I said. I wasn't. I was dreading it. But in spite of discovering how run-down the motel was, in spite of seeing the budding squalor at the Big House, in spite of the confusing encounter with Esther, and in spite of the mysterious conversation in the dark, I still believed in Les and our Big House Family. I still believed I'd come out on the other side of this im pending basement meeting with more clarity, more faith, more *healing.*

"Oh!" Les said before leaving the room. "You journal, right?"

"Yeah, all the time!"

"Bring your latest journal to the meeting. I think it might be helpful."

I cautiously walked down the stained carpeted stairs into Kurt and Lucy's basement living quarters, where us girls were still required to shower. I hated this basement. It was dark and stuffy and violated all my hospitality instincts. The walls were an ugly brown. There weren't any plants. It was even more drab than the motel.

These meetings were routine, I just hadn't been here to experience them. *That's all,* I told myself. *You have nothing to be worried about.*

I reached the bottom of the staircase and saw the lights were even dimmer than usual. A few candles had been lit—by Pam, no doubt—to create a cozy, inviting atmosphere, and the Family were sitting on couches and chairs that had been arranged into a semicircle. It didn't feel cozy; it felt ceremonial.

Emily got up and gave me a hug and rubbed my back as I looked at the folding chair set in the center of the room. That would be my seat until we were done.

"Thanks for letting us do this!" She smiled.

I noticed a few people missing, though. QB, the Barbarians, and Brandon were never a part of these meetings—they were still too young to be of any spiritual "use," I guess. But, notably, Mina, Harker, Dontay, Miguel, Juana, and Lucy were absent.

"Should we wait for everyone else?" I asked.

Les was clear. "This is your group today. Everyone here has been hand selected—*prayerfully* selected—for this meeting." He said it like a chef telling me each of the twenty-five courses I'm about to eat has been customized for my specific taste buds.

"Well, Lord," he said, "we come before you in Jesus's name and we thank you. We thank you for the immensity of your love for us. And we just bring your beloved daughter Joy before you in prayer now, and we ask you to heal her. That her identity would no longer be bound up in her occupation but in who you say she is, who you made her to be, as a child in your house in the kingdom of Heaven. Amen."

"Amen," we all said resoundingly.

"So," Les continued, "Joy was telling me some of her concerns about herself at work. And some childhood wounds and places in her that feel broken. We all know what that feels like, to know we're flawed and not have the tools to fix it. So, Joy, why don't you just give everyone the lay of the land of your heart right now, and then we can start sowing into you."

I swallowed. "Okay, well, thank you guys for taking the time out of your Friday night to come talk with me about this stuff and pray for me."

It occurred to me that I didn't know exactly why I was even here. I didn't call the meeting. I didn't even know what I had done wrong.

"I guess my heart is in a pretty positive place, actually. I'm finally starting to enjoy my life in Wilmington. I don't feel as lonely anymore. I'm getting to be really creative in lots of ways. I'm making friends." *So then, why am I here? Find the problem, Joy. What's the problem?* "I think the problem might be that the more comfortable I get there, the further away I feel from you guys here, and you know, you're my Family! So, I don't want that to happen."

Not having more to say, I stopped and looked around awkwardly.

"We don't want that to happen, either!" Emily said, sunny and positive.

Gretchen added, "You're really important to us, sis." But she said it as she said everything, with an over-the-top intensity that played as a need to feel useful. I chided myself again for being critical.

"Joy, is that your journal?" Les asked, pointing to the hardback book I had set under my chair.

"Uh, yep."

"Can you just open that up for us and share something you've written in the last few days?"

The only acceptable answer was "Sure." But I did NOT want to do this. My journals were full of my deepest, weirdest, most idiotic thoughts—just a way of getting them out of my body. Often, I'd change my mind about something immediately after seeing it on paper. This was going to be excruciating. *Is this what happens in all these meetings?* I opened up my journal and searched for something that could be relevant and not too embarrassing.

"Okay, um, here's one." I read aloud: "'Lord, I'm frustrated about music right now. I have all this creative energy, but I feel like I can't finish anything I start. I want to sing and make an album, maybe even write a musical, but I don't know how to do all the technical stuff to make things *happen*. Ugh, you're so lazy, Joy. Just LEARN HOW! At least I'm inspired, though! Last year I felt so—BLAH, but now, in Wilmington, surrounded by artists, I feel like I'm coming back to life. God, show me how to encourage people to feel your love. Like Sophia. Honestly, I feel like I'm afraid of her rejecting me (and then rejecting YOU, God, because I didn't set a good example!), so I don't even get close to begin with. It's so stupid! Please show me how to love her like you do! And Hilarie . . . she's easier for me to have fun with because we're so similar, but—'"

"That's great," Les said, stopping me midsentence. "You don't have to read the whole thing."

"Oh, okay."

"Anyone sensing anything from the Holy Spirit on that?" Les said, giving Pam a pointed look and a nod.

"You're so precious, Joy," Pam said. "I just love hearing your heart for your costars. You're really a faithful daughter and friend."

"Thanks."

"But, well, I couldn't help noticing there just seems to be a lot of self-focus in that entry. But maybe it's just the one. I don't know. Are most of your entries like that?"

I quickly flipped through the journal. "I guess so. But, I mean, it's my journal. Isn't that what a journal IS? *Myself?*" I chuckled, but no one laughed with me.

"I would just say that perhaps the reason you're feeling more distant from your Family here at home is that you're filling up your thought life with yourself, rather than with God and others."

"Taking our thoughts captive is a very real, vital thing," Les said. "Paul writes in 2 Corinthians 10 that we must be diligent about what we allow into our minds. So, if you're focusing on your professional dreams, rather than trusting that God will open those doors at the right time, then you'll be constantly in rebellion, trying to make things happen yourself. If you're focusing on how you're *behaving* with other people, instead of trusting that God will just show up in the midst of your interactions, then, again, you're trying to play God. Both of these things will isolate you from the people who are here to keep you on the right track: your Family."

I tried to follow his train of thought, but the more he talked the less I understood. I figured it was because I'd been in Wilmington and away from the Family for a while. Like how I'd been excelling in French when I visited Paris but now would embarrass myself if I went back.

"You're letting yourself ask too many illegal questions," he said.

"'Illegal questions'?"

"Thoughts you can no longer allow in, like wondering if you belong in this Family."

Had I been questioning that? I didn't think so.

Then Kurt started talking about covenants, King David professing loyalty to the elders of Israel, and other references I didn't know, but it all somehow tied back to my independence and rebellion.

Then Gretchen jumped in: "It's so easy to slip into double-mindedness, sis, but we're not gonna let you."

Hard to take seriously, I thought, *coming from a Cheetos addict who doesn't know how to make her bed.*

"What was that?" Les pounced on me.

"What?"

"That thought you just had when Gretchen spoke."

"Sorry—nothing. I—"

He pushed. "Not nothing. What was it?"

"I found that hypocritical of her to say. Sorry, Gretch, but I do."

"But everyone is a hypocrite, Joy, including you. You say you want to be a good friend, but you've hardly come home to visit the last few months," Les said.

"Well, the last few episodes have been a heavy storyline for Haley."

"But you've never had a problem coming home before, so . . .

I'm sorry, but I'm just hearing excuses. And I'm not trying to hurt you, baby, but I just find the timing extremely convenient that while you're in a season of budding success, you also happen to be unable to make time for the people you know will hold you accountable. I'm just not buying it."

I was quiet, and Gretchen piped in again: "Yes, we're all hypocrites in different ways. Family is made up of imperfect people, but that doesn't mean we still don't have each other's back."

Then Kurt: "This is the importance of being in covenant relationship with each other. We are not gonna let you get away with this, Joy. You have to stop believing lies about yourself."

Everything was said to me in kind tones, with passion and intention. Les had figured out a way to get everyone in the room, including me, to believe they were being loving by exposing and dissecting my childhood emotional wounds and tying them to current behaviors.

This went on for three hours. There were bathroom breaks, snack breaks, more journal readings, more dissecting. The purpose of the whole meeting was for me to face my demons head-on and "wrestle through."

"Why are you still crying, baby girl?" Les asked toward the end.

"I feel like there's so much I'm doing wrong and I can never keep up."

Pam came near me and pet my knee. "Sweetheart, that's exactly the point. We can never live up to all the things God would require in His perfection."

Jasmine spoke softly: "That's why we need Jes—" but Les cut her off.

"That's why we need *each other*. We're on this ship together. We're not gonna let you fall away. No matter what happens on *One Tree Hill* or your career or anything—we're never letting you go."

By the time my meeting was over, everyone was exhausted and went to bed. I stayed up for a while longer, and in my deep fatigue, I was so grateful for all that this Family was willing to invest in me. Curled up on my favorite beanbag chair, I felt caught up in a spell. The Pacific Northwest had a unique magic. North Carolina felt haunted from the ground up, like everywhere you trod, there were incomplete stories trying to work themselves out from beneath the soil. But Idaho felt heavy in the air, with thick mist—not rising hot from the ocean but pressing down cool, from the sky. The wind moved differently here. The secrets weren't in the graveyards, they slithered through the tops of the trees, taking shelter from endless rain that felt like it was partnering with God to wash away all the old. That's what I needed. A constant cleansing. I opened up my journal and wrote and wrote and wrote until my wrist hurt. I had to document everything I had just learned so I wouldn't forget the truth. I was so quick to forget the truth about myself.

CHAPTER EIGHTEEN

"What in the world is all the commotion?" I asked, looking out the window of the limo. "What, is Britney here, too?"

Hilarie, Sophia, Chad, James, and I were on our way to an appearance on MTV's *Total Request Live* in Times Square. But as we got a block away from the studio, traffic came to a stop—the jam caused by hundreds of kids holding signs and spilling from the street corner into the road.

"Oh my god, I think that's for us." Sophia laughed, shocked.

I looked closer at the signs.

Haley & Nathan 4 EVA!
Marry Me Chad!
OTH is my HOME

"Well, I guess people are watching the show," James said with his typical dry humor.

The show had been picked up for more episodes and moved to a better time slot, so we knew that we were gaining a following, and in Wilmington, we'd started to get a few people asking for autographs when we'd be out downtown. But the *TRL* pandemonium made it clear the show had reached full-blown pop-culture phenomenon status. I hadn't watched a ton of TV growing up, but even I got caught up in the *90210* frenzy. Standing at the big window overlooking Broadway and staring down at the crowd of screaming fans, with another crowd of screaming fans there in the studio, I couldn't believe that this was now happening to us. I was so flustered that in the interview my brain short-circuited. When asked by host Damien Fahey what it was like working on the show, I rambled nonsensically for a few seconds, then apologized: "I'm so not articulate today."

Soon after, we were invited to do a *Teen Vogue* cover shoot. It was the first time I noticed a palpable feeling of competition between the girls. Or maybe it was just me. I was still wrestling with that second-place feeling, especially following Dontay's engagement to Jasmine. The whole photo shoot felt like an awkward dance—all of us wanting to support one another while also really wanting to seize the opportunity for press and exposure. The more attention the show got, the more it felt like we were all thrown into a game of fire dodgeball and everyone just wanted to come out alive. We were all so young and inexperienced, without a mature adult there to walk us through all the nuanced and complex emotions that popped up in our work dynamic.

I should have gone to the hair and makeup Mama Bears for guidance and reassurance, but something ingrained in me from years of being in these charismatic environments was that Christians were supposed to have the ultimate answers, so we shouldn't take advice from nonbelievers. This was compounded by the slow boil I was in, being taught to trust no one outside the Big House Family. On top of it all, I was embarrassed to feel so self-centered. Everyone in the cast and crew deserved accolades and attention for their hard work. The reason the show was so successful wasn't because of the five of us. It was because of all of us—every single person's unique and important contribution. How could I vent about the weirdness of all this attention? *Oh, are your glass slippers too tight?* And I didn't want to share my insecurities with anyone in the Family because none of them had experienced this kind of fame, even Harker. I knew they wouldn't be able to truly understand. Worse, I worried that Les would tell me this was proof that I still deeply wanted to be validated by Hollywood—which I did. I wanted a great film and stage career, to do what I loved—what I knew I was made for. But the new shame cycle that had been introduced by Les around my wanting approval from anyone but God—via the Big House Family— weighed heavily on me. I couldn't figure out the difference between a desire that God had placed inside me and a "sinful desire" that was taking the place of God.

I wanted to call Mina to talk with her about how she'd been feeling now that she'd given up her acting career, but ever since I'd overheard Les tell Kurt over Christmas that she was bipolar, she and I had been growing slowly apart. I didn't really know what "bipolar" meant. This was the early 2000s, when there was a lot more stigma around the word than there is now. And I was still years away from my own neurodivergent diagnosis. More than the word itself, it was the way Les had said it, implying that Mina was unstable and not to be trusted. I didn't know what to believe. I went around in mental circles trying to sort through this career confusion, but the disorientation wasn't just in my professional life.

When the show went to Myrtle Beach to film an episode about a cheerleading competition, I met a cute guy with curly blond hair named Ben who was staying at our hotel. He was a Christian who also lived in Wilmington and was in town on a carpentry job. That's right—I found a cute, Christian carpenter. Jesus similarities aside, it only took a few dates before he was professing his love, and this kind of decisiveness was so intoxicating after all those years of Blue Eyes playing games. While in Ben's presence, it was easy to forget about my dejection over Jasmine's engagement. I hardly knew him, but it didn't matter. We didn't laugh about the same things, but it didn't matter. We didn't like the same music or enjoy the same films or books, but it didn't matter. We both wanted to be in love, so we decided to be in love. A month later he proposed to me with candles and rose petals and a ring I'd never have chosen. And I said yes even though everything inside me said no. I would *will* this into being right.

Ben and I flew to Idaho for a weekend. He met everyone at the Big House, and at one point Les and Pam took him aside for a meeting without me. Ben was classy and didn't mention what they said, and I didn't ask, worried the whole thing might've been too intense and not wanting to make an even bigger deal out of it and possibly give him second thoughts. But the day after we returned to Wilmington, the two of them called me.

"If this is the man that you really love and you're sure about him," Pam said, "then we love and support you. But . . . well, I just don't know how compatible you two are."

"You're from two different worlds," Les said. "You know, you have a lot of life experience, and he's really only ever lived in that small town. And where will you live? He's already got a pretty thriving business, locally. I don't see him moving up here."

"I just don't see it," Pam said.

"Yeah, this doesn't feel right to me, either, baby," Les said. "But it's your decision."

After we hung up, I prayed for courage and immediately went to see Ben. He greeted me with anticipation, knowing their blessing meant everything to me. In shame, I used that to my advantage so I didn't have to say the truth: that I didn't love him after all, that my attraction had worn off now that I had his devotion, that

I didn't know what was wrong with me or why I was so fickle or why I only wanted things I couldn't have. I didn't have to be honest because I had a cop-out.

"Everyone really liked you, Ben. But I talked with Les and Pam, and . . . I think they're right. I think we rushed into this and we should just take a step back."

"A step back or break up?" Ben asked.

"I don't know," I said.

I did know. I didn't want to hurt him more than I already had. No. That's a lie I told myself. I didn't want to face whatever was broken inside me that made it possible for me to be so cold as to change my feelings overnight. Literally overnight. I gave him back the ring, and he was left confused and deeply hurt.

The next week, the cast and crew noticed I wasn't wearing my ring after our visit to Idaho. The Mama Bears asked me about it. As with my insecurities over sharing the spotlight with my costars, I didn't say much and kept my answer vague. But given the timing of it all, it was easy to deduce that I broke up with him because my "family" disapproved. They knew me well enough by this point to know I didn't do anything without the Family's approval.

It was around this time that the real whispers began.

After Ben, I felt more dejected about my ability to make wise decisions, so I started leaning on Les and Pam for more and more advice—not only on my personal life but on my career. Les, especially, was already doing this with everyone else, so even the small act of falling in line made me feel more connected to the group as a whole. When Abe toured with his band, Les always made sure a few Family members went on the road with them. At one point, he convinced Abe to change the band's lineup, replacing the guitar and bass players with Miguel (who was actually very good) and one of the Barbarians (who was not). When Harker booked a movie, Les would join him on set as a "prayer intercessor" for spiritual support, and even started writing a film script with him. It was about warriors, of course. For me, he would offer to read audition scenes with me when I was home for a weekend and was eager to share feedback on any new songs or scripts I was writing to pass the time. He also found a female wedding singer he thought I should start a band with (which I did, briefly).

Les also formed a business management company. It would take over the financials for Ed's medical practice, help Abe's band keep track of tour sales and expenses, and, of course, handle the motel. He named it TRIAD—an acronym for Trinity Redemption Investment and Asset Directors. Now that Les was advising artists, he embraced his own artistic side and drafted up business cards—maroon and gold with that awful Papyrus font—as well as a pretty terrible website. The site's "About" section listed his title as "Leadership Development" and his specialties as "spiritual advising, conflict resolution and vision casting." "Vision casting" was his lingo for whiteboarding or brainstorming. Pam had accounting experience with Ed's practice, and Kurt had run his plumbing business for three decades, so they magically earned the titles of accountants. Juana was also involved, albeit indirectly; TRIAD used the bank where she worked. But most strangely, Gretchen was brought on as bookkeeper and assistant. I didn't know how she would manage anyone's books when, as far as I knew, she'd never had a job or earned a paycheck or balanced a checkbook and couldn't even keep her room clean. But Les wanted to build Gretchen's confidence up, and, as a dyscalculic who'd always had a business manager looking after my money, I didn't want to judge.

I had plenty going on in my work life, anyway. I was writing music in my off time and often sang to myself on set, which led to me being asked frequently to sing on *One Tree Hill*. In one episode, Sheryl Crow made a guest appearance, and Haley is so starstruck she can't form a coherent sentence. I had the same paralysis-in-desire reaction meeting Sheryl as I did the first time I met Moira Kelly. I was so nervous I only managed to say a quick hello, when what I wished I'd been able to say was: *Hi, I know every word in every song you've written and I wanna be just like you.*

As a result of my performances on the show, I met with record labels and played a showcase at the House of Blues in LA. Then in early 2005, I was asked to be the opening act on a thirty-five-city, large-venue *One Tree Hill* concert tour. There would be tour buses, and I had a backing band; I would get to play my own songs in front of thousands of people all over the United States. The tour featured Gavin DeGraw, Michelle Branch's the Wreckers band, and Tyler Hilton, who, fresh off playing Elvis in the Oscar-winning film *Walk the Line*, had recently joined *One Tree Hill* as the hilarious and dastardly character Chris Keller. On tour, Tyler and I took up together like two kids in a potato sack race. We were already singing and recording together in Wilmington for our characters' storyline, but we became good friends on the tour. Writing songs on the bus and in dressing rooms, midnight-on-the-highway viewings of Jim Henson's *Labyrinth* or *The Princess Bride*, post-concert street tacos . . . even though he didn't share my faith (or my Family), I was developing a big crush on him.

At the Portland stop, some of the Big House Family came to see the show. Just like at my twenty-first birthday party, it was a chance for the Family to interact with my non-Family friends. For each tour stop, Warner Bros. flew out a cast member to MC the show. Portland was the city Paul Johansson was sent to. While Lee focused his attention on connecting with Tyler, whom he saw as a threat, fearing I might have a crush, Pam set her sights on Paul.

After the show, Pam, Paul, and I went to a diner attached to the concert venue to grab a burger. I thought the conversation went well. The tone stayed pleasant—unlike Pam's conversations with my mom and Camille's mom—and I was hopeful Paul would now understand how wonderful and harmless the Family was and be able to vouch for me on set when people whispered about the strangeness of the situation.

But after Pam left, Paul said to me, "Boy, she's very careful with her words, isn't she?"

"What do you mean?" I asked.

"It was interesting talking with her. She's very intentional with what she does and doesn't say. Kinda felt like doing a scene with an actor who was well rehearsed. I mean, she's lovely. It's not a criticism, just an observation."

Paul was trying to be nice, but it was clear he didn't see Pam as a warm and sincere friend like I did, which was disappointing. I really had hoped to start merging my two worlds.

As the tour continued on, Tyler seemed to want more space away from me. Instead of staying up talking with me on the bus, he went to bed early. When I asked him to explore the local food scene like we usually did, he said he had already made plans with the other tour members. I didn't understand why until he called me in my hotel room one night.

"Listen, this is awkward, but there's some rumors about you that my tour manager says someone might print in *Us Weekly*, and my name is attached because we've been hanging out so much, and—"

"Wait, slow down," I said. "What rumors?"

"Are you in, like, a religious cult or something?"

I let out a deep sigh. *This world just cannot grasp the concept of a group of people committed to real relationship. It's so sad.* "No, Ty. I'm not in a cult."

"Okay, well . . . All your friends that I met seem nice, but . . ." I could tell this was hard and awkward for him. "I don't know. I just wanted to make sure you're okay."

Us Weekly never printed anything, and Tyler always treated me normally from then forward, but I hated having it hang over us. He had become a good friend, crush or no crush, and it hurt to have people keep distancing themselves from me.

As the tour was ending, one of the final stops was New York. I was so excited to get back to my favorite city, to feel a sense of home again, and even more exciting was the news that my manager called me with prior to our arrival there.

"They're interested in you for Belle!" she said.

"Wait," I said, "on Broadway? Like, *Beauty and the Beast* on Broadway?"

"Yes! I've been pitching you, but this tour selling out has been so helpful for them to see the value of *One Tree Hill* among their demographic. They want to see you read. Can you go in before you leave New York?"

I was giddy over the prospect of satisfying this lifelong dream. "Yes. Obviously. But we leave tomorrow night."

"Okay, I'll tell them. Just work on the material. I emailed it to you. And be ready to go in tomorrow morning. If it goes well, they'll bring you back for a work session and then to see producers in a few weeks when your tour is over."

I performed my fastest set that night so I could get back to the bus and start rehearsing the material. *There goes the baker with his tray, like always* . . . The next day I did my reading and it did go well. I was to come back in three weeks prepared for the final producer session.

The first people I told were the Mama Bears back in Wilmington. Everyone in the hair and makeup trailer stopped what they were doing and yelped with joy and gave me a hug and told me how proud they were. Then I called my mom and dad. They were both so happy for me that they cried.

At the time, it didn't strike me as odd that I told the Mama Bears and my bio-parents before I told Les. My hair and makeup friends were as obsessed with Broadway as I was. That's pretty much all we talked about. I knew they'd get what a big deal it was. And sure, I wasn't speaking much to my parents—especially since in our recent conversations they, too, had started referring to the Family as a "cult"—but they knew this had been a dream of mine since I started acting, and they had been the first people to encourage me to pursue that dream. Now I realize the reason I waited to tell Les was because I was worried what he'd say. And I was right.

"What I feel in my spirit is that you're at a crossroads," Les said on the phone when I finally did tell him. "One direction leads to career, which will be greatly blessed. One direction leads to Family, which will also be greatly blessed. But I'll tell you what's on my heart is that you never had the opportunity to be a part of a Family. You've been on the road for the last few months. This is the longest you've been away from us up here, and we're just waiting with open arms. It's worth considering this might be a tactic of the enemy to keep you from your inheritance as a child of God—your spiritual inheritance of pressing into Family and finding out what it feels like to really be a part of heaven on earth."

We were having this conversation while I was on break from

set. I was pacing in circles on an unused part of our lot, which was right next to the airport and near a military base, so there were always a lot of planes flying overhead.

"I mean, baby, you can't out-give God," Les said.

"What do you mean?" I asked.

"Well, He's the giver of all good things. So, if you make this sacrifice for Him, He's just gonna turn it around and give you something bigger and better. It might not look like what you expect, but He will always turn a tithe into a blessing. Just like we tithe money, we can also tithe our dreams."

I watched an outbound plane, the sun bouncing off the metal. Perfectly white clouds in a blue sky. A slight breeze. I wanted to be on that plane, to have it take me back to New York that instant, with no time to think—because I felt myself giving in.

"That makes sense, I guess."

"If you go to New York, it'll be major for you. Everyone will see how talented you are and your career will take off in ways you can't imagine. But I don't know where that leaves you spiritually. And I don't want to see you receive a gift that you don't have the character to steward properly, which I know being part of this Family can give you. I know you'll make the right decision, and maybe it's selfish of me, but I just want you to stay on the ship with us."

I certainly didn't want to chase after a dream at the expense of my soul. But the thought of sacrificing this after a lifetime of wanting it terrified me. I figured I'd give myself a couple weeks to process, but I didn't even get that long. The following days, every time I called someone in Idaho, they wouldn't pick up or call or text me back. In all my years with the group, I'd never experienced that before. At first I thought people were just busy, until it became obvious they were avoiding me—the way I started avoiding

Mina when I heard Les call her bipolar. *Maybe that's how everyone feels about me now,* I wondered. It was an effective way to show me what I'd be missing if I chose my career over the Family.

So, now I was isolated from both my *One Tree Hill* friends *and* my Idaho Family. In my journal, I wrote: *It's so lonely. I hate being this lonely. What do I want more, which dream is more important, Broadway or Family?*

It felt shallow to even consider. The answer had to be Family. I'd wanted a family longer than I'd wanted Broadway. Family was the bigger dream. If I could let go of Blue Eyes, I could let go of this.

I called my manager. She was dumbstruck and tried to talk me out of it. She said she'd check back in a few days to make sure I hadn't changed my mind. I didn't. She reluctantly called casting, told them there was a problem with my schedule and I couldn't do the role after all. When I told the Mama Bears and my parents, they were just as shocked. They tried to talk me out of it, but, just as with the broken engagement to Ben, I played it off like I was fine. "It's just not in alignment with me right now," I said. But when I was alone in my apartment, I was sick with loss. I wept and screamed harder than I did when I ended things with Blue Eyes because, forget TV, Broadway was THE dream I'd had since I was a child. And it wasn't just my dream: It was Grandma Doris's dream, too. Walking away from that opportunity was an irreversible betrayal of her and my entire ancestry as much as myself.

When I started to come out of my depression over this, the next call I made was to Mina. I didn't know if what I'd heard Les say about her was true, but I did know that she was my friend. I missed her, and if I'd made her feel like I felt when the Family was ignoring me, I had to make it right. She was grateful and admitted she'd been confused as to why we weren't as close lately. I didn't want to betray Les, so I told her I was caught up with work. But when I shared with her about *Beauty and the Beast*, she was devastated for me.

"Joy, why didn't you take it? We would have all supported you! Take it!"

Of course, it was too late.

In the years since I left the Family, I've wondered if the reason Les discouraged me from taking the role was financial. Maybe he thought me taking a role on Broadway would jeopardize my standing on—and paycheck from—*One Tree Hill*. Maybe he thought Broadway was a detour from me getting even more lucrative TV or film roles. Probably that was part of it. But really I think it was a lot simpler than that. If I moved to New York and got to live my Broadway dream, there was a good chance I might never come back. He'd have been right, too! The actress who took Belle in my place got noticed and went on to open another dream role of mine, Mary Poppins, in the Cameron Mackintosh production. I'd have been back on the trajectory Grandma Doris had envisioned, and Les would have had one less person under his control. He couldn't let that happen. Because despite all his shady financial dealings—and they would soon get even shadier—what Les cared about far more than money was control.

CHAPTER NINETEEN

"Did you hear about the swingers?" Emily asked me on the phone one night.

I had not. Apparently, a big group of swingers requested to rent out the conference center as well as the motel for a weekend of debauchery. Despite the money it'd bring in, and how badly the motel needed the money, Emily declined. When Les and Kurt found out, they were furious.

"I don't understand how inviting in a group of swingers is in alignment with the vision of this motel being a ministry," Emily said to them.

"How is it NOT in alignment with our ministry?" Kurt said. "Welcoming in people who don't know the Lord and loving on them? People who are willing to trade their spouse with another person are at the lowest point of self-degradation. Why would we not welcome those people?"

Kurt called the swingers back and agreed to their booking. The Hamoatzah decided to demote Emily to assistant manager and promote Kurt to manager. Les told Emily it wasn't right for a woman to have authority over a man anyway, and that it was his own mistake for trying to set her in a position that was doomed to fail because it was outside of God's leadership structure.

"Kurt's right," Emily said to me. "Those are the people we're trying to reach and show God's love."

"Em, it's not like they're coming for a prophetic conference," I said. "I would have seen it the same way you did."

Especially after what recently happened to Dontay. On an overnight shift, he had been caught watching porn on one of the motel computers. He was fired from his maintenance job. Multiple basement meetings were held for him, in which he had to confess to a porn addiction. He was forced to temporarily move out of the Big House and stay with another family from the church. Jasmine broke off their engagement. She still loved him, but with the past sexual abuse from that college boyfriend, she didn't feel safe to marry someone with a porn habit. She went to the Hamoatzah and told them not to allow him to pursue her until his addiction had been dealt with and he was recovered.

It was interesting that the Family would punish and ostracize one of its most devoted and hardworking members for his sexual behavior, yet had no problem with a bunch of strangers screwing each other. The difference, of course, was the strangers were paying for the right to do so.

Money was so tight that Mina, now pregnant again, sold her beloved BMW that she'd brought with her from LA. In its place, Les suggested she and Harker buy Kurt and Lucy's old Dodge Intrepid, which had only a few more payments on it. Mina shared this news in an email to the Family, and she tried to sound cheery about it. "Praise God!" she wrote. "This Intrepid is so much more practical for our growing Family." But I knew how much that BMW meant to her and how difficult it must've been to give it up.

Soon, the Intrepid started breaking down, once leaving Mina stranded on the side of the highway. With her baby due soon, Ed gave her and Harker his candy-red Fiat.

I heard Les was upset with Ed for stepping in without consulting him.

"There's wisdom in a multitude of counselors," I heard him say often, paraphrasing Proverbs 11:14 to explain why none of us should be making independent decisions. Les felt the car situation had been teaching Harker and Mina a valuable lesson about hard work and how people who didn't grow up privileged lived. That was Ed's son and daughter-in-law—the mother of his grandchildren—Les was meddling with. It would've been perfectly understandable if Ed had told Les to mind his own damn business and worry about his own kids. He didn't, though. Because Pam agreed with Les, Ed accepted Les's edicts and apologized for intervening. If Ed suffered anger at all, he did it silently and without question, like the rest of us.

Well, not all of us, it turned out. Harker was growing increasingly impatient with Les's antics, and this eventually came to the surface.

In addition to TRIAD, Les and Pam opened a counseling practice. At that time, neither of them had a degree or certification in counseling, but because he was a pastor and she was a doctor's wife, it seemed Les had found a loophole.

Ed, as a general practitioner, would see patients for mental health visits and then send the patients to talk for an hour with Les and Pam. We never paid a cent. Was insurance billed for these services? *Someone* was cutting a check to Les for his "chaplain services" or to his ministry for a donation write-off.

With his newfound status as official counselor, everyone in the group started using this method to schedule therapy sessions with Les. He had offered himself to Mina as a sympathetic ear, since new marriages were hard, especially with babies involved. She'd done a few counseling sessions with him. According to Mina, Les repeatedly told her he wasn't sure how trustworthy Harker was and that she should come to him anytime for advice.

It sounded like the same thing I'd eavesdropped on Les and Kurt discussing.

When Harker learned of this, he asked if everyone was accountable to Les, who held *him* to account? When Les answered "the Hamoatzah," Harker held him to it. He called for a meeting with the Hamoatzah and said that it was inappropriate for Les to try to form an alliance with his wife against him. In the presence of the other Leadership members, Les was contrite, and he apologized, even thanked Harker for calling it to his attention. But it was just for show.

As I would learn later, Les had been at this game for a long time. He knew the only way to keep going was to play along for the time being. It was a situation he could use to his advantage later by pointing to this moment and saying, "Look, I can admit when I'm wrong!" That's all his contrition was, though: ammunition for later. Everything changed between Les and Harker after that. It was also the hairline fracture of the fault line that would eventually swallow up the entire Big House Family.

Aside from the swingers conference—where, according to Juana, Miguel had to pile a drunken Kurt into his car after he tried to get a room with one of the female attendees—one of the few other times the conference center was booked was for a weekend-long spiritual workshop led by Les's friend, the Welsh prophet. Let's call him Pirelli, after the snake-oil salesman in Sondheim's *Sweeney Todd*.

Everyone in the Big House Family was expected to help out with Pirelli's event, from the worship team to the cleaning team. Everyone except Dontay. He was still apparently "unsafe" for women to be around (because porn), so Les had him come at

4:00 a.m. to set up the stage and lights with QB and Brandon. There were about twenty-five of us now in the inner circle of the Big House Family, and very few new people were allowed in because of the privacy needs of the "very public figures" Les mentored. He would explain this to church attendees who noticed our little clique and felt left out. As Les liked to keep things casual, the church had no formal membership, no pledge to sign or little card to fill out so someone from the church staff could call and welcome you. We had no church staff. Aside from the Big House Family, Les tried to avoid much interaction with the people he was preaching to. But he did encourage them to purchase tickets to the prophetic workshop and tell their friends. Flyers were passed out and posted around town.

While reading tarot cards, visiting psychics, performing rituals with crystals, and any other secular means of divination are considered to be promoting a "false sense of security" in the Bible, prophecy is seen as very real and is encouraged. According to the Bible, psychics have access to "unknowable information" about someone's past and desires only because Satan or a demon is disguising itself as whatever spirit brings this information—the purpose being to distract people from God with guesses and promises about the future. A prophet would have access to the past, present, *and* the "unknowable future," because only God knows the future, and the purpose of this information is to draw people closer to God.

In the case of Pirelli, and so many other people who claim to be prophets (and psychics!), he was more than happy to use his skills of deduction and knowledge of the Bible to create a large following. His fans had an addiction to the feeling of superiority, just like Les was training us to have. Pirelli would tell people what they want to hear (the "unknowable" future and good news about themselves), and create a subconscious us-versus-them narrative toward anyone on the outside.

Now that Les and Pirelli had joined forces, it gave Les more credibility. It also gave him more exposure. This meant former members of his old church started taking notice and growing alarmed. Every now and then, some of the Family members and I would get random emails from someone warning us and trying to save us from being indoctrinated into Les's new "cult" the way they had been years before. When we shared these emails with Les, he always had an explanation. *This one* wanted to cheat on her husband with him and he wouldn't. *That one* was mistreating their son, and Les had to call Child Protective Services. *This one* was jealous because he wanted to be the lead pastor, so he spread lies about Les. *That one* was stealing money from the church so had to be fired. It was a big conspiracy against him because he was such a mighty man of God. And Les considered the opposition to be a spiritual sign that we were all on the right track. Why would the enemy bother attacking us if we weren't effecting change in the world?

These warnings only fed the us-versus-them narrative that I needed to believe. I was too far in. I'd sacrificed too much by now to start doubting.

So there I sat, in the conference center of our shitty little motel, scribbling in notebooks while Pirelli lectured for hours on seminar topics with such titles as "The Dreams of God," "God Is the Happiest Person You've Ever Met," and "The Truth About You." The cost for attendance was $120 per person, plus $68 (plus tax) per night for a room. This included breakfast but did not include the cost of the course books Pirelli was selling, which was where he really made money. Attendance was capped at 150 people, and it sold out. People came from all across the country—even Tree Hill.

One of the attendees was a pretty, young plus-size blonde named Danielle. She was around my age with a hearty laugh you'd enjoy from across the room, though I didn't hear it that weekend. We didn't actually meet until months later. As she then explained, she'd been too nervous to introduce herself at the workshop. She was there with a friend whom she'd met on something called a "message board" for *One Tree Hill*. I wasn't sure what that was, since I mostly used the internet for music or research on prophetic dream interpretation. Apparently, message boards were places for fans of things like TV shows to connect with one another. Someone on the *OTH* board had mentioned my affiliation with Abe's band. Danielle and her friend went to see a couple of his concerts, where they met Les and had a deep, spiritual conversation in the midst of the bar and the music. This was one of the keys to Les's appeal: He didn't waste time small-talking like the rest of society. He didn't discuss the weather or traffic or sports. He effortlessly dispensed with superficiality and refused to just go through the motions of human interaction. Upon meeting someone, usually one of the first things he'd say was: "How's your heart?" And, often, people wanted to tell him! He encouraged Danielle and her friend to visit the church in Idaho. So, they decided to attend the workshop to see what it was all about, also hoping that they might get a chance to see me there.

What Les didn't know—what apparently not even his friend the great prophet Pirelli could foresee—was that inviting Danielle to Idaho would prove to be another widening of the fault line split that began with Harker.

CHAPTER TWENTY

After six months, Dontay was deemed cured of his porn addiction and readmitted into the Family. His and Jasmine's wedding was back on. Though his mom, Esther, was now disapproving of the Family, she couldn't help but be thrilled her son was getting married and offered to pay for a nice wedding. Instead, the ceremony and reception were held at the motel conference center, with its old carpet and fluorescent lighting. Les thought there might be business in hosting weddings, and he needed wedding pictures for the brochure. Gretchen took their photos and they were terrible.

Soon, two more Family members paired off: Abe and Emily, and the news of this broke me down into tears. I couldn't bear the thought that I'd be alone forever. And so I decided I wouldn't be.

The next time I was back in Idaho, I asked Les if I could meet with him. He told me to come to his office at the motel, where he operated his counseling practice. That morning, I arrived at the motel to find the parking lot mostly empty, except for the usual two or three transient men who hung out there. I also noticed the red Fiat that Ed had given to Harker and Mina. When I knocked on the office door, it was Harker who answered, looking serious.

"Hi, sis," he said, distracted and giving an obligatory smile over the clear tension in the room. It occurred to me that Les and Harker had been having a lot of private meetings. I didn't really put it together until this moment, but suddenly little flashes ran through my mind. Harker and Les emerging from the basement at the Big House, stressed. Passing by other rooms in the house and catching a glimpse of them through a cracked door having a heated conversation. Harker speaking up more at Family meetings, sharing alternative perspectives on various things. Like the word "covenant." Les had been starting to refer to us as a "covenant Family." All the meetings and emails began with "Dear Covenant Family." It was meant as an acknowledgment that we had all been brought together by God's orchestration. I'd heard the word "covenant" many times growing up in a Christian environment and knew that it meant a holy and sacred pact, like a marriage. I hadn't heard of a "covenant Family," but just like I hadn't heard of spiritual parents or Jezebel, it sounded close enough to things I was familiar with, so I never thought to challenge Les—especially because of the way he always used the term so casually. His ability to make bold statements sound harmless was another part of his charm.

But at one Wednesday meeting, Harker did challenge him.

"In the Bible," he said, "a covenant is between two people and usually in marriage, not a group of people with each other."

"Well, what were the Israelites?" Les said. "Were they not a group of people?"

"Yes," Harker said, "but that was between the people and God; the people weren't covenanted to *each other*."

At that point, Pam interjected and steered the meeting in a different direction.

Les was becoming increasingly irritated with Harker, and clearly that was the case in this moment. But Harker left, and Les, sitting at his desk, waved me in, ignoring any sense of strain in the air. Whatever they were sorting out wasn't any of my business, so I put the thoughts out of my mind, took a seat on one of the two faux leather chairs for counseling clients, and focused on the reason I'd come. I needed Les's advice.

"So this is kind of awkward," I said, "but I think I've got a crush on QB."

His whole face changed. Softened. His eyes went wide and the corners of his mouth turned up. Even his voice was gentler. "Really?"

Technically, it was true. During a recent visit to Idaho, I pulled my car into the horseshoe driveway of the Big House and saw QB step out on the front porch in a black t-shirt that hugged his new muscles. He was twenty-one now. Taller than before, it seemed, and he had cut off his long hair. He wasn't unattractive, but I told Les I was worried my crush was more about feeling lonely.

"Everyone else in the group is paired off," I said, "and it kinda feels like I'm probably only thinking about him because he's the last single guy in our Family. I just don't understand why God hasn't brought me a husband yet."

Les leaned back in his leather chair, quiet. His elbows rested on the sides, and his fingers came together in a steeple, a position he frequently assumed. I briefly wondered how the chair had fit through the door since it was bulky at every angle, like a brown throne.

"I don't think you're giving yourself enough credit," he said. "You've been in Hollywood, working with some of the best-looking, most charismatic guys in the world. I don't see you as someone who would settle for being romantically involved with anyone for a reason as desperate as that."

He watched me digest this. I *did* feel desperate, though. I just wanted to be a normal twenty-four-year-old girl with a boyfriend, but it seemed like being a Christian prohibited this—so, what was I supposed to do? Les looked down, pinching a crease in the fabric of his pants.

"I mean, baby, you're a beautiful young woman. You could have any one of those men you work with. I think you have lots of options, and I don't think you'd be interested in someone unless you were honestly attracted to them." He looked down again and smiled shyly. "But I'm biased. I think my son is pretty handsome."

I chuckled with him to keep the mood light, but I was more confused than when I came in. What he said made perfect sense— maybe this wasn't just a phase. Les sensed my unease.

"Let's just pray about it and see what God reveals," he said. "There's no rush. I'm honored that you came to me. Thank you for trusting me with this."

I left his office feeling good. Talking about it out loud made my crush less scary. But it quickly became clear Les told QB. He started paying a lot of attention to me when I would visit. He wanted to go on walks and stay up late talking or playing games at the kitchen table. I accepted the attention because I didn't want to be alone, and because if QB was the man God chose for me, I wanted to embrace that. He *was* very sweet.

It wasn't long before we were officially "dating." He would write me letters—not as familiar and witty as those Blue Eyes wrote me in high school, but still full of kindness. And he was playful, which I loved. Knowing how ticklish I was, he would often start in and get me squirming and flailing and laughing. He would hold my arms down, stroke my hair, and whisper, "Shhh, it's okay, baby. It's okay, it's okay." It was a creepy bit he and the Barbarians used to do to each other when they were wrestling. "It's okay, baby. Shhh, it's okay." He did it because he knew it gave me the heebie-jeebies. I'd finally manage to kick him off me, and we'd both be laughing. The playfulness was a distraction from either of us admitting the lack of physical chemistry or how little we had in common. I loved language and seeing new places.

He constantly used incorrect words and thought people who traveled for leisure were snobs. I valued curiosity, he valued certainty. Once, he asked who Marilyn Monroe was and if Julia Roberts was "the lady with a lot of teeth"—then I seriously questioned the relationship. Still, just wanting what God wanted, trying to be open-minded and open-hearted, I went along with it all. *He's innocent. Innocent is good. I'm jaded. Innocent is what I need.*

After *One Tree Hill* finished its summer hiatus and filming started up again in Wilmington, QB and Les came to visit me in the fall. One afternoon, when Les had gone to the store, QB and I started making out and messing around in my bedroom. Les came back early and unannounced. When we walked out of my bedroom, he was sitting on my couch staring angrily at both of us. He took QB for a walk, during which I suspect he was telling his son that he had to propose to me now because of all the heavy petting. (Can someone please come up with a better term for it than "heavy petting"? I feel like I'm in a 1970s health class video every time I hear that.)

I was right. The next day while Les was out running errands, QB proposed—in spite of me saying, "Don't, Q, don't," as soon as he got on one knee. There was no ring, but he said he'd spend the rest of his life chasing down stars for me, which sounded so lovely, except even now I still have no idea what it meant.

I told him I had to think about it and left. Walking alone in silence for nearly an hour, I felt a wave of hopelessness wash over me. I talked to God, pleading with Him to show up again like He did on that rain-soaked day in the Manhattan café.

I don't want to lose all my friends. This is my Family. This is my tribe. I'm terrified to be alone again, Lord.

Silence.

Please, give me a sign. Is this going to be okay? How do I say no to this? Should I say no, or should I say yes and just let You work it out?

Silence.

I don't trust myself. I don't trust my motives. The Bible says the heart is deceitful above all things. My heart wants to run away from this and hold out for a man that I'm head over heels in love with, attracted to, and adore. But I'm open to the idea that my motives are broken. Are they? Am I just wrestling my flesh right now?

Silence.

Lord, I'm not going to answer him until I hear from You. You have to tell me what to do.

Then came the words. They weren't audible like before, but the feeling in my body was the same. It felt as if God said, *If you choose this, I will make it good.*

It wasn't yes or no. It wasn't a sign or even an answer at all. But it was the response I needed to be able to say yes to Q, simply to alleviate the pressure of this anvil on my chest. Knowing that I had a promise from God to take whatever was about to happen and turn it into something good gave me the freedom to give in to my fear.

"Yes," I told him, when I finally walked back into my house. "I'll marry you."

We scheduled the wedding for eight weeks later during my Christmas hiatus from *OTH*. I was depressed the entire time. We had called my mother from the car the afternoon of the proposal, and I did my best to sound excited. So did she, but neither of us managed to be all that convincing. My dad's reaction wasn't any better, and he tried multiple times over the following weeks to attempt to persuade me to abandon this arrangement.

None of that surprised me. What I didn't expect was the reaction from several of the Big House Family members.

One weekend when I was visiting Idaho and making plans for the wedding, Mina and Harker pulled up and found me outside at the driveway entrance planting a small willow tree I'd found at a local nursery, thinking gardening might help calm my nerves.

"Hey, sis! Harker and I were just about to go for a walk. Wanna come with us?"

We wandered out into the field behind the Big House. When we were far enough away, Mina said, "Joy, we just wanted to check in on you about the wedding. Are you sure?"

"What do you mean?" I said, knowing exactly what she meant.

"I guess I was just really surprised when you two started dating, because, you know, you're very different people, and I just didn't really see the connection."

"Not that you can't have a connection when you're different," Harker said. "But . . ."

Mina finished his sentence. "I've known you for long enough to know your type and the kind of man you imagined yourself with. We just wanna make sure this marriage is something you really want and you don't feel pressured into it in some way."

Harker looked me in the eyes. "Joy," he said, "you do not have to marry QB if you don't want to. You'll still keep your friends. We love you. We're not going anywhere."

In a world where I could have done things differently and my daughter would still exist, I wish I had grabbed them both by the collars and said, *Save me! Get me the hell out of here! I have no idea what I'm doing!* But I was too proud. I absolutely hated giving someone else the satisfaction of knowing that I'd made a mistake and they were right all along. In my asinine, unreasonable pride, I smiled and reassured them that everything was fine.

Somehow this conversation got back to Les. Maybe Harker wanted it to, as yet another sign of his ongoing soft rebellion.

However Les found out about it, he held a private meeting without me and told all the Family members that they were forbidden from speaking against our engagement. Pam was sent to talk to me in an attempt to quell my anxiety.

"I think he's a great person and he's so sweet," I told her, "but I don't feel that *thing*. You know? That *thing* where you just long to be close and to kiss and you just adore the person. There's no real chemistry."

Pam shifted her lips into a smile and tilted her head. "Sometimes God wants us to choose an opportunity based on it being right, not whether or not we want it. He wants to know our obedience before He reveals how deep our desire really is."

"But this doesn't feel right, because I don't feel any desire at all. And I just feel really stuck, because if I don't marry him, I'll lose this whole Family. I really don't want to abandon the ship."

"Sweetheart, you won't lose us."

"No, but I will! He's Les's son. It'll be too weird. And I'm just scared to lose this. I don't want to lose my Family."

I was crying now. Pam reached out a hand to calm me.

"I can just tell you from an outside perspective that I see so much brilliance in God bringing you and QB together. You turned down *Beauty and the Beast* to experience life in a real Family. It's like you offered God a sacrifice of one major desire of your heart, and, in return, He's giving you another one. If you had taken that role, you never would have fallen in love and you wouldn't be getting married!"

But I hadn't fallen in love. Why wasn't she hearing me? I just listened to her and nodded. I wanted to make it make sense. I wanted to believe that all this would be okay. It *had to be* in order for me to keep my life as I knew it. I just needed enough faith to believe that God would make it good.

"Sweetheart, attraction comes and goes," Pam said. "It's what's underneath all that that matters."

When I went back to Les's motel office to further discuss it with him, he said the same thing.

"No one stays attracted to their spouse all the time," he said. "Do you know how many arranged marriages there are where people fall madly in love years after they're married? The Bible is full of those stories!"

(It's not, BTW.)

"You know," he continued, "you grew up seeing Hollywood movies as your example for romantic love, but God wants to show you something deeper and more meaningful than that."

The way he phrased things always seemed so simple and clear.

"I get that. It makes sense. But do I just ignore my emotions?"

"Yes."

I wasn't expecting that. I nearly laughed at his bluntness.

"Jesus never promised that we would always feel good about the things He calls us to do," Les said. "He just asks us to obey and then our emotions will fall in line. We're always called to obey first. Think of all the things you do because you have to: waking up for early call times, eating healthy, showing up for a friend when they call you in the middle of the night. You don't start out feeling excited about these things, but when you do them you see the positive results, and then your emotions line up with the truth of what you really want: a steady job, a healthy body, a loyal friend. First you choose with your mind what you want, and God brings feelings into alignment later."

Again, it made sense. It didn't feel good, but it made sense. By this point I was so used to mistrusting my own instincts. I knew I was led by my emotions. I was a fickle artist who never knew what she wanted. I was all over the place. The more I thought about it, the more foolproof this formula for decision-making seemed.

"You know, baby," he went on, "anyone could marry anybody. Compatibility is made up. People are always changing. If you're not compatible now, you will be in five years. Then you won't be again. Then you will be. It doesn't matter who you choose. You're still bringing yourself into any relationship. And *you're* the one you get to work on. So, it really comes down to if you're ready to work on yourself or not. Marriage only functions as the container for growth. Attracted, not attracted: you just pick someone and let God be in charge of making it work."

The idea was almost freeing. Almost. If I could just get out of my own way. If I could just live in faith instead of in the world that had brainwashed me about romance.

Emotions will fall in line. Obey God first.

So that's what I did. I went through the motions. I gave up my Los Angeles apartment at Les's suggestion. He even *generously* offered to move me out so I'd never have to go back to LA again. I took him up on it, and he and QB drove a U-Haul out to California and packed up my place. I bought a house in Idaho close to the Big House but decided not to move into it until we were married, so it could feel like "our house." I added Q's name to my bank accounts, and they became our joint bank accounts. I officially moved all my financial management from the best firm in New York, Altman, Greenfield & Selvaggi, to the worst firm in Idaho, TRIAD. And I changed Les's name in my phone to "Papa."

Every step along the way I kept thinking something would click and suddenly it would all feel right. As an intentional affront to the feminist defiance I'd inherited from the women in my family, I was choosing to become the damsel, the submissive wife. Why wasn't it working? I kept telling myself I just needed to take one more step. *Just one more. Just one more. Just one more.*

The morning of our New Year's Eve wedding, I woke up in our Quality Inn and Conference Center, where fifteen or so of my friends and family were also staying. This included my mom, stepdad, Nanny Marge, and even Camille, who made the effort to fly up and be supportive in spite of the awkwardness. This did not include Paul Johansson or any of my *OTH* friends, whom I didn't invite, knowing their skepticism toward the Family. It also did not include my dad, who I did invite but who refused to come, apoplectic about the marriage and now fully convinced I was in a cult. I still cringe today about the fact that I put up my friends and family at that dump.

My alarm went off at 7:30 a.m., and I looked around the dingy brown room. I thought about coffee. I thought about how cold it was outside. I thought about my lines for the episode we were going to shoot when I came back. I thought about our mystery honeymoon location, which QB volunteered to plan and wanted to make a surprise. I thought about standing at the altar with him. I thought about whether I left my house unlocked. I thought about how long it takes for ants to build a hill and for cream to churn into butter. I watched the bright red digits on the old clock change minute after minute.

I felt absolutely nothing.

CHAPTER TWENTY-ONE

We were married in a barn on an apple orchard. My dress was designed by Justina McCaffrey, which I'd tried on and purchased alone from famed NYC bridal boutique Kleinfeld. My mom wasn't there with me when I bought it and wasn't there when I put it on, trying not to fall into old space heaters in a cold room off the side of the barn. Pam had inserted herself fully as my spiritual mother, and since the Big House Family took precedence over bio-family, my mom was treated like a guest with no special honors. Contrary to my birthday, Pam didn't speak to her at all at the wedding. There was no need to make nice now. Pam had essentially replaced her.

Whoever was in charge of propane didn't buy enough, so my poor grandmother was shivering the most out of our fifty-plus guests. Thank goodness Juana had the sense the day prior to buy blankets people could grab on their way in.

Walking down the aisle felt like choreography in a play. Standing at the altar while Les married us felt like being in a scene. I thought of how I'd stood at an altar multiple times before. On *Guiding Light* I'd married Paul Anthony Stewart's character Danny Santos. On *One Tree Hill* I'd had two weddings, both to James Lafferty's Nathan Scott. I knew how to play this part.

I looked at QB and looked out at our "audience." *Am I allowed to break the fourth wall in this show?* And then, in the play in my mind, I saw Blue Eyes standing in the back. There, in a t-shirt and jeans and a black duffel coat, his dishwater hair falling into his tan face, waiting for the moment when the minister says, "If anyone has good cause—" And then he was confidently striding down the aisle toward me saying, "I do! I have good cause! Joy, marry me instead." And I grabbed his hand and escaped with him, and we ran and kept running and running through the barren apple orchards covered in snow, never looking back. But this wasn't make-believe. This was my life.

Les never did say the "if anyone has good cause" part. Probably because he didn't want to tempt the several people in the room who legitimately might have stood up on my behalf.

We said our "I dos," walked back down the aisle to Dusty Springfield's "Son of a Preacher Man," and ate some middling lasagna and carrot cake Les had ordered from the Bistro restaurant in town while Miguel spun a decent playlist. This time I ordered a chocolate fountain, but I still drank enough champagne to forget the rest.

QB drove us to the airport for our honeymoon but didn't reveal where we were headed until we got inside. I'd dropped so many hints to him since the engagement: "You know, I've never been to England." "Sophia, Paul, and a bunch of the cast just went to Iceland together. The photos looked incredible!" "The food in Barcelona is supposed to be amazing." "I'm dying to go back to Paris." Only when he handed me my ticket to pass through security did I discover our destination.

We were flying to . . . Colorado?

This was *not* the honeymoon I had been dreaming about since I was a girl. This was the worst idea for a honeymoon that anyone who knew me, even peripherally, could possibly have come up with. No offense if you live in Colorado. Colorado is great if you ski. Which I didn't. Also, gorgeous if you love the cold. Which I hate. *Why the hell did he pick Colorado?*

Naturally, it had been Les's idea. He had gotten a deal at the Lodge & Spa at Cordillera, which was struggling to fill rooms due to it being the hotel where Kobe Bryant had been accused of rape just a year before. What exactly about a public sexual assault case screamed "honeymoon" to this man, I'm not sure. Equally bizarre, Les and QB didn't even pay for it, because in addition to my bank accounts, I had added QB to my credit cards. The least he could have done was use my money to put me on a beach in January! But no, it would have been much more difficult to keep me confined if I was somewhere I actually wanted to be, and Les had raised all his sons to believe that the best thing about marriage was sex.

"We're not really gonna leave the room anyway!" QB said, sensing my disappointment and trying to perk me up with a quote I'm sure he was parroting from his father. I was not perked.

As a good Christian girl saving herself for marriage, experiencing intimacy for the first time with someone I didn't have desire for was extraordinarily confusing for me. The evangelical purity-culture promise of brilliant sex being the ultimate reward for staying zipped up until someone put a ring on it turned out to be a hoax. I couldn't understand why sex made me feel so . . . sad. In fairness, QB was probably just as nervous and disappointed as me. I had hoped sex would bring us closer and produce the chemistry I wanted, but all it did was drive us further apart. I was angry with him for suddenly showing no interest in me besides my body, and he was angry that everything he'd been promised about wives being a personal blow-up doll was false. I was starting to feel the cascade of depression, and by the end of the first week I was actually starting to feel trapped. He didn't want to go sightseeing. He didn't want to try snowmobiling. I even offered to try skiing, but he was determined to stay in the room with me. *F—o—r—e—vvvv—e—rrrr.*

I had to make this fun somehow or I'd go mad.

I convinced him to go for a long walk. We found a hidden, frozen lake and a little brown hut with vintage ice skates in it. They were decorative, but they fit my tiny feet. I told him to wait outside, took off my clothes, and ice-skated around topless, hoping to make him laugh.

"Come on," I said, "let's skinny-skate!"

And he did laugh. At first. Then he started getting anxious, looking around. He was embarrassed, concerned someone would see me and that I (he) would be disgraced.

"Joy! Joy, come on."

"Lose the shorts, loser."

"I'm serious."

"So serious."

"Joy."

"Q!"

He wouldn't budge. His playfulness was the one thing I really enjoyed about his company when we started dating. Now everything was so intense all the time. Everything I did, no matter how benign, created some *reaction.*

I took the skates off, put my clothes back on, and we walked back to the hotel room, hardly leaving for the remainder of the trip.

I had no idea how bad it would get or how exhausted and emotionally stripped I would become, but it was immediately and abundantly clear this whole arrangement was the worst decision I'd ever made.

. . .

After the abysmal honeymoon, QB moved to Wilmington with me and he immediately began the process of "integrating" our lives. He monitored where I went, what I watched, who I talked to. He didn't even want me to own anything that represented my life before marriage. So, I did a big purge of clothes, jewelry, photos— and I definitely couldn't keep the pink brocade couch on which I'd made out with my short-lived fiancé, Ben. Eventually, we traded my charming, color-filled downtown apartment for one that was beige in every way and overlooked a shopping center.

When he met the cast and crew, everyone was cordial, and a few people, like Paul, made an effort to befriend him. But Q resisted. He mistrusted them all. He had never been prepared to face the world on his own. He had been trained to be terrified of the unknown, groomed to need Les there to guide him through everything. On set, he managed his fear by smiling and feigning sweetness and docility. Later at home, he'd wax on about what frauds they all were. Things quickly got worse. He wanted to read every script to see if he was okay with what I would be doing in that episode. He examined photos of my wardrobe choices to make sure there wasn't any midriff or cleavage. Who was I eating lunch with? It better not have been a male cast member. Was I confiding in anyone at work about our relationship struggles? Not if I knew what was good for me! Only Jezebel wives disrespect their husbands by airing dirty laundry.

I was too young to understand all his controlling behavior was rooted in his upbringing, in what Les had taught him. *Man = warrior. Woman = princess. Man be strong. Woman be weak. Woman glad for strong man. Strong man make fire. Man tell woman what to do. Woman thank man with sex.*

For now, I simply found myself erupting on the phone to Pam or Jasmine or Emily multiple times a week, sometimes even multiple times a day. They'd console me with platitudes.

"He's learning how to be a husband, and you're learning how to be a wife."

"Don't ask illegal questions. Accept that you were made for each other and work from there."

"Trust his spiritual leadership. God's given him eyes to see things that you need protection from."

"Marriage is hard work. Don't give up. It's so rewarding."

The only people who seemed to understand me were Harker and Mina. I called them one afternoon while Q was at the gym, which, not having a job, was always where he was.

"I don't know what to do," I said, exhausted. I leaned on my elbows at our round wooden dining table. I had bought the table at Goodwill, because God forbid I should spend any money without his permission, and certainly not on anything as frivolous as clothes or furniture. I picked at the sticky wood lacquer while the Ethan Allen home store taunted me from across the street. "You guys . . . we're not right for each other. QB and I should not have gotten married." My pride had finally broken down enough for me to admit that I had made a colossal mistake.

"I'm so sorry, Joy." Harker's voice was gentle and soothing. "Can we just pray for you before we talk?"

I was becoming weary of people praying for me, but there wasn't another acceptable answer to this question besides "Yeah, of course. Thank you."

"Lord, thanks for giving us the opportunity to know You better through seeing the way You love Joy. She's such a strong, openhearted, thoughtful person, and we're grateful to be her friends. If there's any encouragement or comfort we can offer her right now, please give us the wisdom to hear and speak it. Amen."

Then I started to cry. I didn't realize how badly I needed to hear someone say a few positive things about me. He wasn't praying for me to be delivered from my selfishness or that I would learn the meaning of "submission." Harker carried the same warmth I felt from Mina when we met, and hearing his consolation now reminded me how perfect they were for each other. At the same time, it sent a pang of longing and regret into me. I knew QB and I would never have that.

"I know I made this choice and it's wrong to get divorced," I said. "I'm willing to stay and make it work. But we can't build a marriage on this imaginary story that we were made for each other. We weren't."

"Yeah, I think that's right," Mina said.

"If we can at least acknowledge the truth, that we shouldn't have gotten married, then maybe we could start over from there. If we just had an honest foundation, then that feels like real space for God to come move and maybe make us *into* people who are right for each other. Do you think that sounds crazy?"

"I think that sounds very healthy," Harker said. "It's actually the only way real change can happen."

After hanging up, I anxiously waited for QB to come home so I could tell him this new revelation of mine. I hoped he would feel as relieved as I did at the permission to be honest. When I finally sat him down and shared the big, bad secret that I had been carrying, he was silent for moment. Then he said, "You talked to Harker and Mina about this?"

"Yeah, I just wanted to get some accountability before I—"

"*I* am your accountability," he said. He stood up and began pacing. "I forbid you to talk with anyone else about this until I say it's okay."

"You *forbid* me?"

"Yes."

"Uh. No."

He got louder: "Harker just went behind my back and had a private conversation with my wife about my marriage. Do you not see how inappropriate that is!?"

"It wasn't just me and Harker. Mina was on the phone, too."

"It doesn't matter! It's so inappropriate!"

"Your dad gives spouses separate counsel all the time!"

"That's his job," Q said. "He's a pastor and a counselor."

I wanted to say, *Certified by who?* But I knew that would only make him madder. Instead I said, "Q, you can't tell me who to talk to or not."

"Yes, I can. I am the spiritual authority in this household, and I'm telling you—"

"I'm telling *you*, I don't know what you think this is, but I am not Marti. I am not your mother."

"Ugh, why won't you just *obey* me!?"

I was stunned silent. "Did you just say 'obey' you?"

He glared at me, breathing heavily. And I couldn't help it: I started laughing. I wasn't even laughing at him. I was laughing at myself—at how absurd and cliché the whole thing had become. He stormed out of the apartment.

I didn't know how we were going to move forward, but I knew something had to change. Divorce was not an option—not if I wanted to remain in the Family, which I very much did. So, six months into the marriage, Q had a private meeting with the Hamoatzah and announced to me that it was decided he should move back to Idaho and live in our (my) house there. As much as I wanted a break from our constant conflict, this decision felt wrong. The whole arrangement was starting to feel too incestuous. As a single woman I craved this covenant Family involvement in my world, but being married felt different. I was tired of everyone's hands mixing in our marriage the same way Les kneaded that flop of meat the first time we'd met.

I tried to talk Q out of moving, thinking maybe he just needed something to do, something to build his confidence. I could get him a job with the show's set design department doing carpentry and building sets. We could stop calling home for help and work on the marriage with a local, actually certified counselor to see if it was possible to turn this mess into something good. At least then if it still fell apart, we'd know we gave it our best shot! He declined both offers, saying he trusted his father's guidance on this more than mine and he needed to stay close to his family for his peace of mind.

Later, as I learned more about cults, I would come to understand that Les likely proposed this separation in the hope that by separating us physically he eliminated the possibility of me ending the marriage out of sheer exhaustion. Metin Başoğlu, a psychiatrist and trauma researcher, studied the psychological effects of torture on political POWs and war survivors from Yugoslavia and Turkey by comparing continuous versus intermittent torture. His findings showed that torture with breaks between abuses induced more severe psychological effects than continuous torture. Victims of intermittent torture had higher rates of depression, anxiety, and PTSD. The unpredictability and anticipation of more abuse heightened stress and anxiety, which then caused "learned helplessness," making victims feel powerless and passive over time. This increased compliance because resistance seemed futile.

In hindsight, it appears the physical distance between QB and me was a strategic move to take me from experiencing continuous torture to intermittent. This ensured longevity, which was exactly what Les and the Hamoatzah needed in order to drain my accounts without anyone noticing. These things take time, you know.

As Les expected, there was a lot of relief for me in the sudden absence of constant conflict. But being told, in not so many words, that you're *so* difficult to be around that your husband has to literally live on the other side of the country to manage being married to you was a pretty severe blow to my self-worth. This, I imagine, Les also expected. Since I had been growing more confident and defiant, this move knocked me back down into longing for validation.

Once QB moved back to Idaho, he seemed to be emboldened by the company of his father and brothers as well as the other men in the Family, who had all launched into a "brotherhood" phase. Les was putting them through a marines-style boot camp. Up at 4:00 a.m., heavy training, diet plans. As a symbol of how much in unity they were with one another, nearly all of them got a tattoo over their hearts: a ship in rough seas. The ship itself had a name: *home*.

The distance from me also made QB even more controlling. Instead of being an active part of my life in Wilmington, my day-to-day became his new "unknown" to fear. His demands for my compliance—excuse me, "unity"—became more heightened. He regularly said that my acting career was hurting him and I should quit because he "couldn't see God's purpose in me kissing other men." He hated the fact that I was under contract with *One Tree Hill* for six years and we were only in season three. With the huge success of the show, I was getting more film offers, and he insisted on weighing in on those as well. One day I told him Paul was coming over to help me tape an audition,

"I didn't agree to that," Q said. "What audition is it?"

"*Across the Universe*. That Beatles movie."

"The what?"

"The Beatles. The band?"

"Yeah, I've heard of the Beatles. What is the movie? Did you send this to me?"

"I don't know. I thought so."

"Why does Paul have to be the one to tape you?"

"He's my friend and he's a good director." In addition to acting on *OTH*, Paul had started directing episodes—something I hoped I'd get the chance to do at some point.

"Where does this even shoot?" Q asked. "How long will you be away?"

Away. As though filming somewhere else would be any different from me filming in North Carolina while he lived in Idaho.

"Q, it's just an audition. It's too early to think about any of that."

"Well, I don't feel comfortable with it, so clearly we're not in unity. Are you going to make a choice in direct rebellion of our unity?"

"Unity" was Les's latest buzzword. Everything had to be done "in unity." Like all Les's buzzwords, it was just a synonym for "control."

When I told Les about Q's continued interference in my career—he was, after all, my financial manager—he said, "Just because Q is young and doesn't know Hollywood doesn't mean he can't hear from the Lord to make decisions. He might be the *best* person to discern things because he's not emotionally tied in the way you are."

Because of my independence and rebellion, the Hamoatzah decided I needed more frequent basement meetings to give me a "safe space to grow," as Pam said (i.e., learn to quit screwing up my marriage). It got to the point where Q would even dictate what I wore. Not that I had many options. I had always dreamed of a walk-in closet, and that's one of the things that sold me on the Idaho house: a long and deep closet with plenty of shelves. Except most of it sat empty because I wasn't allowed to spend my money on vanity like shopping.

One night we had plans to go out to dinner. I put on a pair of Levi's and a white tank top with a black bra underneath.

"Ah, no," Q said.

"No what?" I said.

"You're not wearing that. A black bra under a white shirt? It's so trashy."

"It is not trashy! Besides, we're just going to dinner with your parents. Who cares?"

"Yeah, dinner in public! I don't want my wife to be drawing attention from random men because your bra is showing."

I was too tired of fighting. "Fine. I'll change my shirt."

"Those jeans are too tight, too."

"What?"

"They show off every curve of your body."

"I hate to break it to you, but that's kind of unavoidable. I have a curvy body."

"Yeah, but that's for me. You don't have to show it off to everyone."

"They're literally jeans. This is how they're made. What do you want me to wear, a skirt?"

"Depends on which skirt."

"Omigod." I rolled my eyes and walked back into the closet, reemerging a minute later in a black crop top and tailored sweatpants.

He put his hands out as if to say, *What the hell?*

"What's wrong with *this?*"

"Your midriff is showing. And those are, like, soft pants."

"'Soft pants'?"

"Yes, they're cozy and intimate. Look, you're not a man. You don't understand how guys think. You look like you should be lounging at home on the couch, and that's inviting for men. It makes them think about being intimate and cozy with you."

I stared at him. I knew what he was saying was absolutely ridiculous. But I doubted myself. It was true: I *wasn't* a man. Was this a reality to which I'd been forever oblivious? Were men walking around all day dreaming about the possibility of spotting a woman in pajamas?

I opened my mouth to respond but didn't know what to say except that I would go back into my closet and try again.

An hour later, Q had called to push dinner back twice. Most of my clothes were off the hangers in a pile. I had tried on everything. Skirts were "easy access." Button-down shirts could be "ripped open." Yoga pants were a definite no-no.

I sat on my closet floor crying under the LED overhead lighting, hungry, beaten down, and hopeless. I was left with an oversized t-shirt tucked into an old pair of khaki cargo pants I had bought at a thrift store in 1997 after they finished trending.

Q walked in. "I'm sorry, honey," he said. "I know this is hard."

My mind was a haze.

"Come on," he said, helping me off the floor. "You look great. Let's get some food."

He kissed me and walked out.

I pulled a sweatshirt over my head and looked in the mirror.

Who dresses like this? I thought. And then it hit me. *Oh. Right. I'm becoming his mother after all.*

CHAPTER TWENTY-TWO

Since Q was being so strict about my appearing in other people's projects, I decided to develop my own. For years I had been working on a staged, musical adaptation of the Nicholas Sparks novel *The Notebook*. *The Notebook* ruined me—both the book and the movie version. After seeing the movie, I sat in the theatre for twenty minutes after the credits rolled and just wept. Most love stories are unrealistic and exaggerated fairy tales. As much as I loved *Beauty and the Beast*, even I could admit Belle had Stockholm syndrome. *Braveheart*, she dies. *Titanic*, he dies. *Romeo + Juliet*, double suicide. *An Affair to Remember* always got me, but what are the odds of meeting a Cary Grant type on a European cruise? In all the romances I'd seen in movies, it was always easy to say, *Yeah, but that's not real life*, and go off to accept a normal, good-enough relationship.

What was so devastating about *The Notebook* was its plausibility: the possibility that two average people who didn't always get along could experience decades of sacrificial, wild, passionate, pure love like THAT!!??? *Wrecked* me.

Whenever I had a shooting break from *One Tree Hill*, or even a few moments to myself in my trailer, I'd work on my libretto and score for a classical/bluegrass/swing music version of *The Notebook* that I dreamed of taking to Broadway. I told myself that this—not my marriage to QB—would be God's reward for passing on *Beauty and the Beast*.

I've always been a composer, going back to high school writing songs for Blue Eyes, but I didn't read music and I couldn't write for instruments. I needed someone I could sing my song to, tap out the beat and explain where the song gets big and where it gets small, and they would translate that to actual instrumentation. For that, I enlisted the help of Ron Aniello, a wildly successful Grammy-nominated songwriter and producer who would go on to produce multiple albums for Bruce Springsteen and other huge artists like Shania Twain. I'd linked up with Ron shortly after the *One Tree Hill* concert tour, when Epic Records signed me to an album deal and appointed Ron as my producer. We'd quickly recorded the album at a Los Angeles studio (where I ran into Prince in the hallway and he said I had a great ass—something I didn't tell QB about, as hard as he was working to make me feel ashamed of my body. Fuckin' PRINCE! I backed into mirrors for a month). Now we were waiting for Epic to decide when they wanted to release it. Ron and I enjoyed working together so much, and Ron believed in my artistry. When I presented him with my ideas, he immediately recognized the project's huge commercial potential and was eager to help.

When we finally finished writing this massive musical on spec, I contacted Nicholas Sparks, sent him the material, and implored him to grant us the rights. After inviting Ron and me out to his beautiful home in New Bern, North Carolina, and me giving a passionate pitch on why I was the right person for this gig, Nicholas gave me permission to mount a workshop of it in Wilmington and invite Broadway producers to see if we could get it picked up. Ron and I were ecstatic, but there was still one more hurdle: getting QB's permission.

He wasn't thrilled that I was working so closely with Ron but felt better when I told him local Broadway vet Judy Greenhut would be codirecting with me. While he agreed to let the workshop go forward, he refused to let me play the lead role of Allie. I begged him. I had written this part for myself. I knew this character inside and out. I needed to get back onstage.

"No! I don't want you being romantic with some guy playing Noah," he said, slamming his hand down on the Goodwill table during one of his infrequent visits to Wilmington.

I was too exhausted to keep fighting, and I comforted myself with knowing this was just the first production of many. We would need to workshop it several times to get it right. Maybe once he saw it and realized how innocent it was, and how *good* I could be onstage—that God really did build me for this—maybe he'd reconsider and let me play the role in a later version.

I launched into production, casting, sets, costumes. We had an incredible group of talent to choose from in artistic Wilmington, including one of our very own *One Tree Hill* producers Beth Crookham and my old friend Allison Munn from *The Outsiders* musical in LA, who was now a recurring character on the show and lent her voice to our demo recordings. It all felt like the joyful sense of belonging I knew from childhood. With QB living in Idaho and out of my way, I was writing nonstop, singing, *playing*; I was coming back to life. Les caught a whiff of this and started to call me to help "vision-cast" for the future of the musical. Then he and the other members of the TRIAD staff—Kurt, Pam, and Gretchen—came to Wilmington toward the end of the workshop rehearsals. They weighed in on creative choices. They also took over the financials, which meant misplacing contracts and failing to pay bills on time. The production cost $100,000—all of it paid for by me and Ron Aniello. Les was concerned I was spending so much money on this venture. He pressed me to sell tickets to the performance to try to recoup some of the cost. I explained to him we couldn't sell tickets because the show contained a few things that were in the movie but not the book, and we didn't want to get sued by Warner Bros.

"So, you're just spending all this money to put on a free show for people?" he asked.

"Well," I said, "the hope is that the response to the show is enthusiastic enough that some producer would want to take it to Broadway."

"And so then you'd make a lot of money?"

"Possibly. But that usually only happens if a show runs for years. Most shows run for, like, three months. And only, maybe, one out of five make back their investment."

"So why do it?"

I wanted to say, *Because it's Broadway, and because I've always dreamed of performing on Broadway, and I've always loved musicals and acting and telling stories that move people. And isn't that the point of life: to try to do what you love and make the world a better place by achieving one unique dream at a time?* But I had a feeling that answer would only result in rehashing the same conversation we'd had about me marrying QB—how emotions shouldn't be a consideration in decision-making. So, I just said, "Because if you are one of those one out of five, you can really get rich." That answer satisfied him and ended the conversation.

Everyone in the *Notebook* crew was confused as to who these random people from Idaho were and why they suddenly had a say in everything. I worked hard to run interference between the two camps and successfully kept the TRIAD group from completely derailing things. We had six performances and rarely a dry eye in the house. There were some elements that needed fixing before it could succeed on Broadway: the show was about forty minutes too long and could use a few more pop songs (since I'd composed with Rodgers & Hammerstein in mind and modern Broadway audiences don't have the same attention span that we used to). But that's what workshops were for and we were ready for that next phase. A handful of major Broadway producers came down to watch it, and five of them made us an offer. They loved the script and commented that what Ron and our pianist, Chad Lawson, did with the 1940s swing/bluegrass music was absolutely beautiful. Ron and I went to New York for meetings with the bidding producers, and everything was looking auspicious. All we needed was the next batch of rights from Nicholas and from Warner Bros., which should have been easy, just a few documents that needed signing.

But the weeks dealing with legal turned into months and months into years. I couldn't understand the delay. We had Broadway-producing superstars waiting to sign a contract, but we couldn't get the lawyers to just *send it*. I found out later that the offers made to us by producers were sideswiped by someone on the other side of legal, who apparently took great pains to convince all parties involved that because Ron and I didn't have any Broadway experience, we couldn't be trusted with this. Plus, there were all these rumors flying around that I was in a cult. The whispers had reached far beyond Wilmington by this point. Casting agents, managers, and producers in LA and New York were starting to share the gossip and cut back on the offers. A cult wouldn't be good for anyone's business. *The Notebook* was an iconic property, and it could not be tangled up with something as aberrant as a cult. It simply could not. A few years later, the stage rights were sold to a different Broadway producer who I was informed happened to be very good friends with the person who'd cut us out.

I'm still so proud of what Ron and I and that wonderful group of actors and crew accomplished. Even then, I was proud of myself for not letting QB and Les erode my confidence to the point where

I just gave up. I was heartened to know that I was capable of seeing something I created through from start to finish. But one hundred thousand gut-wrenching moments have passed through my body since then. The heartbreak and shame of losing that was so massive, I could only deal with it by ignoring it. With all the turmoil I was already suffering, I didn't have the energy to grieve that, too. Even now, years later, I can't honestly say I've grieved it. Anytime I see the name, the poster, ads for the Broadway show that isn't mine, I have to turn my head and think about happier things.

I soon understood why Les seemed so concerned about my spending so much of my own money on the *Notebook* workshop. During one of my weekend visits to Idaho, a few of us were hanging in Les and Marti's bedroom watching an old episode of *The Sopranos*. Les also identified with Tony's love of food and thought it was so cool that Tony always hung out at his friend Artie Bucco's restaurant, Vesuvio. Les loved the idea of being a regular at a restaurant and treating it like a kind of clubhouse.

When Dontay arrived home from his shift at the motel and came into the bedroom, Les muted the TV and spun his old recliner around toward the rest of us on the couch and the bed.

"I have some exciting news," he said. "The Bistro is for sale!"

Located on Main Street, the Bistro was the only nice restaurant in town—though mainly by default, because there were only two or three restaurants in town total. "Nice" meant it had cloth napkins and served steak, though the odds of it being cooked properly were even lower than a Broadway show making back its investment.

"I talked with the owner," Les said, "and he really wants to sell it to us. I think we should buy it."

"All of us, together?" Dontay asked.

"Well, I just wanted to do a little vision-casting with you guys and see how we felt about that," Les said. When he next said he'd like to see QB in the managerial position, it was clear this was as much his motivation as his *Sopranos* fantasy of being a spiritual gangster, minus the white-collar crime (or so I thought). Q had no direction in his life. He didn't have the charisma or elocution of his dad and showed no initiative. He wouldn't even help out with yard-work. Neither would the Barbarians, who mainly just sat around the Big House all day playing video games. So, the ministry paid a landscaping company to mow the yard. Les knew his eldest son needed to gain a sense of purpose and take on some responsibility. He thought managing a restaurant could be the answer. In spite of being resentful that Q was still choosing to live on the other side of the country and make me do most of the traveling to see him, I did want him to build his confidence and find a purpose.

"Joy, I think this is just the perfect opportunity for you and Q to work on your marriage as a team," Les said. "You know, to have a project to do together."

I looked around the room. Everyone seemed excited. *Is this the final step of faith I take that will finally make my marriage work? What else do I have to lose?* My dreams were dead, my relationships outside the Family were dead, my marriage was on a ventilator.

A restaurant? Sure, why not? Of course, Q wouldn't be the only one with a job there. "Lucy has a nice voice," Les said. "She could be in charge of live music. Miguel loves to cook. He could be chef—with me consulting on the menu, of course." He went on to list all the other jobs the Family could take on.

I wasn't sure how this would be possible, given most of those Family members already had jobs at the motel, but I soon discovered that wouldn't be an issue.

. . .

During another of my Idaho visits, this time for Jasmine's baby shower, we had a Family meeting. Les usually led these meetings, but this time Kurt was the first to speak. He was hunched over on a chair, leaning his elbows on his knees. His neck always reminded me of a plucked chicken, the way it wobbled when he talked.

"Well," he said, "we've come to the end of our journey with the motel."

The room was silent.

Kurt went on: "We did the best we could, but we just weren't able to raise the money we needed to pay the mortgage the last few months, so we're gonna have to pack it in."

How were the investors—including Dontay's mom and myself—going to get our money back? *And* we were buying a restaurant? How much of my money was QB signing checks for to make this happen? TRIAD now had full access to my accounts. I knew there was no point in asking. The few times I'd asked for an update on my portfolio, TRIAD would set a meeting, Kurt would scribble on a yellow legal pad while Pam presented me with dozens of pages of numbers I didn't understand, and Les would say something to the effect of "that's the whole point of having a financial manager, so you don't have to think about that stuff."

Les could see how dejected the Family was by this motel news. We thought with that enterprise and now a restaurant, we were on our way to building a kind of Christian utopia. The failure of the motel meant a failure of our mission. Les quickly tried to reassure us.

"This is not a discouragement, Family," he said. "This is a victory, and I think we should all go out and celebrate! And I really want you to get this. Money will always come and go. Just look

227

how God brought us the Bistro. Sometimes we dream something one way, but God has another purpose for that dream. In this case, we were able to introduce so many people to Jesus through our time on that property. There were junkies we got to help get into a program; there was someone who checked in to commit suicide, and I was able to talk with him and he's turning his life around. Even Danielle, who so many of us have come to know and love— the fact that, Joy, you were the motivator for bringing her to us is just a miracle."

A few months after that Pirelli prophecy workshop, where she was too nervous to say hi to me, Danielle emailed Les and said she felt her heart tugging toward this new group of friends who seemed so open and connected. With Les's encouragement—and a promise of a job at the motel—Danielle moved to Idaho. She'd overcome her intimidation, and we'd become friendly. I still kept my distance, somewhat, at Les's advisement. "You don't want it to be a Selena situation," he said. "You know, how her assistant became obsessed and killed her." I chuckled, thinking Les meant it as a joke, but he was serious, and it added to my growing paranoia of anyone who wasn't in the inner circle of the covenant Family. Later, I realized Les wanted me to keep my distance not for fear of Danielle, but because by keeping me at bay, he could use me as an incentive to exploit her. *Do more work for us, submit more fully to the Family, and you'll be rewarded with an invitation to the inner circle and even greater access to Joy.*

"What about Danielle?" I asked. "Where is she gonna live now?"

"We'll help her figure something out, of course," Les said.

What was figured out was that she'd stay in Dontay and Jasmine's spare bedroom while they waited for their baby to arrive. Danielle felt awkward about it, but the motel hadn't actually paid her a wage. She was working for her room. Now she was broke and needed to earn a real paycheck. Luckily, we were about to buy a restaurant, so the church paid for her to go to a local baking school in anticipation of hiring her once the Bistro reopened.

Not long after the motel meeting, she emailed Les and me with some unsettling news. *One Tree Hill* message boards were filling up with the cult rumors. It wasn't just an "industry secret" anymore. "I don't believe this is true, obviously," Danielle wrote. "But I felt you should know what's being said." Les, of course, brushed it off in his usual way, saying such attacks by the enemy simply proved we were on the right course.

The rumors were also growing more noticeable on set. A few times I walked into a room where a group of people were talking and immediately they fell silent. These conversations were different from the ones I'd overheard when I began the show—people making fun of me and my "weird, religious group of friends," which was something I'd once overheard. Back then, the whispers were accompanied by stifled giggles. Now, they were accompanied by looks of alarm, even slight fear. People were courteous enough when the cameras were rolling. My on-screen chemistry with the cast was still good. My TV marriage was better than ever! James had grown up a lot as the years went on, turning quickly from a shy boy into a kind and interesting young man. I'd go to work, someone would say "Action!," and I'd be in a loving, healthy relationship, feeling the warmth of spousal affection and encouragement. Then it would all fade away. After work, there was no more antiquing or sleepovers or philosophical discussions over dinner. More and more, I felt shunned. It was easier to see myself as a victim rather than someone who entered a place full of open arms and chose to turn my back. Regardless, the isolation felt awful, so I handled it by convincing myself I didn't need them anyway.

Eventually the rumors reached Epic Records. One day while on set, I got a call from my A&R guy there. I thought he was calling to tell me they'd finally decided on a release date for my album. Instead, he said I was being dropped from the label. The excuse was that a new boss came in and wiped the slate clean so he could raise up all his own artists.

"Unfortunately, it happens all the time," my A&R guy said.

"Doesn't the fact that I'm on a hit TV show carry some value?" I asked.

"It does," he said. "But . . . honestly, your personal situation seems really complicated. The more we've worked together, the more it feels like I'm not just working with you but with your husband as well, and . . . to be frank, we didn't sign him. We signed you."

"I mean, we try to do things in unity, so I just like him to be a part of things . . ."

"I understand, and you gotta do what's best for you. But this is what's best for Epic."

I put the phone down, and tears started to well up. The assistant director poked his head into the empty set where I had taken my call.

"Joy, they're ready for you."

I composed myself, followed him to the shooting set, and stepped onto my mark.

"A camera up!" the PA called. "Scene nineteen, take three."

The clapper board snapped. The cameras rolled. I smiled and did my job.

The Bistro purchase required a large infusion of cash for the down payment. TRIAD suggested they pay me back on the motel by rolling over the ten they owed me into my first restaurant invest-ment. I agreed to this and assumed they were adding up the num-bers correctly.

It was only a matter of weeks before the keys were in Les's hands and he could finally live his Tony Soprano dream. Tak-ing my ownership role seriously, and as a nod to Les's "fun" Mafia obsession, I commemorated the occasion by commission-ing a Family photo shoot inspired by Annie Leibovitz's *Vanity Fair* portrait of the *Sopranos* cast and hung it over the fireplace right in the center of the restaurant. I wasn't going to let this place become a dump like the motel. I was going to get involved! I wanted to be on the phone *at least* during creative and plan-ning meetings. I made my opinion known about decor and wine, organized weekly floral deliveries. When I was home, I tasted every dish and strategized on the menu with TRIAD, but I also noticed Les gave away more food than he sold. Comped menu tastings and wine were doled out to Family members more often than counseling prescriptions at Ed's office. QB's role as man-ager consisted of small-talking with people in the front of the house while Kurt and Les actually ran everything in the back, and badly. The staff was overworked, underappreciated, and also subjected to lengthy, pointless meetings about teamwork and feelings. I'd talk with QB about it, he'd say, "I'll deal with it," and then nothing would change. I was getting frustrated, but I didn't live there, and I had a real job to focus on in Wilming-ton. Soon, the creative and financial meetings seemed always to occur on days I was on set. QB had his own opinions that clashed with mine, and after about six months of trying and being stone-walled, I backed off.

Occasionally, they'd come to me with requests for more large sums of money.

"The vinyl booths are just so tacky. We really need to reuphol-ster them in fabric if people are going to take this place seriously."

"The walk-in fridge is just so old."

"We need a swamp cooler."

"We need an industrial ice-cream maker."

"We need an espresso machine."

Initially I would question the essentialness of these purchases, but I quickly realized such debate was futile and just said yes—even to their proposition of refinancing my home to give the restaurant a needed cash infusion. It was the same with my mar-riage. I was so buried underneath the exhaustion of arguing over every little thing.

The spell of emotional numbness would be briefly broken only in moments when I was confronted with desire. I'd see a movie that I'd turned down an audition for and get hit with a wave of sadness that I was giving up my career. Or I'd see an attractive man who reminded me that I had a reservoir of pent-up longing and romance and zero desire for my husband. Then I'd resent Q, and my mood toward him would shift in an instant without him having any idea why. Given how he'd reacted to my confession in Wilmington, I didn't see him being receptive to a discussion about it, so I'd put on a poor performance of contentment and journal my shameful feelings instead. Pages and pages and pages of me trying to convince myself of what everyone kept telling me was true. Why couldn't I ever actually believe it? Then I'd feel guilty for disrupting our unity by keeping secrets and I'd finally tell him what was wrong. As I expected, he'd get angry, I'd go numb to not have to fight, and the cycle would start all over. We were grasping for excuses to just have one nice day. Even sex was roped into this. It had always been a struggle, but since I was al-most never interested, QB brought it up to Les, who counseled us to schedule sex as a "duty" we (I) performed. This gave QB a marker to track and hold me accountable to—another example of how I was failing as a wife. So, I complied and fell into a state of numbness with that, too.

The more I complied, the more numb I became, and the easier things got. I found out that when the numbness lasts for long enough it bears a striking resemblance to peace.

The next three years were a loop of this. Then things on *One Tree Hill* changed.

Chad and Hilarie would be leaving the show. QB wanted me to leave, too, so I agreed. I knew something had to change, but I wasn't ready to admit that it should be my marriage. I declined multiple offers to return for season seven, dealings I discussed at length with TRIAD. Then, one day (when the paycheck was high enough), Les brought it up over lunch at the restaurant with QB, Dontay, and Jasmine.

"I don't think the Lord is done with you at *One Tree Hill*," he announced.

QB stopped chewing his sandwich and looked at his father.

"What?" I asked, shocked.

"I've been praying about this, guys, and I gotta say, I think you're really close to seeing a lot of people give their life to the Lord because of the hard work you've been putting in. I just think it would be a shame to abandon ship before you get to reap the rewards of what you've sown."

Jasmine sipped her coffee. "That's called a mixed metaphor, Pop."

Les laughed. "You know what I mean."

I didn't want to go back. I didn't want to keep doing twelve-hour travel days, flying across the country every other weekend. I didn't want to stay in the cycle I was in. But Les had rehearsed his pitch, I was numb, and he was very convincing. So, I accepted the offer, got back on the August flights to Wilmington in 2009, and the loop of learned helplessness continued.

By 2010, I thought the lack of constant external conflict meant QB and I were doing well enough to try to have a baby. It was pure delusion. I had never been less healthy and happy or further from God. It was hell.

Then, just as my dad told me all those years ago in my bedroom, a light began to slowly turn on, and the cracks started to show.

PART THREE

CHAPTER TWENTY-THREE

Another basement meeting was called, this time for Gretchen. She sat in the middle seat surrounded by the Family.

"As you guys know," Gretchen said, "I've been in charge of bookkeeping for TRIAD. And, um . . ." She started to cry. Pam went and sat at Gretchen's feet and stroked her legs. Gretchen spoke slowly. "I'm so sorry. I have been, um, using the money to gamble. I kept thinking I could turn it into more, and then it just got worse." Her crying turned to sobbing.

Pam continued petting her, saying, "I'm so proud of you."

The room was silent. Gretchen continued: "QB and Joy, I took the most from you."

By now I'd been sufficiently groomed that the only correct response was to forgive her. Immediately. I was sure I was so full of selfishness that I had no right to look down on anyone else. I had no right to get angry. I gave no thought to my own feelings or emotions. On the contrary, I wanted to emulate the compassion I thought was expected from a Christian. Pam was modeling the behavior we were expected to display for Gretchen at this moment. I watched her cry and knew how it felt to be ashamed. But as I started to speak, QB spoke first.

"It's okay, Gretch," he said. "We all make mistakes. I forgive you."

I became furious.

It wasn't Q's money. It was mine. There was nothing for him to forgive. And why wasn't he angry on my behalf? So often I'd seen him become vicious for some small perceived infraction. I disrespected him by asking too many questions. I failed to communicate my plans and he felt disregarded. I'd refuse to give in on an argument because I so fervently wanted him to just understand me instead of demanding my compliance. More and more he was starting to adopt his father's method of throwing or breaking things when I wouldn't listen or understand him the way he wanted. But that was when it was just the two of us. When it was just us, he was a tough guy. Now that he was surrounded by the rest of the Family and faced with a legitimate offense that actually deserved his hysteria and aggression, all he offered was meekness. I was more enraged by his trite statement than I was about the theft itself. Yet, even in my fury, I was afraid to make the moment about "our" problems.

Almost robotically, I stood up and went to Gretchen and hugged her. "Love you, sis," I said.

Her confession seemed to be over before it began. No one asked how much she stole. I still don't know. It had to have been big, otherwise I'm sure TRIAD would have just covered it up. There wasn't any talk about repayment. There was no outrage at the betrayal of a close friend and confidante, using our money to feed her addiction. It was just, *Let's move on.*

Perhaps as a result of this theft—and the realization that the more people let into the Family, the harder it'd be to monitor them all and the easier it'd be for such deception—Les soon after declared that no more people would be allowed into the Family.

"I've been praying about this," he declared, "and I feel like the Lord is telling me that this covenant Family is complete and whole now. No one new will come in unless they're married or born in."

The timing of this particular decree was surreal and made me wonder if Les was even more of a prophet than his Welsh friend Pirelli. Just a few days later I found out I was pregnant.

The metal laundry basket incident happened when I was six months pregnant. Who knows what we were fighting about that time. It was probably the state of our house when I arrived home on one of the last flights I'd be able to take while that far along in the pregnancy. The beautiful new house I had bought was looking more and more like the Big House. The floors were grimy, the bathroom sink was coated with weeks of toothpaste spit, laundry piles littered the bedroom, and the kitchen had a pile of dishes and pots so dirty the crusted food was molding, leftover from a dinner he'd made weeks prior.

Whatever caused the fight, QB had thrown a fit and heaved that metal laundry basket against the wall, leaving dents in the drywall and feces on the floor from our terrified Yorkshire terrier, who, after relieving himself, scampered into the bedroom to hide. I called Emily to come over because I was so shaken up. She arrived to broken pots and planters all over the front porch, which Q had smashed before driving off.

When Emily walked inside, she found me sweeping up broken glass from picture frames.

"Oh my god, Joy," she said. "Are you okay?"

I really wasn't. I'd endured this for five years of marriage. Now I was pregnant and scared, and I just couldn't hide it anymore.

Emily picked up a small end table that had also been knocked over in the mess of a room. "I had no idea he got angry like this," she said.

No one does, I thought. *He's a quiet boy. He's the nicest guy in the world.*

I burst into tears. I dropped onto the couch, still holding the broom and dustpan, my belly pressing into my thighs.

She sat next to me. "Does this happen a lot?" she asked.

"It's not usually like this," I said, trying to protect him. "This is the biggest mess he's ever made."

"I don't think it matters if it's *usually* like this or not. This is a serious problem. This is not okay, Joy."

She put an arm around me.

"I'm so sorry," she said. "I had no idea."

"You've got your own stuff to deal with," I said. Abe had been having weird bouts of vertigo lately and was diagnosed with something called "pars planitis," in which his retina would randomly detach and cause vision loss and vertigo. "How is he doing?"

"He just needs to be careful," Emily said. "It's not loss of vision that's the biggest danger, it's him falling down when his eyes black out and hitting his head. The doctor said that's the biggest thing he needs to avoid: sharp blows to the head. That could severely worsen the condition, even cause permanent blindness. So I'm gonna have to stop beating up on him."

She grimaced as soon as she said it, forgetting for a moment why she was there. I gave her a smile that made it clear I took no offense.

At that moment I felt a sharp pain in my stomach, as if all my muscles were clenching together around the baby. I winced and let out a groan and tried to breathe through it.

"What is it?" Emily asked.

"I don't know, I don't know. Oh, God, this really hurts."

"Can you walk to the car?"

"Yeah, I think so. Yeah." The fear and pain were all mixed together now. We made it to Emily's car, and she drove me to the hospital. Coldplay's "Fix You" came on the radio like a ridiculous movie cliché, and I stared out the window trying to be strong and not succeeding.

The baby was all right. The pain had been caused by early Braxton-Hicks contractions, likely brought on by stress. Emily dropped me home a few hours later, and Q's car was back in the driveway. When I came in the house, the first thing I saw was the pile of dog shit that he hadn't bothered to clean up.

Rosie was born in Wilmington. I wanted Pam to be there for the birth because Pam had been there for all the Family births. Mina, Jasmine, Emily—none of their bio-moms were allowed in the room, but Pam helped with every delivery. Except mine. She was busy with her own grandkids, so Les and Marti came out to help. Les came into the birthing room to pray over me, and the nurses gushed about what an *amazing* man he was. "Your baby is so lucky to have a grandfather like that."

Martine's presence was helpful and calming. Wanting photographic memories, I asked Shantel VanSanten to film the birth. Shantel played my sister Quinn on *One Tree Hill*. She had been warm and open from the day she joined the cast in Season 7. I never felt judged by her, and we'd gotten so close. QB was great, too. He'd learned all the pressure points and sat by the bed massaging me. In my lucid moments of noticing him bring me water or hold my hand, I had quick flashes of the good times we had together. Staying up late drinking wine and laughing at a TV show. A short trip to the Bahamas where we swam with dolphins and actually saw Julia Roberts in the hotel, so I could clarify her name for him in real time. Playing board games. The occasional flower bouquet. The letters he used to write me on parchment paper with a real quill and ink. He was a romantic at heart—if only I'd stop getting in the way. *It's not all bad*, I reminded myself, fervently hoping we'd settle into more of those nice times, now that we had a baby to care for.

It's a terrifying feeling to have someone hand you this fragile little human, all soft and gooey with a million working parts, any one of which could stop working in a fraction of a moment and it's up to you to do the things that keep the gears moving. I started to trust God in a new way. Different from handing over my dreams and hoping He'd bring something else back around. Different from trusting Him to answer prayers for my marriage to be good.

This kind of trust was like waking up every single day in an abandoned well—like the kind kids used to fall down in the '80s—and praying someone will find you. I felt utterly helpless in my reliance on a God I'd lost so much faith in to give me daily wisdom, patience, peace, and rest. But I had no other choice, and by the end of every day, however messy, I did always feel like I'd been thrown the rope I needed.

Mom came out to visit after the birth. She stayed in Wilmington for several weeks, helping patiently while I took out all my frustrations with QB on her. My hormones didn't help. I was an emotional grenade, but she swallowed all her desires to scream back at me like she had when I was younger. She was deferential instead of demanding, curious instead of critical. It was a shocking display of self-control, and it went a long way toward me really starting to trust and lean on her. During that time, I turned thirty. No champagne fountains. Just an evening at home with Mom and Rosie and QB. He gave me a card—not handmade this time, store-bought.

We were only three months away from wrapping *One Tree Hill* forever. The Mama Bears had an impromptu baby shower for me when I returned to work to finish out the remaining episodes. I was gifted the beautiful rocking chair that my character Haley had nursed her baby daughter in during the last season. Sophia and Austin Nichols (who played her love interest, filmmaker Julian Baker) gave us an impossibly soft blanket with Rosie's name and birthday embroidered on it. Daphne Zuniga, another '90s TV icon who had joined the show to play Brooke Davis's sensational mom, gave me a very character-appropriate gift of a bottle of champagne. "For later," she said with a wink. And there was so much more—an outpouring of affection for me and my new girl. I remember being surprised at the support I received since I had built an emotional wall up against everyone. It was a humbling moment.

Q moved back to Wilmington full-time, planning to take care of Rosie while I was at work. She had to stay close since I was nursing her, and she had that tongue-tie, which made it extra difficult. Q had to be with her in my trailer most of the day in order to keep her schedule. I'd take breaks and come nurse or pump, then go back to work. Q occupied his time with video games and taking walks with the baby. After a few weeks of that, he said he "wasn't a babysitter" and that he was hiring a nanny so he could go "do stuff" during the day. When I asked him what "stuff"—knowing that meant going to the gym—he said "restaurant stuff." It was hard not to laugh.

Based on conversations I had with Danielle, Dontay, and other Family members, the restaurant was proving to be a debacle. Les never anticipated how much money it took to operate a restaurant, and he and Kurt were always complaining about the cost of things. Miguel was a good cook but wasn't qualified to run a professional kitchen. There weren't a lot of other options. Few experienced chefs were eager to move to middle-of-nowhere Idaho. Les finally found someone, but the chef didn't have enough money to move or credit for a mortgage. Les offered to buy him and his family a nearby house to live in! This I found out from Les himself, because of course "we buy" meant "Joy buys." By now, I wasn't surprised he told me rather than asked. No, what surprised me was that he even told me. I guess for the same reason as Gretchen's confession of theft: a sum that large was likely to be noticed eventually.

On a catch-up call with Jas and Dontay, they explained the chef was a disaster. He was verbally abusive to the staff, way too slow getting dishes out of the kitchen, and had a drug problem. When several of the staff complained, Les responded: "This restaurant is a place of ministry, and rather than judging this man, we should be helping him get his life together."

"We're working our butts off, but it feels like quicksand," Jasmine said.

"And everyone is freaking out about money," Dontay added. "Danielle got asked to cater a dinner for twenty-five people for Pop's Rotary Club meeting, and Pop gave her a hundred dollars to do it. He even yelled at me last week when I deposited the cash from the night instead of leaving it for Kurt to do."

"Just pray for us out here, Joy! I think we're all getting tired of Pop being in charge of literally everything," Jasmine said. "He's gotta be exhausted, too!"

When I thought of the awful circus that awaited me back in Idaho, I was even more sad *One Tree Hill* was nearly over. The show had been the buffer between me and QB, and I was afraid to face a life just with him, finally together. I had spent nearly a decade in Wilmington, almost all my twenties, under contract with Warner Bros. and playing Haley James Scott. I had even proven my mettle as a director and been invited back to direct multiple episodes, discovering creative joy in a totally new arena. Now that it was drawing to a close, I realized how rare and special this entire experience was, and how I hadn't appreciated it properly in the years gone by. I vowed for those last few weeks to put my concerns about my personal life aside and really savor the remaining moments.

• • •

During the last week of filming, fans flooded the set, crowding outside the stages with their cameras. Cast members also showed up to the stages, even if they weren't filming, just to watch and cheer for whoever was completing their last-ever scene. Mine took place on a rooftop overlooking downtown Wilmington. My on-screen son, played by Jackson Brundage, pulled a loose brick out of a wall, where Haley and Lucas used to store predictions for the future and hide them away from the rest of the world. Now Haley was reflecting on all the time that had passed and was writing new predictions with her little boy.

"It's a magical place, son. I've seen that magic in your eyes for the past nine years. There's only one Tree Hill, Jamie Scott, and it's your home."

Those were my last words as Haley James Scott. Before they said cut, I sang a verse from the musical *Sunset Boulevard*, not for the episode but for all the people who had made their own sacrifices to be a part of this show over the years, including the writers and editors who'd be watching all this in LA.

I don't know why I'm frightened,
I know my way around here,
The cardboard trees, the painted scenes, the sound here.
. . . .
We'll have early morning madness.
We'll have magic in the making.
Yes, everything's as if we never said goodbye . . .

And that was it. Our executive producer and regular director, Greg Prange, said, "Cut! Ladies and gentlemen, that is a series wrap on our wonderful, beautiful Bethany Joy Lenz." He may have said more, as it was custom for him to give a few short words, but I can't remember them. I only remember holding back the tears. I wish I had let myself weep the way I wanted to, but I had gotten so used to numbness that when I felt the tears welling up, I tamped them down, afraid if I let them out I'd never be able to stop.

An hour or so later, after wrapping out my trailer, I climbed into Paul's car. Though QB's disapproval meant we couldn't stay as close over the last few years as we'd been earlier in the show, we both thought it would be nice to have one last dinner. QB granted me permission, though I'd asked only performatively. I was going whether he liked it or not.

"Jesus, what a day!" Paul said. "Oh, sorry for using that word. 'Day.'" He smirked. A dad joke on curse words that he always did (and still does).

"How do you feel?" I asked him.

"Oh, Joy. You know." He paused and took in a sharp breath—his reliable signal that an eloquently phrased thought was coming forthwith. "... We're all fucking tired."

I laughed.

"How do *you* feel? You're the one with the new baby! You're about to go back home and start a whole new chapter in your life!"

I watched pretty, charming Wilmington speed by. Historic homes, Spanish moss, graveyards I had wandered through and envied their occupants on rare occasion. "It feels right for the journey to be ending," I said. "Yes, we're all tired ..."

"But? You sound like there's more."

Of course there's more! I want you and every person I've been say-

ing goodbye to over the last few weeks to take hold of me and say, *"We're your family. Don't go back to that awful place."*

"No. It'll be nice to go home." Saying the word "home" didn't feel the way it felt when I used to talk about Florida or Texas or New Jersey or New York or LA. Home was now a wayward ship with terror-stricken passengers. I changed the subject. "Sophia gave me *The Alchemist.*"

"Brilliant book. You get her anything?"

"Yeah, I found this small wooden suitcase, so I decorated the whole inside like a—whaddya call those school projects inside a shoebox?"

"Diorama?"

"Yes! Like a diorama, kind of, with . . ." I stopped. There was something I wanted to keep secret about this one. Even though we never managed to arrive at the friendship we wanted with each other—that sisterly, yell-it-out-and-it's-still-okay friendship— my heart still turned into a giant bear hug around her. I loved Sophia and hoped we might get there one day. I told her not to open the suitcase but put it on a shelf until she needed it. Whenever the occasion should arise, she would know.

"Saying goodbye on projects like these is so hard," Paul said. "This is the longest I've been on a series, but I came in old already." He laughed. "You guys grew up on this show! You were pretending to have a husband for ten years! How do you just say goodbye to that?"

"I don't know. James was the hardest one to say goodbye to."

"Oh, I thought it would have been me." He smiled.

"Ha, well, ask me in an hour when dinner's over." I rolled down the window and the cool beginnings of winter blew in. "I was married to James longer than I have been to QB. Well, Haley was married to Nathan. You know what I mean."

"You get him anything?"

"I wrote him a card."

Even though James and I had a platonic real-life relationship, my time on set with him pretending to be in a happy marriage had given me a reprieve—maybe even an example of what a happy life could be like. Bottling up these feelings just as I always did, wishing I knew how to express ten years of gratitude, I just gave him a hug and a card.

"Jesus, you coulda at least bought him a bottle of tequila," Paul said. "Sorry, there's that word again. 'Tequila.'"

When Paul dropped me off at my apartment after dinner, we both promised to keep in touch. But I suspected that might be the last words we ever exchanged. Fortunately—both for myself and my daughter—I was wrong.

CHAPTER TWENTY-FOUR

"They fucking LIED to me!"

On the first weekend I arrived home, the big top was up and the circus was in full operation. Jasmine was the angriest I'd ever seen her, pacing my living room while QB was out with the baby.

"What? What happened?"

"Pop and Dontay, and whoever else knew."

"Knew what? Jas, what happened?"

She stopped pacing and looked at me. "Dontay cheated on me a month before we got married."

"What!?"

"He went to Pop WEEKS BEFORE THE WEDDING and confessed that he was out late at a bar after work and we had been in a fight. So, he started talking to this girl and he *went home with her,* and he says they didn't have sex but WHATEVER, that doesn't even matter! After the whole porn thing, he still—*UGGHH!*"

"Jas, wait. Les knew about this and didn't tell you and let you go through with the wedding?"

"You're not gonna fucking believe this." I had never heard Jasmine curse! "Dontay was literally *on his way* to tell me and Pop ordered him to keep it a secret."

I blinked. "No . . . no, that doesn't—"

"He told Dontay to keep quiet and that *living with this for the rest of his life* would be his punishment."

That sounded insane. There was nothing even remotely biblical about that. "I'm so confused. Why?"

"Because he had promised Dontay that he would find him a wife, and nothing was going to get in the way of what 'God' had ordained. Joy, I didn't even tell you what happened when I went to them about the porn stuff."

"There's more?"

"I told Pop that I didn't want to be with Dontay until he was healed from this addiction, and he said, 'Well, that's not your call to make. It's not a woman's place to hold a man accountable.'"

As compliant as I had become, even I knew this was just plain wrong.

"It's like he's sitting around pulling puppet strings! I don't even know what to do, Joy. I'm so furious. They trapped me into this! I was supposed to be here *temporarily* and then transfer to Stanford, but Pop convinced me I needed to stay and learn to be a part of a family first!"

"Wait—what?"

"Yeah! He gave me this whole speech about being at a 'crossroads' in my life, whatever the hell that means. I was gonna go to Paris, too! I had all these plans, and instead I left them all behind to work at a shithole motel and marry a guy with a porn addiction who cheats on me and lies to me. We've got two kids. I just don't know what to do."

She kept talking, but all I could think about was Les convincing me to turn down Broadway using the same words nearly seven years prior.

I asked QB about it all later that night, and he said we didn't know what really happened between Dontay and Jas and it was likely just a big misunderstanding.

"And what about the whole 'you're at a crossroads' and 'you need to learn how to be a part of a family' thing?" I pressed.

"What—Pop gave you both similar advice because you were in similar situations?"

"No . . . no, I don't think it's the sa—"

"Look," he cut me off, "it's not really my place to tell you this, but . . . Pop thinks Jasmine might be bipolar."

I stared at him. My body went still the way it does when you wake up at 3:00 a.m. and think someone's broken into your house. "What did you just say?" I asked quietly.

"He's trying to help her. I just—I don't think you can believe a lot of what she says right now."

I couldn't keep looking at QB without him noticing my alarm, so I looked down and nodded.

"Okay," I said with a shallow breath. "When did Pop tell you this?"

"A couple weeks ago."

Right around the time Jasmine and Dontay were getting fed up with him. I was trying to rationalize it—*I'm missing something, I shouldn't be questioning this, it's none of my business*—but didn't have much time. The next circus act was about to start.

It was 1:30 a.m., and I was up nursing Rosie, watching *Friday Night Lights* on my iPad, when my inbox pinged with the arrival of the email that would begin the unraveling of the Big House Family.

Dear Beloved Friends and Confidants,
  Thank you for taking the time to read this.

It was from Harker's account, though at the bottom it was signed by both him and Mina. It was long. It took about ten minutes to read. Then I read it again, making sure I understood exactly what they were saying.

Four years ago, Harker realized that, despite the hours upon hours of sermons he'd listened to throughout his life, he'd never read a book about the history of our faith. "If my faith was to be truly mine," he wrote, "I needed to boldly question the information I'd been taught." So he started reading. And reading. And reading some more. And then, still curious, he and Mina and the kids started attending services of other denominations.

From the beginning, Harker had shared all this with the Hamoatzah: "Not because I enjoyed making my loved ones nervous or fearful, but simply because I valued the transparency of relationship so much." The Leadership asked him to keep this exploration to himself and not share it with any of the other Family members, so as not to erode their confidence in our group. Harker agreed. But over the last month or so, he noticed active resistance from not only the Hamoatzah but other Family members. He had kept his promise not to share what he was doing, but clearly the Hamoatzah had not. They were poisoning other members against Harker and Mina. I was not one of them. This was the first time I was hearing any of this. But now those little glimpses of tension I'd seen between Harker and Les made sense. "The sense that my Family were uniting against my expedition," he wrote, "instead of entering into the discourse with an open mind, was difficult for my heart."

The email went deep into theological history and was hard to follow, especially for someone who prior to that very moment had been happily engrossed in the saga of Tim Riggins and Lyla Garrity. He referenced the five pillars of the early Christian church, the great schism of 1054, the apostolic succession, the Ninety-Five

Theses, and the historian Justo L. González. But there were several lines in the email that I understood all too well, most of all: "I do not want 'unity' at the expense of truth." So, as a result of his long journey—and no doubt the Family's ensuing antagonism—he and Mina had decided to leave us and enter into full communion with the historical Orthodox Church. In closing, he wrote, "Our only request is that you not judge these things without truly looking into them with an open heart."

It was clear how unlikely this was the next morning at breakfast.

"This is a covenant Family," Q said. He was pacing the kitchen, fuming. "Do you even understand what that means? It's like a marriage. We commit to each other and we don't leave. We're supposed to be on this ship together!"

"I don't care if they wanna be Catholic or Orthodox or whatever," I said to Q while feeding Rosie. "They've been some of our best friends for, like, ten years. If it wasn't for Mina, I wouldn't be a part of this Family. Who cares where they want to go to church?"

Rosie spit out some of her banana onto the tray. We were at the six-month marker and finally starting solid foods.

"They didn't say they wanted to stop being friends or doing life with us," I continued. "They just want to worship a little differently than we do. It's not a big deal."

"I'm calling Pop," he said, and stormed out.

After a few days, the Hamoatzah had drafted and sent a lengthy response to Harker and Mina—a dissertation, really—about why they were so lost. Aside from Dontay and Jasmine, who were dealing with the fallout from his confession, the email was signed by nearly all the members of the Family, including Ed and Pam. Though I was hearing Ed had done so reluctantly, and that this incident—as well as how close Pam was with Les and Kurt—was causing tremendous strain on his marriage. I not only signed the response but followed it up with my own three-page letter, doubling down on how important it was they trust "spiritual leadership and accountability and not go off on their own." I was humiliatingly clinging on to my need for sanity.

The truth was, however, that Harker and Mina's email unlocked something in me. It gave me permission to think differently. Not right away, but in the weeks that followed it got me thinking, *Maybe one day we can do what they did*. "We" meaning me and Rosie.

Abe was one of the few Family members who didn't sign the response to Harker and Mina, and seeing how poorly his brother had been treated made him start to push back on things he normally would've stayed silent about. For instance, during one Family meeting, Les gave a whole spiel on how we all needed to be tithing more.

"I've been covering the bills for cable, electricity, water, and garbage," he said. "I've had to take my van in multiple times to get the paint fixed from everyone borrowing it and driving too fast over the gravel road. Also my cell phone bill, even though most of my calls are counseling related. You know, this is a ministry that we're all in together. Your donations should pay for this stuff."

Abe spoke up. "I guess I'm just confused, Les. We're all tithing. Emily and I are. I *know* Joy and QB are. My parents are. Dontay, Jas, and Gretchen are working *for* the ministry, and I think they get half their paychecks in free food from the restaurant Joy bought . . ."

Les squinted at this, but Abe continued.

"I grew up in this house, and Harker and I mowed the lawn

every Sunday. You've got three able-bodied sons, but they never mow and the ministry pays a gardener to come do those things. And nobody else here needs HBO for *The Sopranos*. So, when we tithe, what *exactly* is the money being used for? Because the hotel is gone and the restaurant is doing well, right?"

Les went red-faced. I hadn't heard any of that put so plainly before. *Abe is absolutely right*, I thought.

Les leaned toward him. "If you can't see the value of what the Lord is doing here and you need a full nickel-and-dime accounting of how your money is being spent, then please feel free to give to another organization," Les spat out. "I don't need donations with strings attached."

He stormed out of the room as Abe called out, "What organization? There's nothing organized about any of this!"

The tension and anxiety that had consumed the Family since Harker and Mina's email finally boiled over one evening at the nearby softball field, where the men showed up for their scheduled game and the wives watched as usual. Jasmine was notably absent. As the dusk sun was sending its last streaks across the sky, I sat on a blanket with Rosie, Danielle, and Emily, close enough to the fence to hear Dontay say, "Well, fuck you, then." He'd directed it at Brandon, Kurt's son, who was now seventeen if-he-was-a-string-bean, and who apparently wouldn't high-five Dontay after the game.

Hearing Dontay cuss at his son, Kurt charged at him, but Dontay had just walked off the field and the fence was now between them.

"Say that again, motherfucker," Kurt said. "You're gonna pick a fight with my kid!?"

Dontay ignored him and kept walking away. Miguel came up beside Kurt and put a hand on his shoulder. "It's not worth it, man," Miguel said. "Just let him walk it off."

"Get off me, fuckin' spic," Kurt spat out.

Miguel's eyes went wide and his hands went up in a bewildered surrender. Brandon ran up to his dad and got between the two of them, holding out his scrawny arms to try to keep Kurt at bay.

"Dad! Stop. What the heck?"

"Oh, now *you're* gonna come at me?" Kurt said. "After I just stuck up for you! Huh?" Brandon backed up as Kurt towered over him, his voice getting louder. "I try to defend you and now you're gonna come at me!" He poked Brandon in the shoulder, goading him. Pushing. Poking.

"Dad! Stop!" Brandon swatted Kurt's hand away, which set Kurt off even more. He balled up his fist and raised his arm like he was about to punch his son. Suddenly, Abe was there between them. Abe wasn't a match for Kurt's height and weight, but he was serious. Abe didn't touch Kurt, he just stood in front of Brandon.

"Back off, Kurt. You're not gonna punch your son."

It was all happening so fast that it was hard to track, but I had never seen Abe angry. He seemed to have endless patience for everyone, everywhere. When *Abe* ran out of patience, you knew the situation was bad.

Emily stood up next to me and started to cautiously approach the fence. Out of the corner of my eye I saw Lucy still lounging in her foldout chair beside Martine, Gretchen, and Pam. Her legs were crossed, her lacquered claws wrapped around a Styrofoam soda cup, and she was shaking her head. There was no urgency in her. It was like she was just moderately embarrassed that these silly men were being so *uncouth*.

There was a moment where Kurt seemed to be backing off.

He dropped his arm for a split second, and Abe turned around to check on Brandon. Then Kurt hauled off and sucker punched Abe in the back of the head. Hard. Abe stumbled forward.

I stood up. *His eyes,* I thought. He was moving like he had blacked out for a minute. *Oh my god, his eyes!*

I didn't even notice Emily until she landed clumsily on top of Kurt from the top of the dugout fence, which she had just scaled out of sheer adrenaline. They both went down into the dust. Emily straddled him, her fists pumping and slamming into his face over and over again. "That's my husband!" she yelled as Kurt tried to put his arms up and deflect the blows.

Brandon had his hand on Abe's shoulder, concerned. Just as Abe seemed to snap back to life and see his wife pummeling Kurt in a cloud of red dirt, Les grabbed him and pinned both of his arms down in a bear hug, completely eliminating Abe's ability to defend himself or Emily. As Abe rapidly blinked and struggled to get free, Les pressed his whole body into him, his face against Abe's head, whispering in his ear delicately, almost romantically.

Miguel stepped in and pulled Emily, still swinging, off Kurt, who then scrambled to his feet and stood over her. He was growling in her face when Miguel put his body in between them.

"You need to get the fuck away from her, right now. Back the fuck off, Kurt!"

"FUUUUUUCK!!!!" Kurt screamed as loud as he could, in a park with a dozen kids running around. But after some huffing and puffing, he finally did back down.

I glanced down at Rosie, who was playing happily on the blanket, totally unaware of the violence around her. I looked around for Q and saw him and the Barbarians just outside of the fray. They looked like players waiting to be tagged into a game, and they were all focused on Les. He had them trained like puppies.

"What the hell was that?" I said on the car ride home.

"Whatever, it's just a fight," Q said. "It's not a big a deal."

"Did you SEE what happened? Kurt just *attacked* them!"

"We don't know exactly what happened."

It was the same thing he said when I told him about Dontay cheating on Jasmine.

"I do!" I said. "Q, he punched Abe in the back of the head, while Abe is having all these vision and brain issues right now. He could have just caused some serious damage! And then he was threatening Emily."

"Emily was on top of him, punching him in the face!" Q said, as if Kurt were somehow the victim.

"Wait, are you serious? She was defending Abe after Kurt sucker punched him! And Abe couldn't defend himself 'cause Pop was holding him down! I saw it with my own eyes. There's no excuse."

My phone pinged with a message from Gretchen on the Family group text:

Hey Everyone! We're all meeting at the restaurant for pizza in a half hour! See ya soon!

"Is this a joke?" I said. "Gretchen is saying we're all meeting for pizza at the restaurant. Like nothing just happened."

"Good," Q said.

"Good?"

"What kind of a Family would we be if we let dumb fights break us all up. We're not that weak."

I didn't know how to respond. I texted Emily:

Is Abe okay? I'm freaking out about his eyes. Are you okay? That was insane.

Emily texted me back:

Headed to the hospital now for scans. Ed meeting us there.
Pam apparently going for pizza. What the hell???

I texted her:

I don't know. She's lost her mind. Everyone has lost their
minds. We are not okay.

I didn't go for pizza. I dropped QB off at the restaurant and took the baby home.

Abe's retinal and cranial scans came back okay. The doctor asked if he wanted to involve the police and press charges. He decided not to. I asked Abe later what Les had been saying in his ear while he was holding him down on the softball field. Abe looked like he was going to be sick at the memory.

"I think I was more disturbed by that than by Kurt punching me," he said. "Les was squeezing me so tight with all his body weight, so I couldn't fight back, and he just kept whispering, 'It's okay, baby. It's okay, baby. Shhh, it's okay.'"

CHAPTER TWENTY-FIVE

The week after the softball game, I was bombarded with dreams about being rescued from catastrophes and natural disasters. Always by helicopters and always at the last minute. One would swoop in just as the building I was standing on crumbled. Or Emily would be hanging by a rope, holding out her hand to catch me as the boat I was on capsized in a tsunami. I didn't have to be Freud to interpret their meaning. I was done with Les. I knew too much and I didn't trust him anymore. Or Kurt. Maybe even Pam. I needed a break, and I knew convincing QB that we needed space from *his* bio-family was critical, or I'd have to leave him. I knew that much. I just needed a plan of action.

Since *One Tree Hill* paychecks weren't coming in anymore and the restaurant was still failing spectacularly, Les had told QB that he supported us living part-time in LA so I could continue to work. I used this as an excuse to arrange for QB, me, and Rosie to fly to LA for a week. I would meet with new acting managers and hopefully be able to start the conversation about extracting ourselves from Les's influence.

I never got to broach the topic because of the conflict between us. The trip was ruinous, I fled the hotel with Rosie, and Q flew back to Idaho on his own, forcing me to face the realization that— as my parents had been saying for so long—I was indeed in a cult and needed to get out.

I didn't want Rosie to grow up in a split household. I told Q where

I was at and begged him to not ask for advice from anyone in the Big House Family for one year. Just one year, for me. He refused.

Eventually, I found myself making the same phone call I had made to Blue Eyes ten years prior.

"If you're not going to choose me and prioritize me, I can't stay here in second position. It's hurting me. Are you willing to make *any* changes at all?" I asked.

"I'll do what I have to do and you do what you have to do," he said.

Whatever kind of nonanswer that was, it was exactly the answer I needed in order to make my decision. So, I finally said the other word besides "cult" I'd been so reluctant to utter:

"Divorce."

That week in LA I stayed with Daphne Zuniga in her peaceful Brentwood home with a pool and passionfruit growing over an arbor. Paul Johansson was there for me as well. He had a son Rosie's age, so the kids played while we talked and I unburdened myself of so very many secrets that I had been holding in for years. He and Daphne both listened without judgment, but it was still frightening to feel like I was betraying my husband and my Family. *His* Family? I wasn't sure. So much was still inside the haze.

I asked my mom to come stay with me at Daphne's for a few days. I told her the marriage was over. She let out her own tears of relief and shared with me how long she and my stepdad had been praying for this day. She had never stopped calling and texting and emailing and trying to engage with me, putting aside all her outrage and fears and concerns and depression. She didn't question. She didn't bait. She just waited patiently, trusting that the girl she'd raised, however imperfectly, would one day come to her senses.

My dad was different. I hadn't talked to him since he'd refused to come to my wedding. He'd apologized later and desperately tried to stay connected, except he had been so insistent that I was in danger, and I couldn't allow in a catalyst to that kind of doubt. I had to *believe* to survive, so I told him he had to talk and make peace with Q first—which he tried to do. But, of course, Q cut him out and Dad was left for years making fruitless communication attempts via email, voice messages—even snail mail. One of the photos he'd recently sent was of my little brother, who was almost ten by then. I had missed family weddings, kids' birthdays, and milestones, and I wasn't willing to miss any more.

Making that phone call to my dad was so difficult and shameful, but hearing his voice full of warmth was all the reassurance I needed.

"Listen," he said over the phone. "I want to tell you that I'm sorry." His voice kept pinballing up high behind his nose, as though he might burst at any moment. Dad, who always seemed so even-keeled. "When I got remarried, I was in bad shape, and I focused more on making her happy than I did on protecting you and taking care of you. And I need to apologize. It wasn't right, and I'm so sorry that I hurt you. I just wanted to say that, and I wanted you to know I love you."

"I appreciate that," I said, and promised to introduce him to his granddaughter as soon as I could.

Q wasn't returning my calls, and I was officially on the outs with anyone left in the Family. I was in touch with Danielle, though, who shared two pieces of news. The first wasn't all that unexpected: Miguel and Juana left the Family. The softball nastiness was just too much for them to get over, and they always seemed a bit ambivalent about the Family anyway. The second, though, was quite surprising. For months, Danielle had been sensing something shady was going on with the restaurant's accounting. The prices on the menu didn't make sense based on the amount we were being charged by our vendor for the ingredients. Then Dontay confided to her how one night he was in charge of locking up and took the day's cash to the bank to deposit it. Kurt and Les went ballistic on him, which made Danielle wonder whether they were pocketing the cash and not reporting the income on their taxes. She hadn't said anything to anyone, since questioning the Hamoatzah was strongly discouraged. But seeing the way Harker, Mina, and now I had defied the Family had empowered her.

She approached Les in his office at the restaurant. She asked if he was aware of the discrepancy with the menu prices.

"Sorry, did someone ask you to take care of bookkeeping this week?" he asked, annoyed.

"No," Danielle said. "I just had to fill out the order form for my baking ingredients, and when I realized what they cost, my brain just kinda did the math."

Les quickly changed his look from annoyance to a phony cheeriness. "Well, I appreciate you looking out," he said. "I'll double-check with Kurt and Pam, but I know there's all kinds of tax breaks and reasons for why we chose these prices."

I had been abysmally irresponsible with money, given how willingly I gave control of my finances to TRIAD. But even I knew that the business structure of the restaurant meant if it lost money, Les would be able to claim a big tax write-off, while I'd still have to pay taxes on the money I put in.

If my defiance had inspired Danielle, hers now further inspired me. I knew what I needed to do.

CHAPTER TWENTY-SIX

I walked into the bank, trembling. Juana greeted me with a smile and a handshake and led me back to her glass-walled office, acting as if she were meeting me for the very first time, as if she and I weren't members of the same cult. I could say the word now.

I hadn't spoken to Juana since the softball game. The kind way she looked at me once we'd taken a seat in her office indicated we didn't have to discuss it. That had been another life. She looked nice in her black blazer and striped top. I was reminded that we were the only two women in the Family who'd had jobs outside of Les's ministries: the motel, the restaurant, and TRIAD. We had never talked about or even acknowledged this, but seeing the ASSISTANT MANAGER nameplate on her desk made me realize it'd always been a kind of unspoken bond and source of respect between us.

I wondered if she'd ever watched an episode of *One Tree Hill* and had that same feeling seeing me on the screen. I wondered if anyone in the Family besides Danielle had ever watched an episode of the show. If so, no one ever said so. No one ever told me what a good job I'd done acting a scene or performing a song. Not once did I ever walk into Les's bedroom to find him in his recliner watching *One Tree Hill*—only *The Sopranos*. Compared with a "prestige" show like that, I knew the Family probably thought *One Tree Hill* was cheesy. Hell, sometimes I thought it was cheesy. But that didn't mean I wasn't proud of our work. Sitting in Juana's office, in the company of another hardworking woman, I thought just how proud

I was and how severely the Family had diminished that pride, taught me that pride of any kind was wrong, instilled in me an omnipresent shame. It made what I was about to do much easier.

"Okay," Juana said, "so I just need your ID, and I'll pull up your account."

I handed her my driver's license. She made a few keystrokes.

"How much do you need to withdraw today, Ms. Lenz?"

She knew that wasn't my married name. But that was the name that was still on my driver's license. Again, she was treating me as if I were any other customer. I understood. It was better that way. So I did the same. I didn't say, *I'm not trying to leave Q high and dry. I just can't let him keep pouring my money into the restaurant.* I simply said, "What is the balance?" Then, with a smile, I added, "Mrs. —."

She couldn't resist giving me a slight grin as she turned the screen around to face me. I scanned the numbers. When I arrived at the total, my heart started racing and my throat got tight.

"What am I looking at, Juana?"

She could tell by my tone and the use of her first name that something was very wrong. She, too, dropped any pretense of professionalism.

"This is your checking, Joy. What, is there a problem?"

"Is there another account?" I asked, already knowing the answer.

"No," she said, confused. "Just this one."

It couldn't be right. I had been making around a million dollars a year for several seasons. I grabbed her calculator and focused through my dyscalculia.

Okay, the government took 40 percent, agents took 10 percent, lawyers 5 percent, manager 5 percent. Subtract, what? $120k for yearly expenses? Travel, mortgage, rent in North Carolina, $10k into that *stupid motel, 10 percent tithe, $200k into the restaurant. If this math is right, that still should leave $2.4 million.*

I looked at the screen again.

$220,000.

"There's two million missing," I muttered.

"What do you mean?" she said.

"I mean there's two million dollars missing."

Juana let out a heavy exhale and turned the screen back to her.

"I'm gonna open up a new account for you right now," she said, attacking her keyboard.

I knew $220,000 was more than many people would see in their whole lives. But I'd spent twenty years building a career. I'd spent thousands of hours of prep on thousands of auditions that went nowhere to reach the few that did. Painstakingly, I'd inched up my contract value year after year, job after job, to earn the negotiating leverage for a formidable paycheck on multiple pilots that didn't get picked up, and finally I landed a dream job with a steady salary. I spent the next decade working hard, late, early, always. I hadn't traveled or mentored anyone, hadn't become a philanthropist or even made large donations to a *real* charity. I hated myself. What a waste of space I was. A waste of talent. Of time. I had thrown away what little spare time I had chasing a God I was now not even sure existed, enduring years of abuse in a pathetic cult of selfish people, and living in a place where every dream I had went to die. At least if I had money I might feel like it was worth it. I could create my own projects. I could make sure Rosie had a college fund. I could pay off my house.

Oh my god, my house. How would I pay the mortgage? There was $800,000 left on it due to the refinancing for the restaurant. The house wasn't even worth near that now—not after the housing collapse and recession. I would have to do a short sale. And

I'd been looking into the cost of divorce attorneys. The first retainer was $20,000. I was told unless I settled, it would likely take years, and there was no way I was going to settle because I wasn't letting Rosie anywhere near those people, and so I would have to prove why. That meant dozens of depositions, hiring a cult specialist and a child psychologist and now a forensic accountant to comb through my financial records for the last few years and find out where the two million went. If, of course, TRIAD didn't first happen to burn all those records and claim there was a fire. Did they even pay my taxes? What if I owed the IRS, too?

I gasped for air. A guttural moan of agony shot out of my mouth involuntarily, followed by tears. Juana reached across her desk and grabbed my hands, stroking them and breathing with me until I gathered enough air to calm down.

She spoke calmly and directly. "Ms. Lenz, I need you to tell me how much to put into the new account."

She was back to using my last name. Back to being a professional. I didn't know it at the time, but later I would learn what she was about to do was absolutely out of bounds. With a joint bank account, both parties had to sign off on withdrawals over $10,000. By allowing me to make this withdrawal, she was risking her career and reputation.

I wiped my eyes, my nose. I stiffened my posture and tried to match her stoic demeanor.

"Let's leave thirty thousand," I said, figuring that with Q living rent-free in the Big House, that should be enough for him to live off of for a year. "Move the rest over."

Juana nodded, indicating that yes, that was sensible. She then pressed the button to initiate the transfer.

CHAPTER TWENTY-SEVEN

Pam called and said she wanted to come over to check on me.

I opened the door, and she stepped in and gave me a big hug that made me go stiff. I didn't know how involved she'd been in TRIAD's "loss" of my money. I was still conditioned to try and assume the best, but Pam was getting more suspicious by the day. Then QB appeared behind her on the porch, as though they had arrived together, which was confusing until she reached into her purse and handed me a manila envelope. With a sincerely sympathetic smile, she said, "You've been served."

I didn't even understand what this meant. Despite my research on what a divorce would cost, I didn't know anything about who was supposed to serve whom and for what reasons. I did know Pam was a certified notary public, so that must've been why she was the one to serve me. But I was so confused that I actually thanked her, and she in turn pet my arm and nodded. Somewhere in her twisted mind, I think Pam believed she was doing me some great favor. In a way, I suppose she had. Her delusional performance here erased whatever little ambiguity was left about my future with these people, and with Q. Now there was no more deliberation or waffling. Now we really were over. But just in case there was any doubt, the next day I came home from a doctor's appointment with Rosie to find the house cleaned out: computer, couch, dresser, dishes—all gone. He even took the dog.

Now I set about finding a lawyer of my own. My priority was

moving with Rosie back to LA, which Google told me would require something called a "relocation request." The legal world was so terribly intimidating to me. My only foray into it was that short stint on a CBS drama called *The Guardian*, where I played a paralegal for Dabney Coleman and Simon Baker. I met with several lawyers. All men. None of them were interested in the cult dynamic of my case. They either thought I was exaggerating or didn't see the relevance or both.

I would say, "Listen, I was subjected to hours at a time of 'group therapy' in a basement where everyone sat around telling me what was wrong with me and I would cry and repent for all my 'mistakes,' and then, at the end, everyone gathered around me and prayed and told me how much they loved me in spite of my flaws. And I felt so grateful that these people would take so much time out of their lives to help me 'work on myself.' Isn't that so fucked up?"

And they would say, "Uh-huh. Uh-huh. Do you know the ratio of judicial rulings by the State of Idaho family courts on custody disputes due to assertions of emotional abuse by one or more parties in favor of the party asserting such assertions versus rulings against the asserting party?"

Later, as my case dragged on for years, I would come to learn more about the legal system and how in family court any abuse besides physical is completely dismissed and ignored. Courts don't like things that aren't concrete evidence. They can't rule on feelings. Veteran lawyers have a saying for this: "No bruise, no case." The control and manipulation experienced by victims is so hard to explain, and when each case of psychological abuse is explained out of context, it often elicits a response like, *Well, I can see the other side of it, too.* There is even less sympathy for cult members: *Hey, lady, you're a grown-up. If you wanted to turn over your autonomy to some sociopath leading a little religious club, that's on you.*

. . .

Eventually, I found an attorney who got it. A woman. She filed the relocation request, submitting a comprehensive brief explaining why I needed to leave the state, but she said it usually took a few months for the judge to rule. In the meantime, I'd have to stay in Idaho and deal with the awkwardness of living near my old Family. And it wasn't like I could avoid them, having agreed to let Q take Rosie a few times a week.

On those days, Q and I met at a neutral location, usually a parking lot. He would arrive accompanied by at least two other Big House members—typically one of the Barbarians and Gretchen. They would get out of the car and flank Q. They wouldn't speak. They just stood to either side of him and stared at me stone-faced. What did they think was going to happen? As though all 115 pounds of me were scary enough to warrant three adults bullying me—*intimidating* me—in front of our child. The worst part was that these were people I had called my best friends for ten years of my life. I trusted them with everything, and now they were treating me like an enemy simply because I didn't want to stay in an abusive marriage or go to church with them anymore. I tried to make sense of it, and the only consistent thing that kept coming back to me was: *These people don't like to lose.*

To them, losing would mean they'd failed God and He wasn't on their side. And if God wasn't on their side, then their whole belief system would disintegrate and everything they'd been doing for decades would become meaningless. They had to double down, again and again, until everyone else submitted. This way they wouldn't ever have to question themselves or doubt their righteousness. Objectively, I understood their dilemma. It was classic narcissism, only in a group format.

Even Q's mousy mom, Marti, was roped in. She rang my doorbell one afternoon. When I answered, she said, "Q is on his way to pick up Rosie. I'm just gonna wait for him here."

She started to move past me into the house. I stopped the door with my foot and blocked her from entering. It was one thing for Q to bring goons to a parking lot, but I was not going to be monitored and bullied in my own home.

"I'm not comfortable with that, Martine," I said. "You're welcome to wait on the porch, and I'll bring Rosie out when Q arrives."

Marti moved toward me again and started to push open my front door. "This is QB's house, too, and he's invited me in."

"Actually it's not his house," I corrected her, wedging myself harder into the door gap and pushing back against her. "I bought it before we were married."

She got close to my face and pressed her body into mine, leaning her weight onto her right side to try to force it open. "His name is on the deed! This is his house, too!"

I had never, in ten years, seen Marti assert herself. I was almost proud of her. Almost.

"Martine, you're incorrect," I said. "I bought this house on my own, and you are not welcome here."

We both weighed about the same, so this was a farce of an arm wrestle. Then she started pleading as she pushed: "Don't abandon ship, Joy, we love you! You're always getting in your own way— but we're not gonna let you go! We're pulling you into the ship with us—"

"I DON'T WANT TO BE ON YOUR FUCKING SHIP!" I quickly brought the arm I had in the doorframe down, swiping in front of my chest and knocking away her wrists from pushing on me. She stumbled backward and, after a split-second pause, clumsily slammed herself onto my porch railing.

"You pushed me!" she said, eyes wide.

I tried to stay measured, channeling Juana at the bank. "You were trying to force your way into my home," I said.

"You just shoved me into the railing and my wrist is bruised! Do you see this?" She held up her wrist, on which I saw nothing. "That's assault! I'm gonna report this!"

Her beady eyes bulged with a mixture of rage and fear. More than anything, she looked like an animal in a trap. I slammed my door shut and dead-bolted it.

Everyone has lost their goddamn mind! I thought. *Who the hell are these people?*

I thought of that photo I'd commissioned that hung in the restaurant. In my mind, the image morphed and fangs began to sprout from everyone's smile. I'd been dining with vampires. *No,* I realized. *I am the dinner.*

My lawyer warned me that there was a possibility that the judge would deem Rosie part of Q's and my "community property" that hadn't yet been divided and therefore might be ordered to remain in Idaho until such time. With each passing week, I grew more nervous. But when the ruling was finally delivered, it was in my favor: I could take Rosie to Los Angeles.

Danielle had recently helped Jasmine and Dontay pack up their kids and move in with Esther for a while, so she offered to help me move as well. She'd also been fired from the restaurant. Les told her it was because of "budget cuts," which was hilarious, considering it was probably the first time Les had ever spoken the word "budget." Obviously, the real reason was that Danielle had asked too many questions. She was one of the most capable and generous women I knew. I was so ashamed that I'd gotten her involved in this mess and relieved she had the wherewithal to say piss off to the Family. She came from a long line of strong women, too. The same day they fired Danielle, I hired her to help with my move. I could barely function enough for Rosie's day-to-day. She saw the state I was in and took charge.

"Here's how much the move will cost you," she said, showing me a breakdown on her phone. Why couldn't she have been working for TRIAD instead of Gretchen? *Oh, yeah, because she wouldn't have let them get away with robbing me blind.* "I'm coming over this weekend and boxing up your things into a U-Haul. And Monday, while you're in your preliminary custody meeting, I'm driving your life to California. Okay?"

I couldn't remember having ever been more grateful. I hugged her tight. "Okay."

A week later, I flew to LA to meet her with Rosie and the dog. I have to at least give Q credit for voluntarily returning the dog to me.

That generosity, however, would not last. Now that the relocation request was settled, custody of Rosie had to be decided. And while I never doubted Q's seriousness and knew full well the Family's commitment to winning at all costs, I still underestimated their ruthlessness when Q told me in that LA hotel room all those months ago, "I will fight for custody and I'll win. I will take. Her. Away from you."

Thing is, they underestimated mine, too. And I had one thing they did not: my bio-dad. My *real* father.

CHAPTER TWENTY-EIGHT

That first time I talked to my dad again, he was so overcome with emotion that the conversation was mostly just him saying how much he loved and missed me over and over again. That was all that mattered to him: reassuring me how much I meant to him. He didn't even mention Q or the cult. He didn't want to bring any negativity or anger into our reunion. But that didn't mean he wasn't angry. And the cause for that anger was even greater than I realized.

A couple months after I relocated to LA, Dad came to visit me. I had rented a house in West Hollywood that supposedly Errol Flynn kept his mistresses in. I couldn't afford it, especially with my quickly mounting lawyer costs. But I thought for sure, given the success of *One Tree Hill*, I'd book another show and money wouldn't be an issue. Surprise, surprise, an actress in her thirties coming off a CW teen drama wasn't exactly in high demand. As Ava Gardner once said: "Actors get older, actresses get *old*." The only kind of auditions I was getting was for "Mom of Ten-Year-Old" on *Law & Order*.

I was so stressed I started smoking—well, attempting to smoke. It was the first time since briefly in high school during my "Jersey Girl" phase, and I'm not sure I knew how to properly inhale any more than I did then. Nevertheless, I'd snag the odd gas station pack of Nat Shermans or extra-long Virginia Slims or, if I got lucky and they were in stock, the rainbow-colored ones with the gold filters. Because if I'm going to pick up a bad habit, god-damn it, I'm going to do it with glamour! And, no, I never smoked in front of the kid or in the house. I'd savor them late at night on the back balcony, watching the palm trees sway in the breeze and the cars whip past on Sunset Boulevard. Holding a stick of fire made me feel in control of *something*.

Before my dad arrived, I made sure to hide the cigarettes and clean up any butts on the balcony, reverting to my teenage self, afraid of getting busted, not grasping the hilarity of this. *You just spent ten years of your life in a cult, but yes, totally worry about your dad being disappointed in you for using tobacco.*

I didn't have to worry. My dad likely wouldn't have noticed if the house was full of ashtrays. He barely even glanced around when he walked in. He went straight to the dining room, unzipped his suitcase, pulled out a red folder, and dropped it on the table. It made a massive thud, sending the dog scampering into the bedroom—though fortunately this time without shitting the car-pet first. The folder was stuffed so full of papers it barely stayed closed.

"What's this?" I asked.

"The last six years of my life," my dad said.

After I cut him out, I thought he'd simply tried to forget about me and moved on with his life. Instead, he'd devoted his time to studying cults, learning how they worked, and chasing down any information he could find about Les. I was so moved I burst out crying. Then, as I flipped through the folder's contents, I felt like crying for a different reason, realizing how little I knew about Les and how gullible and naive I'd been.

It was page after page of emails, letters, newspaper clippings—all about how Les had wrought destruction in the lives of every-one who came into his path. It started small—he had exaggerated his military experience. Decorated sniper, my ass. He also apparently (obviously) never co-pastored a church with Dr. Tim Keller. I later called Dr. Keller's office to double-check, and his secretary confirmed after talking with Tim that they had only rented space in the same building, once. Then the allegations got dark. Witness after witness referred to purported sexual misconduct that bled into his congregations, supposed lawsuits for me to look into, financial "wrongdoing," and a tendency to destroy marriages and split apart families. There was even the story of some guy who was so enraged by whatever Les had done that he drove a van from New York all the way to Idaho with LES—IS A FALSE PROPHET painted on the side of it, among other accusations.

My dad had mapped out a timeline. He had compiled lists of known associates and those with one terrible story after another. All these years he had been planning for this day.

"This is how we get this motherfucker," he said.

I shared it all with my attorney, who seemed to agree that this could be the thing to prove how dangerous it'd be to grant custody to Q and his family. My attorney also jokingly offered my dad a research job at the law firm. But for me, the folder was only the start. It made me want to reach out to these people who also had their lives destroyed by Les. It made me want to connect with them and know that I wasn't the only one. I saw in them a different kind of family into which I'd unwittingly been inducted.

Cold calls, snail mail, emails, Facebook friend requests: I tried to contact anyone and everyone who I was sure or even suspected had been associated with him. It consumed me. Obsessed me. There were many dead ends—not always because there was nothing there

Sometimes the person was too afraid to say anything. I heard a lot of "I'm sorry, but I don't want to have anything more to do with that man. He's done enough damage." The consensus seemed to be that Les was a relentless monster who would come after anyone who wanted to hold him accountable.

"Are you sure you know what you're doing?" they always asked when I told them about the custody case.

"No," I always said. And we always laughed.

I was surprised that there was usually some laughter on those calls, though I suppose I shouldn't have been. Like me, they were relieved to hear the voice of someone else whose life had been damaged in the same way. They were all saddened and outraged to hear Les was doing the same thing to people, in some cases decades later—yes, of course, saddened and angered—but also comforted to know that they weren't just some stupid idiot who had been duped, that they were human just like me and made a terrible error in judgment. Because sometimes that's what humans do. It's what makes us human. Almost always before getting off the phone or in our last correspondence, they thanked me. We both thanked each other.

There were a few people more than willing to tell me exactly what awful things he had done to them. A conversation with a former leader at one of Les's defunct churches—and there were many—was one of the most revealing. He had worked alongside Les for a few years. His wife and kids were very close with Marti and her sons.

"We loved them," he said.

But the closer they worked together, the more Les's behavior became questionable. He would refuse personal accountability from the church board and treasurer. When the Leadership team challenged him, he simply recruited new leaders who wouldn't.

He paid a tae kwon do instructor friend a $45,000 salary to be an associate pastor, even though he did nothing for the church. One afternoon in a closed room of the church, Les was found with the female worship leader's head in his lap. When confronted, Les said nothing was going on and that she was suffering from a migraine headache. He had so many issues with women. "Women who didn't fall in line, he labeled as bipolar or schizophrenic. The list goes on and on," the man told me, as I lowered my head into my hand. "And the stuff he covered up, too. There was a congregant named Kurt—"

"Wait, Kurt and Lucy?"

"Yes. Did you meet them?"

"They lived in the Big House with Les and everyone else. Me and all the other young women were required to take showers in his basement apartment."

"Oh my god."

"What?"

He was quiet for a moment. "You need to talk with Alice Burke."

"Who is she?"

"It's not my story to tell, but you need to talk with her. What I will say is that I wouldn't allow my daughter anywhere near Kurt. He's the most vile person I've ever met, and I hate myself for not seeing it sooner."

He gave me Alice's phone number and email.

It took a few weeks to get Alice on the phone. She was more scared than anyone I'd talked to. I spent the first fifteen minutes of the call explaining my story, trying to gain her trust, still not knowing why I was talking to her

Finally, she spoke up. Her voice was shaky and soft, barely audible. "I didn't think I'd have to talk about this ever again," she said. "Honestly, I . . . I don't know if I can do this."

I said nothing, not wanting to say the wrong thing to push her either way. One thing years of acting had taught me was how to be quiet and listen.

"Did anything bad ever happen to you with Kurt?" Alice asked me.

"No," I said. "I mean, he clearly had anger issues." I gave her a quick recap of the softball story. "And he always creeped me out. Les made all the girls living in the house shower in Kurt and Lucy's bathroom."

"Les made you?"

"That was his request. None of us wanted to, but he had reasons that seemed valid, so we didn't push back and eventually just got desensitized to it."

"And Marti and Lucy were fine with it?"

I hadn't thought about that. "I guess so," I said.

She took a deep breath. "I was Kurt and Lucy's foster daughter. Lucy was friendly and pretty caring toward me. But Kurt . . . he was always leaving his hands on me too long. He'd hug me and press his body . . ." She paused, then went on. "There was a weekend Lucy was gone, doing someone's makeup for a wedding or something, and Kurt drove me out to some lake house he'd rented. He said we should take a vacation."

She paused again, for longer this time. So long that I felt compelled to break the silence.

"Alice? Are you okay?"

"You know what? I can't. I can't talk about this. Is it okay if I write it down? Can I just write it and email it to you?"

"Yes. Yes, absolutely. I hate asking you to relive something traumatic, and I don't want to push you, but Kurt is still heavily involved in Les's and QB's lives, and I'm scared for my daughter if QB were to be granted visitation with her in that home."

"I understand," she said. "I'll do it."

The next morning I woke up to an email from her. She detailed how Kurt had taken her to the lake and given her medicine for a cough. She'd passed out for an unknown number of hours. She only remembered waking up naked in a bathtub with Kurt over her.

All I could think about was that red bottle of hydrocodone on my first visit to the Big House and how I had been knocked out for more than twenty-four hours. I felt pretty confident Kurt hadn't done to me whatever he'd done to Alice. I had been sharing a room with Jasmine and Gretchen, and there were too many people in the house. When would he have had the opportunity? I continued reading as Alice went on to describe the most horrifying part of all, which she also alleged in her testimony in my court case.

Alice said that after she confided in Les, her church pastor at the time, he and Martine took Alice into their own home. She thought it would be a safe haven, but there she experienced more aggression, where "church leadership" had many, many meetings with and about "how to handle" her, until finally—unbelievably—Les sent her back to live with Kurt and Lucy. *He sent her back.* According to Alice's testimony in family court, "it was decided that Kurt had a repentant heart."

Months later, with the help of social services, Alice applied for and was granted permission to transfer across the country.

As I would learn in family court, so much of any witness testimony is considered "hearsay." I didn't know how I would prove all this, but one thing I did know for sure was that there was absolutely no way in hell I would allow Rosie in that house *ever* again.

It took three years, about twenty trips back to Idaho for court appearances, and roughly $360,000, but the judge ultimately agreed. I was awarded custody of Rosie, with Q receiving visitation rights. It wouldn't have happened without the material my dad had supplied and written statements from Alice and several other of Les's victims. This included Emily and Abe, plus Emily's father; Harker and Mina and Mina's parents, too. Dontay, Jasmine, and a few former employees of the Bistro also spoke up for me, as well as Esther—who especially jumped at the opportunity to speak out against Les and TRIAD after being swindled out of $75,000 and losing a close relationship with her son for over ten years. I even had written statements from a few *One Tree Hill* friends, such as Paul Johansson, Daphne Zuniga, Allison Munn, and producer Joe Davola. Since they weren't fully aware of what was happening at the time, their statements mostly supported my claim that it was necessary for my career to be based in LA. Later, though, I'd learn from a conversation with Paul that the cast and crew had been very concerned for me. I'd misread those whispered conversations. They weren't making fun of me, and they weren't scared of me. He said they sensed I was being taken advantage of and might even be in danger. They were trying to figure out how they could help me.

"I loved you," Paul told me one evening. We kept our late-night wine and philosophy conversations going in LA for many years after I left the Big House Family. "I thought we could stay close friends. But you made it very clear to me that, yes, our friendship is important, but *these* are my people. That's how you spoke. And when I first met Q, I just didn't get it. I even said that to you. I said, 'Everybody has to bring something to the party. What's he bringing?' And you said, 'He's bringing his Family. I'm not just in love with him. I'm in love with his Family, I'm in love with the church, I'm in love with God. And God told me to do this.' I tried to be happy for you, but it was a very odd time. Even when you were pregnant in that episode I directed, I wanted to put my arms around you. You looked so wrecked. You looked so beat down and alone and struggling. When you acted, you lit up. But in between, sitting in that chair and waiting for your turn, I could see this turmoil in you, and it broke my heart every minute. But you don't just walk up to somebody and say, 'What the fuck is wrong?' I didn't want to do that to you, especially when you were pregnant. But you were my closest friend, and I lost you for those years."

I also had testimonies from a cult specialist and a forensic accountant I hired. The cult specialist helped me better understand what I'd been through. She shared a number of studies done on self-indoctrination dating as far back as the 1950s. In one study, Stanford professor of psychology Leon Festinger had participants do a boring task but then lie to the person going after them and say the task was fun. Some were paid a dollar to lie; others were paid twenty dollars. The people who were given only a buck felt worse about lying because a dollar wasn't a good enough reason for being dishonest. These participants then convinced themselves that the task was actually kind of fun in order to ease their own consciences. In contrast, the people who got twenty dollars weren't terribly conflicted about lying because they had a good reason: the money.

This was what Les was doing, the cult specialist explained: training our neural pathways to adjust our attitudes rather than our actions.

She also helped me see my ex-husband differently. The more I learned how grooming worked, the more I felt bad for Q. He never had a chance to be his own person. He wasn't taught to have agency and ideas. He was taught to obey and conform. Loyalty above all. QB had been merely a vacant lot for Les to park all his own thoughts, ideas, and desires. I tried to remind myself of this as he made my life hell over those three years. I would book a job that required me to travel with Rosie, and he would "forget" to sign court-ordered paperwork needed for such travel, causing the producers to scurry and consider recasting the role. Or when he'd come to LA and take Rosie for a weekend—staying at an Airbnb—and would change her clothes in the car immediately after the parking lot handoff, a signal of his refusal to acknowledge she had a life with me.

Every day of those three years was emotionally exhausting. Every day I felt like I was sinking deeper and deeper into a tar pit of fatigue. At my lowest point, I stood one night on the balcony after smoking a cigarette, thrust up two middle fingers into the air at God, and screamed, *"FUCK YOU!"* Tears poured out of my eyes. I couldn't hold in my anger anymore. *"FUUUUUUCKKKK YOUUUUUU!!!"* I did everything right. I did everything You asked me to do. And this is what I get!? Well, fuck that. And fuck Jesus and fuck church and fuck-fuck-fuck-fuck-fuck YOU!"

On the street below, the traffic whizzed by under the neon billboards. A montage of all the things I'd done "right" started to attach itself to the passing cars.

Committed my life to God
Went to church
Prayed for people out loud

Had a private prayer life
Went to counseling
Kept a repentant heart
Sacrificed my dreams
Forgave people who hurt me
Studied the Bible
Tried to keep a clear conscience
Didn't have sex till I was married
Didn't curse
Didn't use the Lord's name in vain
Tried to be a submissive wife
Took my husband's name and trusted my money to his
    "spiritual authority"
Humbled myself for correction
Reached out for counsel when I was confused
Became vulnerable so I could receive love
Trusted church Leadership to guide me
Trusted my friends to look after my money for "Kingdom
    purposes"
Trusted my husband to hear from God
Gave endless amounts of my time, money, energy, ideas, and
    emotional space in order to be "healed" and "used by
    God"

"It's bullshit," I said, talking to a God I didn't know or trust and wasn't even sure was listening. But I was angry, and I was going to be heard by whatever was in charge of the bullshit little board game it seemed like we were on down here. "You know, you're either not there or you're really fucking cruel. What the hell kind of God asks people who follow Him to do all this stuff and follow all these fucking rules and then, when they do, just allows their life to fall apart? What, is this amusing to You? Just watching us down here all wandering around on Your little Life board game? How DARE YOU!? I fucking did EVERYTHING You asked me to. I have always tried my very best. I deserve better than this. Asshole. I deserve better. So, fuck You!"

On and on I went as anger took over my whole body. I was sweating and crying and yelling. It was a terrible-twos temper tantrum of the highest order. Rosie—across town with Q for the weekend—would have been impressed.

Eventually, I collapsed onto a chair. No tears left to cry. No one left to blame. I had finally done the unthinkable and cursed God, made demands, and stopped being so goddamn obedient. I sat, ready to let hopelessness wash over me; ready to embrace it, really. But for some reason, the only thought that flooded in was the sound of rain and the smell of bacon and coffee wafting over red vinyl.

Never doubt that I am real.
Never doubt that I am real.
Never doubt that I am real.

Did I make that up, too? Just another manufactured manifestation of the "Holy Spirit" in a moment of need? I seemed to be capable of convincing myself of so many things.

Except I was sane then. Wasn't I? I wasn't in crisis. I wasn't even bothered. There was no need for me to have imagined that moment. There was no trauma or psychotic break or, besides my routine, unrequited love for Blue Eyes, even a remote longing for help in any way. I was just a nineteen-year-old kid enjoying a rainy day. That had to have been real because . . . because what other explanation is there?

Then the voice came again. Not that it was audible or inside me or even coming from me, but rather like I was inside the voice. And it was the same warm, loving presence it had been all those years ago. I'd know it anywhere. I had been chasing it for ten years in all the wrong places.

That's why I said it <u>then</u>, so you'd know I was real now, when you needed me most.

CHAPTER TWENTY-NINE

Part of the judge's ruling was separating custody from the financial issues. There would have to be a new trial to untangle all that. When we subpoenaed all financial records from TRIAD, they were delivered in fifteen bankers boxes stuffed full and out of order.

"I've been doing this a long time," my forensic accountant said to me on the phone after the ruling. "I know what I'm looking at. There's no doubt these people are crooks who absolutely robbed you blind."

I had moved to a cheaper rental in Studio City. It was on the corner where my bedroom window backed up against the Oyster Bar parking lot and the lid to their dumpster bin was often left open, hanging over the rose bush in our front "yard" (LA patch-of-grass). Rosie was four years old and helping me fold laundry, one of her favorite "grown-up" activities. I stepped away so she couldn't hear the conversation.

For ten minutes, the forensic accountant explained the intricacies of how it worked—or tried to, anyway. My brain short-circuited as she talked about what sounded in my mind like a spaghetti bowl of maneuvers. She explained a world I was an alien to—since I was twelve, I'd just had business managers (or my mom) taking care of anything that had to do with money. I didn't even know I had a retirement account! Through my discombobulated haze floated phrases like "falsified checks" and "501(c)(3)" and "cash infusion" and "guise of tithing" and "shell corporations" but I couldn't be sure I understood it all. The machinations were so tangled that my mind is still boggled today when I look at the archives of paper trails. My confusion was compounded by my self-loathing over having been so naïve and cowardly—to have been *so* afraid to live my own life that I completely turned over my autonomy and let someone else be in charge of me. Yes, while the means weren't completely clear to me then, the financial end result was: more than $2 million had been siphoned from my savings. And, even with that realization, I was still thinking the way Les had taught me: exculpating him and, instead, blaming myself.

"I've already sent a letter to the Idaho state district attorney's office, requesting they take on the case as a matter of public safety," my accountant said, snapping me back into the moment. "But even though we have the overall numbers and basic trails to be able to put together the story, we still need to *show* the concrete evidence, receipt by receipt, bank statement by bank statement. Based on how many bank accounts there were, how much money was moving around, and all the other people involved, I estimate it's going to take me and my team somewhere between two hundred and five hundred hours to sort through all this and present an airtight case. I would LOVE to take this on, but I have to tell you, even at a discounted rate, you're still looking at spending over one hundred thousand dollars minimum, maybe significantly more. And that isn't including legal fees for requesting subpoenas, taking more depositions, and actually presenting in court."

I wasn't even sure how I was paying rent in a couple months. I'd been getting two or three small roles per year: short arcs on *Dexter*, *Colony*, and *Grey's Anatomy*; a Lifetime Christmas movie; a small-budget action film that failed to get distribution. The forensic accountant read my silence and continued.

"Look, I will take this case and I'll get these people. What they did to you is unconscionable, and I'd be happy to see every one of them locked up. But can I offer my advice on a personal level?"

"Of course," I said.

"Walk away," she said. "You got your daughter. You've been fighting these monsters for three years—nearly all her life. You know the toll that's taken on your health. I'm sure it's taken a toll on your relationship with your daughter, even subconsciously. Going after them like this will not be short. You're looking at another year at least, possibly more. And they are litigious and contentious. They'll probably try to make your life worse than they already have. Don't let them rob you of any more of your peace. Take your beautiful girl and start your life over."

I looked back at Rosie folding laundry. Her husky little voice called out to me: "Mama! I found a button!" She was giggling and waving it in the air.

"So, just let him get away with it?" I said. "Give him even more money in mediation—money that should be for Rosie?"

Q's attorneys had proposed a mediation offer in which he would get half my retirement account, the one my mom and *professional* business managers had apparently been paying into since I was twelve and started acting professionally. He'd also get roughly ten thousand dollars annually until Rosie was eighteen in order to "repay" half the money I took when I separated our accounts. And he'd get one of the cars, and I'd assume the debt for the short sale of the house.

"There's always a chance the DA's office will take the case," the forensic accountant said. "Some of the money has been wired across state lines, which might even make this a federal case. You can let this go on your end and leave it up to the authorities."

My stomach churned and my throat was hot. Rage flooded

through me. Then, across the room, Rosie slipped off the stool she was standing on and bumped her elbow on the way down. A silent cry bubbled up, and I ended the call.

I sat with her on the kitchen floor. *Octonauts* Band-Aid, Popsicle from the freezer, and she was laughing again. As I watched those bright eyes, the rage in me quelled. I thought of the last lines I'd delivered as Haley. *It's a magical place. I've seen that magic in your eyes. There's only one Tree Hill, and it's your home.* I wanted Rosie to be able to feel that kind of magic and peace. I had her. I had her. Nothing else mattered. I called my attorney back.

"I'm sorry, Joy. It's a tough pill to swallow."

"It's fine. I have nothing left to protect but her," I said. "Sign it."

EPILOGUE

I'd recognize that one-of-a-kind shade of auburn hair anywhere. I was at an *Entertainment Weekly* party for some awards show when I spotted Camille across the room. She was smiling and catching up with Katharine McPhee, a new LA acquaintance of mine at the time.

It'd been months since the custody ruling, and I was trying to get my life back to some kind of normalcy. This meant going to social events like this one and catching up with people I hadn't seen in years. Of course, they'd always ask what I'd been up to. Initially, I tried to talk around what happened. I'd say I'd gotten married, had a child, gotten divorced—but keep it vague.

But these interactions were starting to feel weird. Any kind of subterfuge—even something small and seemingly harmless like this—reminded me too much of how Les had deceived me. I also remembered what I'd learned about humility and self-acceptance from my conversations with Les's other victims. Pretending nothing happened wasn't just a betrayal of myself; it was a betrayal of them, too. Mostly, though, I was just exhausted at being ashamed and embarrassed all the time. If God had allowed me to become a feast for bloodsuckers, only to pull me out alive, I was going to take every chance I could to make it good. I sidled up to Camille at the bar.

"Cam!" I said, touching her shoulder. Soft skin, toned arms. She'd become a Nantucket girl. She turned around, and I could see the immediate reaction in her eyes: *Oh no, this is awkward. Is she gonna try and convert me again?* But Hollywood propriety prevailed, and she quickly recovered with a convincing smile that reminded me what a good actress she was.

"Hi, Joy!" She gave me a half-hearted side hug, then—like a waitress who uses "we" when she means "you"—asked, "How are things?"

"Well, I'm not in a cult anymore."

Camille gasped and choked on her champagne, then threw her arms around me in a real hug. It felt great to be honest.

Kat was bewildered. She put her hand on my arm. "Wait, you were in a cult?"

"Yeah," I said. "Bible study went sideways."

Camille laughed. "Sure did," she said. "Oh my god, I'm so happy for you. Are you okay? You have a little boy now, right?"

"A girl. And, yes, I'm okay."

"Let's get together soon." Her eyes were tearing up as she squeezed my hand. "I missed you, Joy."

Not everyone was so generous. Around the same time I found myself standing in the grass at a backyard birthday party in Los Feliz with an old friend from New York. Her tan skin was coated in glittery highlighter. Professional-dancer body. Black hair. Green doe-eyes. It'd been years since I'd seen this woman. I was looking up at her because she was five nine and in heels that were somehow deftly avoiding what my own heels were doing—sinking into the grass like golf tees.

"I went to one of those churches for a little while once," she said, her perfectly varnished nails clutching a martini. "I mean, until I figured out what was going on. Then I was like, 'Yeah, I'm not stupid enough to fall for this.'"

She laughed and sipped her drink, totally unaware of what she'd just said. But I was burnt out on people-pleasing.

"Would you call a woman who got into an abusive relationship 'stupid'?" I asked.

She paused, suddenly realizing I wasn't laughing with her. "No. I mean . . . No, of course not."

"Why not?"

"Well, those women are looking for love and they get taken advantage of. It's not their fault these guys pretend to be someone they're not. But, like, a *group*—"

"And once a woman gets hit, is she stupid because she doesn't leave?"

"I don't know," she said. "I've never been in an abusive relationship. I don't know why someone would stay."

"Come on, you went to Juilliard," I said. "Use that well-trained imagination—you paid tuition for that! Why do you think someone would stay in an abusive relationship?"

She looked down and shook her head, searching for an answer that wouldn't make her seem even more callous and small-minded. "Maybe they think they deserve the abuse? Or they don't understand they're being abused because they believe what the guy is telling them? I mean, I don't know, I guess they probably think it's normal because of whatever in their childhood?" She was talking herself through it now. "They probably, like, see the best in people and think eventually things will get better. I mean, they *have* to believe it's gonna get better, right? They have to believe the pain is worth it in the long run. Like there's some great redemption on the other side."

"Yep," I said. "Those all sound like very human, understandable reasons for staying somewhere unhealthy."

"Yeah," she said softly, looking into her cocktail.

"That martini looks great," I said with a smile. "Gin?" She nodded. "I'm gonna go find one for myself. Glad to see you again."

She was just saying out loud what most people thought. But rather than discourage me from sharing my story, it showed me how important it was to continue to do so. The only way people change their perception of abuse survivors is if they are challenged—if they hear about what it's really like from someone who experienced it, rather than have the usual cult stereotypes and clichés reinforced by whatever trashy true-crime podcasts they listen to and documentaries they love to watch.

Typically when I tell someone I was in a cult, their first response is: "Which one?"

I know they're hoping I'll say NXIVM or the Children of God or the Branch Davidians or another group they've heard about on some salacious podcast or Netflix show. I know this because I see the disappointment on their faces when I say, "Just a small Bible-based group in the Pacific Northwest. You wouldn't have heard of it."

The first few times encountering this disappointment made me feel insecure, worried my cult wasn't cult-y enough. After all, there was no branding, no strange rituals with psychedelics, no polyamory—though I had some suspicions about Les and Pam. I got the sense Ed did, too. Feeling like I needed to prove my cult's legitimacy, I learned to tell people straightaway, "They stole over two million dollars from me." This always perked them up.

After doing that a few times, though, I realized this was what made Les so smart and his cult so dangerous. I call Les "smart" because, even though it's easy to look at him and his financial ineptitude and think, *Worst cult leader ever*, he was savvy in a few key ways—especially with how careful he was to make sure his cult didn't have the usual hallmarks and signifiers. That way it was easier to deny and sow doubt. A cult? No, of course not. Cults wear the same monochrome dresses and carve swastikas into their foreheads and play Beatles records backward. Those *home* ship tattoos all the men had? How were those any different from college fraternity tattoos? In fact, that was one of the ways Les seemingly managed to avoid prosecution. The DA did consider pursuing a case against him, but apparently because fewer than seventy people were involved, they didn't deem him a public threat. I'm not sure who came up with that arbitrary threshold, but it does make me wonder if that had something to do with Les's decision to end new membership after Danielle joined.

My best guess is that threshold is related to financial crimes. Because psychological abuse and manipulation is so hard to prove in court, perhaps the DA thought, from a legal standpoint, their best and maybe only chance at prosecution would be to treat this like they would, say, a Ponzi scheme. But this kind of approach reinforces the idea that the only way to define a cult is by the metrics of sordidness and sensationalism. And this definition reinforces the perspective of so many people like my martini-sipping, high-heeled friend: *I would never be so stupid to fall for something so crazy.*

The less tabloid-friendly truth—and the reason I'm now so willing to tell my story—is that cults can come in multiple guises and anybody can fall for one—it just depends on your blind spots. In fact, someone like martini girl, whom most people—foremost herself—would consider "intelligent," is a prime target. Intelligent and ambitious people want to be challenged, and someone having high expectations of you is a turn-on. High demand is a motivator, success is a drug, and before you know it, you're rationalizing anything in order to meet the demand and get your high. The demand has become your god.

There *is* one indisputable way to identify a cult, one characteristic they all share. It is not a belief in alien spacecraft or a plentiful supply of Flavor Aid. It is the notion that anyone who does not agree with the group's beliefs or choices, who expresses concerns, who simply dares to ask questions, is deemed "unsafe." Every good thing about that person must be subsumed by the fact that they disagree with me, so I can boil down their character into something vilifiable. For mind control to work, there has to be heroes and villains. It has to be us versus them. In a cult, it isn't good enough for you to say, "I love you, but I disagree with you." You must affirm my choices and beliefs. Only then can you be considered "safe." In a cult, safety means agreement.

The irony, of course, is that while you are not allowed to have your own opinion about my beliefs, I am allowed to have an opinion about yours.

Technically the last time I saw Les was a few months after the custody verdict, when he came with Q to LA to see Rosie. But when they picked her up in the parking lot, Les stayed in the car, so I saw only his shadowy figure in the back seat. The last time I got a good look at him was in court toward the end of the trial.

It was the first time he appeared in court. Throughout the preceding couple of years, he'd been depicted in testimony by myself and others as to who he was in private. When he was "Papa," he was an overbearing presence; whether playing "sweet" or being aggressive, he resembled a much less compelling version of his hero, Tony Soprano. When he arrived in court, he'd lost so much weight he looked more like Uncle Junior. He wore a geeky sweater vest over a shirt and tie and slouched as he shuffled up to the witness stand. To complete the unassuming and unthreatening affect, he sported a pair of wire-rimmed glasses, which I suspected he'd bought at the drugstore on the drive over. When he spoke, his voice was low-key and his answers were brief—almost apologetic. He seemed *utterly* confused about why he was there. He complimented me from the stand and talked about how much he loved me and wished I didn't have such hard feelings. *Divorce is hard for everyone. We just hope for this to end amicably and soon. For Rosie, of course. She's who matters most.* It was a tour de force performance. The skilled orator and emotional manipulator I'd been explaining him as to the judge was nowhere to be found. As much as I despised Les, as an actor I had to appreciate his commitment to the bit.

After the verdict, I lost touch with most of the Family. Harker and Mina, Abe and Emily, Dontay and Jasmine, Miguel and Juana: most of them scattered to find their own healing in different ways. The Hamoatzah remained, but there wasn't anyone for the Leadership to lead except for Les's kids, Brandon, and Gretchen.

I did stay in touch with Danielle. I learned from her that once access to my money was cut off, Les defaulted on the restaurant, and the building was sold at auction to the local fire department and used for training exercises. I heard from friends that Les set up a portable grill, cooking and selling hot dogs to the firefighters and local spectators, laughing and joking as he forked the meat, trying to give the impression that it was no big deal seeing his dream burn down.

The Van Hewitts eventually sold the Big House as well. To Danielle. She did a complete renovation and was able to flip it for a nice profit. She sent me the online listing, and I barely recognized it. The ratty carpet had been pulled up and the wood floors beneath refinished. The '80s wallpaper was stripped and the stairs stained in a lush cherry wood. The kitchen was gutted and gleaming countertops installed.

I smiled at God's sense of humor. I had become a part of this "Big House Family" before *One Tree Hill*, and Danielle became a part of it *because* of *One Tree Hill*. In the end, our sweet, hometown TV show became the crucible for all of it, including Danielle helping me break free. Thinking of how faithful the fans of the show have been in the years that followed the series finale—showing up for fan conventions, staying engaged on social media, and supporting our continued professional endeavors—I laughed to myself at the thought that a "cult TV show" outlasted an actual cult.

As I scrolled through the listing, I saw my old bedroom with the tall windows had been staged with another set of bunk beds, but one clearly intended for children. A game room had been put into the basement, now brightened with white paint and wall-sconce lighting. Out front, the driveway was lined with rose bushes and the willow tree I planted was taller than I remembered.

It was a beautiful home. A big house, for a real family.

ACKNOWLEDGMENTS

In July 2023, when I mentioned on *Drama Queens*—the *One Tree Hill* rewatch podcast I cohost—that I should write a book about having been in a cult for ten years, I was simply musing in my living room as we recorded, thought nothing of it, and went on with my day. I was gobsmacked when it got picked up by media outlets around the world. "A slow news day," I joked to myself. Several of these outlets reached out wanting more details, but I knew there was too much to my story to condense it into an article for soundbites and clickbait that *might* last a week. I decided to write a book, but I needed a literary agent to guide me through the publishing world to which I was an alien—one who viscerally understood the sensitive nature of the topic. Jonathan Merritt came in clearheaded, empathetic, and incredibly savvy. I wish every agent had your bedside manner and strategic abilities, J. You're a secret weapon! Let's do more and more and more. Thank you for guiding me and encouraging me to trust my instincts every step of the way, including the next best choice I made, Simon & Schuster.

Sean Manning has spoiled me. I don't know how I'll ever work with another editor after experiencing his care, humility, brilliance, and dedication. He made me feel so safe and capable during the very scary process of writing a memoir about a time in my life I never wanted to revisit. Without him, this book would be full of tangents, scattered thoughts, and more clichés than a TV

rom-com. ;) I couldn't have asked for a better champion. Everything I write from here on out will have your mark on it, Sean.
"Thank you" is what we say when a friend treats us to coffee, or
the server brings an extra side of ketchup. The only thing that
seems to approach a full expression of my gratitude would be to
say that you've made another human feel seen, known, accepted,
and enjoyed—if we're not on this planet to do just that, I don't
know what else we're here for.

My heartfelt thanks goes to everyone at Simon & Schuster for
choosing and believing in me, including Omesha Edwards, Han-
nah Bishop, Ingrid Carabulea, Tzipora Baitch, Irene Kheradi,
Beth Maglione, Amanda Mulholland, Lauren Gomez, Zoe Kaplan,
Jonathan Evans, Morgan Hart, Samantha Hoback, Nancy Tan,
Kate Lapin, Dominick Montalto, Paul Dippolito, Emma Shaw,
Jackie Seow, and Felice Javit. Also, thank you to Ed Klaris and
Sam Borenzweig, as well as Christopher Ferebee.

Joanna Ng, your help was a lifejacket as I attempted to organize all the pieces. I hope we can work together again.

Anne Woodward, Cheryl McLean, Hailey Helms, and Adam
Kaller—each of you have kept me sane in one way or another, and
you work your asses off. Thank you.

Mom and Dad, Pop Pop, Candace, Matt, Sam, Anna, and all
my family who waited for me . . . "Thank you" will never be
enough to say for all your years of patience amid the turmoil.
Your grace and continued encouragement are gifts I cherish. I'm
proud to have been raised by (and around) such loving and resilient people.

Kyle Negrete, Paul Johansson, Kim and William Paul
Young, Amy Young, Eric Williams and Dawn Smith, Nathan
Johnson and Laura Osnes Johnson, Nicholas Sparks, Nikki
Dyani, Holly Goline, Ron Aniello, Tori Fillat, Danny Shyman,

Acknowledgments

Susan May Pratt and Kenneth Mitchell, R&R, Erik Palladino, Aleque Reid, Sarah Drew, Kelly Viavattine, Stephanie Ike, Eli Goree, Beth Crookham, Anthony Evans Jr., and the Yungs—you all showed up for me in enduring friendship during my years in the group and/or in recovery. I wouldn't be here without you.

Aunt Diane, I'm glad to have a public forum to thank you for the years of time and care you selflessly put into helping me wade through the financial abuse, restructure my life, and gain fiscal confidence. You display such generosity of spirit, and my life wouldn't be the same without you. I love you.

To properly write this book, I spoke to many former members of the Big House Family and people who were otherwise involved, who were bravely willing to dive into past dark days. They did this because they believed in this project and wanted to contribute whatever they could if it would bring hope and healing to someone out there. I wish I could list all these names, but I hope each one knows my gratitude. Especially Emily and Jasmine . . . I could weep. Thank you for supporting and collaborating, and for sharing your memories, laughter, and tears with me. And most of all, for trusting me. Thank God we all jumped off the ship.

One of the most valuable resources to me after I left the group and began untangling my immense internal conflict around Christianity, Jesus, the Bible, the patriarchy, church, "relationship," and trust in general was going back to a place I knew was solid. Tim Keller was a voice of faith through *reason* whose books and catalog of sermons made me feel sane and empowered me to scrutinize, question, and understand what I believe. I'm overwhelmed with emotion and gratitude for the late Dr. Keller and his wife, Kathy, and their continued ministry at the Gospel Coalition.

Acknowledgments

• • •

In closing, I'd like to address *you*, Reader.

I took a trip to Paris again recently, and for the first time went inside the Sacré-Coeur in Montmartre. I have deep, personal conflicts with Catholicism, so I was bewildered by the thick, peaceful presence inside those walls. As I admired—*marveled at*—the craftsmanship, the impossibly beautiful paintings, the meticulous mosaics that would catch a small light from an east window and illuminate the entire cathedral, I was caught in a trap. Even if I could discard the beauty as "misguided devotion," I couldn't deny the familiar, warm presence of God. It made me think of a question I'd asked myself many times in the years that followed my exit from the cult. While most people tend to wonder why God would allow so many bad things to happen, I wondered why God allowed so many *good* things to happen to me while I was involved in something so damaging. *Lord, I would have gotten out so much sooner if there hadn't been a steady stream of good things I could point to as signposts that I was "on the right track"!* I learned how to be vulnerable there, I learned how to put others before myself (a big deal for an only child), I learned how to serve, I learned how to have deep friendships, and best of all, I got an incredible daughter out of it.

I sat in a pew, frustrated, and—as I tend to do—wrestled with God until I got an answer. Looking around the church, unsettled by my inability to reconcile how something so beautiful could come from something so corrupt, I finally felt that recognizable voice in my spirit say:

This place is you. This place is humanity.

I think we're all little cathedrals of contradiction. Terrifying darkness and shocking beauty coexist in everyone, and God

302

doesn't wait for us to clean out all the bad before celebrating the good. It's scandalous, really—that kind of love.

So, my acknowledgment of you is that I appreciate you taking this journey with me and holding space for all these complex themes. No matter who you related to the most in this story, I thank you for coming to the table.